The Big Sea

The Big Sea

An Autobiography by

LANGSTON HUGHES

Pluto  Press

This edition first published in 1986 by Pluto Press Limited,
The Works, 105a Torriano Avenue, London NW5 2RX
and Pluto Press Australia Limited, PO Box 199, Leichhardt,
New South Wales 2040, Australia

First published in 1940 by Alfred A. Knopf, New York

7 6 5 4 3 2 1

90 89 88 87 86

Made and printed in Great Britain by the
Guernsey Press Co. Ltd., Guernsey, Channel Islands.

British Library Cataloguing in Publication Data
Hughes, Langston
   The big sea : an autobiography. — (Liberation
   Classics)
   1. Hughes, Langston — Biography   2. Authors,
   American — 20th century — Biography
   I. Title   II. Series
   818'.5209   PS3515.U274Z

ISBN 0 7453 0134 7

TO

EMERSON AND TOY HARPER

Life is a big sea

full of many fish.

I let down my nets

and pull.

CONTENTS

〜〜〜〜〜〜〜〜〜〜〜〜〜〜〜〜〜〜〜〜〜〜〜〜〜〜〜〜〜〜〜〜〜〜〜〜〜〜〜

I · TWENTY-ONE

CONTENTS

II · BIG SEA

CONTENTS

III · BLACK RENAISSANCE

I

Twenty-One

BEYOND SANDY HOOK

Melodramatic maybe, it seems to me now. But then it was like throwing a million bricks out of my heart when I threw the books into the water. I leaned over the rail of the S.S. *Malone* and threw the books as far as I could out into the sea—all the books I had had at Columbia, and all the books I had lately bought to read.

The books went down into the moving water in the dark off Sandy Hook. Then I straightened up, turned my face to the wind, and took a deep breath. I was a seaman going to sea for the first time—a seaman on a big merchant ship. And I felt that nothing would ever happen to me again that I didn't want to happen. I felt grown, a man, inside and out. Twenty-one.

I was twenty-one.

Four bells sounded. As I stood there, whiffs of salt spray blew in my face. The afterdeck was deserted. The big hatches were covered with canvas. The booms were all tied up to the masts, and the winches silent. It was dark. The old freighter, smelling of crude oil and garbage, engines pounding, rolled through the pitch-black night. I looked down on deck and noticed that one of my books had fallen into the scupper. The last book. I picked it up and threw it far over the rail into the water below, that was too black to see. The wind caught the book and ruffled its pages quickly, then let it fall into the rolling darkness. I think it was a book by H. L. Mencken.

You see, books had been happening to me. Now the books were cast off back there somewhere in the churn of spray and night behind the propeller. I was glad they were gone.

I went up on the poop and looked over the railing toward New York. But New York was gone, too. There were no longer any lights to be seen. The wind smelt good. I was sleepy, so I went down a pair of narrow steps that ended just in front of our cabin—the mess boys' cabin.

Inside the hot cabin, George lay stark naked in a lower bunk, talking and laughing and gaily waving his various appendages around. Above him in the upper bunk, two chocolate-colored Puerto Rican feet stuck out from one end of a snow-white sheet, and a dark Puerto Rican head from the other. It was clear that Ramon in the upper bunk didn't understand more than every tenth word of George's Kentucky vernacular, but he kept on laughing every time George laughed—and that was often.

George was talking about women, of course. He said he didn't care if his Harlem landlady pawned all his clothes, the old witch! When he got back from Africa, he would get some more. He might even pay her the month's back rent he owed her, too. Maybe. Or else—and here he waved one of his appendages around—she could have what he had in his hand.

Puerto Rico, who understood all the bad words in every language, laughed loudly. We all laughed. You couldn't help it. George was so good-natured and comical you couldn't keep from laughing with him—or at him. He always made everybody laugh—even when the food ran out on the return trip and everybody was hungry and mad.

Then it was ten o'clock, on a June night, on the S.S. *Malone,* and we were going to Africa. At ten o'clock that morning I had never heard of the S.S. *Malone,* or George, or Ramon, or anybody else in its crew of forty-two men. Nor any of the six passengers. But now, here were the three of us laughing very loudly, going to Africa.

I had got my job at a New York shipping office. Ramon got his job at another shipping office. But George just simply walked on board about supper time. A Filipino pantry boy got mad and quit at the last moment. Naturally, the steward didn't want to sail short-handed. He saw George hanging around the entrance to the pier, watching the stevedores finish loading. The Filipino steward said: "Hey, colored boy! You, there! You want a job?" And George said: "Yes," so he walked on board, with nothing but a shirt and a pair of overalls to his back, and sailed.

Now, he lay there in his bunk, laughing about his land-lady. He said she intended to put him out if he didn't find a job. And now that he had found a job, he wouldn't be able to tell her for six months. He wondered if she knew Africa was six months away from Harlem.

"*Largo viaje,*" said Ramon.

George commented in pig-Latin—which was the only "foreign" language he knew.

I might as well tell you now what George and Ramon were like. Everybody knew all about George long before we reached the coast of Africa. But nobody ever knew much about Ramon.

George was from Kentucky. He had worked around race

horses. And he spoke of several white gentlemen out of his past as "Colonel." We were all about the same age, George, Ramon, and I.

After Kentucky, George had worked in a scrap-iron yard in St. Louis. But he said the work wasn't good for his back, so he quit. He went and got a job in a restaurant near the station in Springfield, Illinois, washing dishes. A female impersonator came through with a show and took George with him as his valet. George said he got tired of being maid to the female impersonator, so as soon as he got a new suit of clothes, he quit in Pittsburgh. He found a good job in a bowling alley, but had a fight with a man who hit him with one of the balls because he set the pins up wrong. George claimed he won the fight. But he lit out for South Street in Philadelphia to avoid arrest. And after that, Harlem.

George had a thousand tales to tell about every town he'd ever been in. And several versions of each tale. No doubt, some of the stories were true—and some of them not true at all, but they sounded true. Sometimes George said he had relatives down South. Then, again, he said he didn't have anybody in the whole world. Both versions concerning his relatives were probably correct. If he did have relatives they didn't matter—lying there as he was now, laughing and talking in his narrow bunk on a hot night, going to Africa.

But Ramon of the upper bunk didn't talk much, in English or Spanish. He simply did his work in the morning. Then he got in bed and slept all the afternoon till time to set up the sailors' mess hall for supper. After supper, he got in bed again and laughed at George until George went to sleep.

Ramon told us once that his mother was a seamstress in

Ponce. Ernesto, the Puerto Rican sailor aboard, said "seamstress" was just another name for something else. Anyhow, Ramon was decent enough as a cabin mate, and practically always asleep. He didn't gamble. I saw him drunk only once. He seldom drew any money, and when he did he spent it on sweets—seldom on a woman. The only thing that came out of his mouth in six months that I remember is that he said he didn't care much for women, anyway. He preferred silk stockings—so halfway down the African coast, he bought a pair of silk stockings and slept with them under his pillow.

George, however, was always saying things the like of which you never heard before or since, making up fabulous jokes, playing pranks, and getting in on all the card games or fights aboard. George and I became pretty good pals. He could tap dance a little, shuffle a lot, and knew plenty of blues. He said he could play a guitar, but no one on the *Malone* possessed a guitar, so we never knew.

I had the petty officers' mess to take care of and their staterooms to make up. There was nothing hard about a mess boy's work. You got up at six in the morning, with the mid-Atlantic calm as a sun-pool, served breakfast, made up the rooms, served luncheon, had all the afternoon off, served dinner, and that was all. The rest of the time you could lie on deck in the sun, play cards with the sailors, or sleep. When your clothes were dirty, you washed them in a bucket of soapsuds and lye. The lye made the washing easy because it took all of the dirt out quick.

When we got to Africa we took on a full African crew to supplement the regular crew who weren't supposed to be able to stand the sun. Then I had an African boy to do my washing, my cleaning, and almost all my work—as did everybody on board. The Africans stood both work and sun without difficulty, it seems.

Going over, it was a nice trip, warm, calm, the sea blue-green by day, gold-green at sunset. And at night phosphorescent stars in the water where the prow cut a rift of sparkling foam.

The S.S. *Malone* had been built during the war. It was a big, creaking, old freight boat, two or three years in the African trade now. It had cabins for a half dozen passengers. This trip the passengers were all Nordic missionaries—but one. That one was a colored tailor, a Garveyite who had long worshipped Africa from afar, and who had a theory of civilization all his own. He thought that if he could just teach the Africans to wear proper clothes, coats and pants, they would be brought forward a long way toward the standards of our world. To that end, he carried with him on his journey numberless bolts of cloth, shears, and tailoring tools, and a trunk full of smart patterns. The missionaries carried Bibles and hymnbooks. The Captain carried invoices and papers having to do with trade. We sailors carried nothing but ourselves.

At Horta, our only port of call in the Azores, we anchored at sea some distance from the rocky shore. Everybody went ashore in rowboats or motor launches. Some of the boys made straight for women, some for the wine shops. It depended on your temperament which you sought first. Nobody had much money, because the Captain didn't permit a draw. I had an American dollar, so George and I bought a big bottle of cognac, walked up a hill to the top of the town, and drank it. The sun was setting. The sea and the palm trees and the roofs of Horta were aglow. On the way down the hill in the amber dusk, George smashed the cognac bottle against the wall of a blue house and said: "I wants to holler."

"George, don't holler right here on the main street," I cautioned.

George said: "This town's too small to holler in, but I got to holler, anyhow." And he let out a tremendous "Yee-hoo-oo-o!" that sent children rushing to their mothers' arms and women scurrying into doorways. But a sleepy-looking cop, leaning against a wall with a lantern, must have been used to the ways of sailors, because he paid George no mind. In fact, he didn't even stir as we went on to the center of the village, where there were lots of people and lights.

We came across the bo'sun and some sailors in a bar, emptying their pockets, trying to get enough together to pay for a round of drinks that Slim—who didn't have a penny—had ordered for all. I had four cents to contribute. Chips had a quarter. But, all told, it didn't make enough to pay for the drinks, so the bartender said they should give him the rest when the S.S. *Malone* came back to Horta in five months. So everybody agreed they would settle then. Whereupon, the bartender set up another round of drinks for nothing.

The *Malone's* whistle began to blow. The bo'sun said: "Come on, you bloody so-and-so's, the Old Man's calling you!" We went down to the wharf. Some other boys were there. An Irish kid from Brooklyn and his cousin had two girls on their arms, and the wireless man, Sparks, was in the middle between the two girls. Sparks said they were the best two girls in town and that he always traded with them. The Irish kid said his was the best girl he ever had.

His cousin said: "Aw, nuts! You never had one before!" (The Irish kid was just out of high school and this was his first trip to sea. He looked like a choirboy, except that he couldn't sing.) We waited for the launch that we had paid to take us back. Finally it came. At seven bells we went on toward Africa, the engines chugging soft and serene.

The next day was Sunday and the missionaries wanted everybody to come to prayers in the saloon, but nobody went except the Captain and the Chief Mate. The bo'sun said he'd go if the missionaries had any communion wine, but the missionaries didn't have any, so he didn't go.

When we got to Teneriffe, in the Canary Islands, it was mid-afternoon and very bright. The Canaries looked like fairy islands, all sharp peaks of red rock and bright sandy beaches and little green fields dropped like patchwork between the beaches and the rocks, with the sea making a blue-white fringe around.

The Captain let us draw money—so Las Palmas seemed a gay city indeed. Ashore, three or four of us, including Ernesto and a Norwegian boy named Sven, had supper at a place with very bright lights, where they served huge platters of delicious mixed fish with big bottles of cool, white wine. Then we all went to a white villa by the sea, called *El Palacio de Amor* and stayed all night. In the morning very early, when the sun was just coming up, we drove back to the wharf in an open carriage. We kept thinking about the girls, who were Spanish, and very young and pretty. And Sven said he would like to take one of them with him.

But all those days I was waiting anxiously to see Africa. And finally, when I saw the dust-green hills in the sunlight, something took hold of me inside. My Africa, Motherland of the Negro peoples! And me a Negro! Africa! The real thing, to be touched and seen, not merely read about in a book.

That first morning when we sighted the coast, I kept leaving my work to lean over the rail and look at Africa, dim and far away, off on the horizon in a haze of light, then gradually nearer and nearer, until you could see the color of the foliage on the trees.

We put in at the port of Dakar. There were lots of Frenchmen, and tall black Senegalese soldiers in red fezes, and Mohammedans in robes, so that at first you couldn't tell if the Mohammedans were men or women.

The next day we moved on. And farther down the coast it was more like the Africa I had dreamed about—wild and lovely, the people dark and beautiful, the palm trees tall, the sun bright, and the rivers deep. The great Africa of my dreams!

But there was one thing that hurt me a lot when I talked with the people. The Africans looked at me and would not believe I was a Negro.

NEGRO

You see, unfortunately, I am not black. There are lots of different kinds of blood in our family. But here in the United States, the word "Negro" is used to mean anyone who has *any* Negro blood at all in his veins. In Africa, the word is more pure. It means *all* Negro, therefore *black*.

I am brown. My father was a darker brown. My mother an olive-yellow. On my father's side, the white blood in his family came from a Jewish slave trader in Kentucky, Silas Cushenberry, of Clark County, who was his mother's father; and Sam Clay, a distiller of Scotch descent, living in Henry County, who was his father's father. So on my

father's side both male great-grandparents were white, and
Sam Clay was said to be a relative of the great statesman,
Henry Clay, his contemporary.

On my mother's side, I had a paternal great-grand-
father named Quarles—Captain Ralph Quarles—who was
white and who lived in Louisa County, Virginia, before
the Civil War, and who had several colored children by a
colored housekeeper, who was his slave. The Quarles
traced their ancestry back to Francis Quarles, famous
Jacobean poet, who wrote *A Feast for Wormes*.

On my maternal grandmother's side, there was French
and Indian blood. My grandmother looked like an Indian
—with very long black hair. She said she could lay claim
to Indian land, but that she never wanted the government
(or anybody else) to give her anything. She said there had
been a French trader who came down the St. Lawrence,
then on foot to the Carolinas, and mated with her grandmother, who was a Cherokee—so all her people were free.
During slavery, she had free papers in North Carolina,
and traveled about free, at will. Her name was Mary
Sampson Patterson, and in Oberlin, Ohio, where she went
to college, she married a free man named Sheridan Leary.

She was with child in Oberlin when Sheridan Leary
went away, and nobody knew where he had gone, except
that he told her he was going on a trip. A few weeks later
his shawl came back to her full of bullet holes. He had
been killed following John Brown in that historic raid at
Harper's Ferry. They did not hang him. He had been
killed that first night in the raid—shot attacking, believing
in John Brown. My grandmother said Sheridan Leary
always did believe people should be free.

She married another man who believed the same thing.
His name was Charles Langston, my grandfather. And in

the '70's the Langstons came out to Kansas where my
mother was born on a farm near Lawrence.

My grandfather never made much money. But he went
into politics, looking for a bigger freedom than the Eman-
cipation Proclamation had provided. He let his farm and
his grocery store in Lawrence run along, and didn't much
care about making money. When he died, none of the
family had any money. But he left some fine speeches
behind him.

His brother, John Mercer Langston, left a book of
speeches, too, and an autobiography, *From a Virginia
Plantation to the National Capital*. But he was much
better than Charles at making money, so he left a big house
as well, and I guess some stocks and bonds. When I was
small, we had cousins in Washington, who lived a lot
better than we did in Kansas. But my grandmother never
wrote them for anything. John Mercer Langston had been
a Congressman from Virginia, and later United States
Minister to Haiti, and Dean of the first Law School at
Howard University. He had held many high positions—
very high positions for a Negro in his day, or any day in
this rather difficult country. And his descendants are still
in society.

We were never very much "in society" in Kansas, because we were always broke, and the families of the Negro
doctors and lawyers lived much better than we did. One
of the first things I remember is my grandmother worrying
about the mortgage on our house. It was always very hard
for her to raise the money to pay the interest. And when
my grandmother died, the house went right straight to the
mortgage man, quickly.

I was born in Joplin, Missouri, in 1902, but I grew up
mostly in Lawrence, Kansas. My grandmother raised me

until I was twelve years old. Sometimes I was with my mother, but not often. My father and mother were separated. And my mother, who worked, always traveled about a great deal, looking for a better job. When I first started to school, I was with my mother a while in Topeka. (And later, for a summer in Colorado, and another in Kansas City.) She was a stenographer for a colored lawyer in Topeka, named Mr. Guy. She rented a room near his office, downtown. So I went to a "white" school in the downtown district.

At first, they did not want to admit me to the school, because there were no other colored families living in that neighborhood. They wanted to send me to the colored school, blocks away down across the railroad tracks. But my mother, who was always ready to do battle for the rights of a free people, went directly to the school board, and finally got me into the Harrison Street School—where all the teachers were nice to me, except one who sometimes used to make remarks about my being colored. And after such remarks, occasionally the kids would grab stones and tin cans out of the alley and chase me home.

But there was one little white boy who would always take up for me. Sometimes others of my classmates would, as well. So I learned early not to hate *all* white people. And ever since, it has seemed to me that *most* people are generally good, in every race and in every country where I have been.

The room my mother lived in in Topeka was not in a house. It was in a building, upstairs over a plumbing shop. The other rooms on that floor facing a long hall were occupied by a white architect and a colored painter. The architect was a very old man, and very kind. The colored painter was young, and used to paint marvelous lions and tigers and jungle scenes. I don't know where he saw such things in Topeka, but he used to paint them. Years later, I saw him paint them on the walls of cheap barrooms in Chicago and New York. I don't know where he is now.

My mother had a small monkey-stove in our room for both heating and cooking. You could put only one pot on the stove at a time. She used to send me through the downtown alleys every day after the stores closed to pick up discarded boxes to burn in our stove. Sometimes we would make a great racket, cutting kindling with a hatchet in our room at night. If it was a tough box we could not break up, we would put a whole piece of board in the stove, and it would stick out through the top, and my mother would call it "long-branch kindling." When she would go away and leave me alone, she would warn me about putting "long-branch kindling" in the stove, because it might burn until it broke off, and fall, and catch the rug on fire.

My mother used to take me to see all the plays that came to Topeka like *Buster Brown, Under Two Flags,* and *Uncle Tom's Cabin.* We were very fond of plays and books. Once we heard *Faust.*

When I was about five or six years old, my father and mother decided to go back together. They had separated shortly after I was born, because my father wanted to go away to another country, where a colored man could get ahead and make money quicker, and my mother did not want to go. My father went to Cuba, and then to Mexico, where there wasn't any color line, or any Jim Crow. He finally sent for us, so we went there, too.

But no sooner had my mother, my grandmother, and I got to Mexico City than there was a big earthquake, and people ran out from their houses into the Alameda, and the big National Opera House they were building sank down into the ground, and tarantulas came out of the walls—and my mother said she wanted to go back home at once to Kansas, where people spoke English or something she could understand and there were no earthquakes. So we went. And that was the last I saw of my father until I was seventeen.

When I was in the second grade, my grandmother took me to Lawrence to raise me. And I was unhappy for a long time, and very lonesome, living with my grandmother. Then it was that books began to happen to me, and I began to believe in nothing but books and the wonderful world in books—where if people suffered, they suffered in beautiful language, not in monosyllables, as we did in Kansas. And where almost always the mortgage got paid off, the good knights won, and the Alger boy triumphed.

Our mortgage never got paid off—for my grandmother was not like the other colored women of Lawrence. She didn't take in washing or go out to cook, for she had never worked for anyone. But she tried to make a living by renting rooms to college students from Kansas University; or by renting out half her house to a family; or sometimes she would move out entirely and go to live with a friend, while she rented the whole little house for ten or twelve dollars a month, to make a payment on the mortgage. But we were never quite sure the white mortgage man was not going to take the house. And sometimes, on that account, we would have very little to eat, saving to pay the interest.

I remember one summer a friend of my mother's in Kansas City sent her son to pass a few weeks with me at my grandmother's home in Lawrence. But the little boy only stayed a few days, then wrote his mother that he wanted to leave, because we had nothing but salt pork and wild dandelions to eat. The boy was right. But being only eight or nine years old, I cried when he showed me the letter he was writing his mother. And I never wanted my mother to invite any more little boys to stay with me at my grandmother's house.

You see, my grandmother was very proud, and she would never beg or borrow anything from anybody. She sat, looking very much like an Indian, copper-colored with long black hair, just a little gray in places at seventy, sat in her rocker and read the Bible, or held me on her lap and told me long, beautiful stories about people who wanted to make the Negroes free, and how her father had had apprenticed to him many slaves in Fayetteville, North Carolina, before the War, so that they could work out their freedom under him as stone masons. And once they had worked out their purchase, he would see that they reached the North, where there was no slavery.

Through my grandmother's stories always life moved, moved heroically toward an end. Nobody ever cried in my grandmother's stories. They worked, or schemed, or fought. But no crying. When my grandmother died, I didn't cry, either. Something about my grandmother's stories (without her ever having said so) taught me the uselessness of crying about anything.

She was a proud woman—gentle, but Indian and proud. I remember once she took me to Osawatomie, where she was honored by President Roosevelt—Teddy—and sat on the platform with him while he made a speech; for she was then the last surviving widow of John Brown's raid.

I was twelve when she died. I went to live with a friend of my grandmother's named Auntie Reed. Auntie Reed and her husband had a little house a block from the Kaw

River, near the railroad station. They had chickens and cows. Uncle Reed dug ditches and laid sewer pipes for the city, and Auntie Reed sold milk and eggs to her neighbors. For me, there have never been any better people in the world. I loved them very much. Auntie Reed let me set the hens, and Uncle Reed let me drive the cows to pasture. Auntie Reed was a Christian and made me go to church and Sunday school every Sunday. But Uncle Reed was a sinner and never went to church as long as he lived, nor cared anything about it. In fact, he washed his overalls every Sunday morning (a grievous sin) in a big iron pot in the back yard, and then just sat and smoked his pipe under the grape arbor in summer, in winter on a bench behind the kitchen range. But both of them were very good and kind—the one who went to church and the one who didn't. And no doubt from them I learned to like both Christians and sinners equally well.

SALVATION

I was saved from sin when I was going on thirteen. But not really saved. It happened like this. There was a big revival at my Auntie Reed's church. Every night for weeks there had been much preaching, singing, praying, and shouting, and some very hardened sinners had been brought to Christ, and the membership of the church had grown by leaps and bounds. Then just before the revival ended, they held a special meeting for children, "to bring the young lambs to the fold." My aunt spoke of it for days ahead. That night I was escorted to the front row and placed on the mourners' bench with all the other young sinners, who had not yet been brought to Jesus.

My aunt told me that when you were saved you saw a light, and something happened to you inside! And Jesus came into your life! And God was with you from then on! She said you could see and hear and feel Jesus in your soul. I believed her. I had heard a great many old people say the same thing and it seemed to me they ought to know. So I sat there calmly in the hot, crowded church, waiting for Jesus to come to me.

The preacher preached a wonderful rhythmical sermon, all moans and shouts and lonely cries and dire pictures of hell, and then he sang a song about the ninety and nine safe in the fold, but one little lamb was left out in the cold. Then he said: "Won't you come? Won't you come to Jesus? Young lambs, won't you come?" And he held out his arms to all us young sinners there on the mourners' bench. And the little girls cried. And some of them jumped up and went to Jesus right away. But most of us just sat there.

A great many old people came and knelt around us and prayed, old women with jet-black faces and braided hair, old men with work-gnarled hands. And the church sang a song about the lower lights are burning, some poor sinners to be saved. And the whole building rocked with prayer and song.

Still I kept waiting to *see* Jesus.

Finally all the young people had gone to the altar and were saved, but one boy and me. He was a rounder's son named Westley. Westley and I were surrounded by sisters and deacons praying. It was very hot in the church, and getting late now. Finally Westley said to me in a whisper:

"God damn! I'm tired o' sitting here. Let's get up and be saved." So he got up and was saved.

Then I was left all alone on the mourners' bench. My aunt came and knelt at my knees and cried, while prayers and songs swirled all around me in the little church. The whole congregation prayed for me alone, in a mighty wail of moans and voices. And I kept waiting serenely for Jesus, waiting, waiting—but he didn't come. I wanted to see him, but nothing happened to me. Nothing! I wanted something to happen to me, but nothing happened.

I heard the songs and the minister saying: "Why don't you come? My dear child, why don't you come to Jesus? Jesus is waiting for you. He wants you. Why don't you come? Sister Reed, what is this child's name?"

"Langston," my aunt sobbed.

"Langston, why don't you come? Why don't you come and be saved? Oh, Lamb of God! Why don't you come?"

Now it was really getting late. I began to be ashamed of myself, holding everything up so long. I began to wonder what God thought about Westley, who certainly hadn't seen Jesus either, but who was now sitting proudly on the platform, swinging his knickerbockered legs and grinning down at me, surrounded by deacons and old women on their knees praying. God had not struck Westley dead for taking his name in vain or for lying in the temple. So I decided that maybe to save further trouble, I'd better lie, too, and say that Jesus had come, and get up and be saved.

So I got up.

Suddenly the whole room broke into a sea of shouting, as they saw me rise. Waves of rejoicing swept the place. Women leaped in the air. My aunt threw her arms around me. The minister took me by the hand and led me to the platform.

When things quieted down, in a hushed silence, punctuated by a few ecstatic "Amens," all the new young lambs were blessed in the name of God. Then joyous singing filled the room.

That night, for the last time in my life but one—for I was a big boy twelve years old—I cried. I cried, in bed alone, and couldn't stop. I buried my head under the quilts, but my aunt heard me. She woke up and told my uncle I was crying because the Holy Ghost had come into my life, and because I had seen Jesus. But I was really crying because I couldn't bear to tell her that I had lied, that I had deceived everybody in the church, that I hadn't seen Jesus, and that now I didn't believe there was a Jesus any more, since he didn't come to help me.

THE MOTHER OF THE GRACCHI

My Auntie Reed cooked wonderful salt pork and greens with corn dumplings. There were fresh peas and young onions right out of the garden, and milk with cream on it. There were hoe-cake, and sorghum molasses, and apple dumplings with butter sauce. And she and Uncle Reed owned their own home without a mortgage on it, clear.

In the spring I used to collect maple seeds and sell them to the seed store. I delivered papers for a while and sold the *Saturday Evening Post*. For a few weeks I also sold the

Appeal to Reason for an old gentleman with a white beard, who said his paper was trying to make a better world. But the editor of the local daily told me to stop selling the *Appeal to Reason,* because it was a radical sheet and would get colored folks in trouble. Besides, he said I couldn't carry his papers and that one, too. So I gave up the *Appeal to Reason.*

On Saturdays I went to football games at the University of Kansas and heard the students yelling:

> *Walk-Chalk!*
> *Jay Hawk! K. U.!*

And I felt bad if Nebraska or Missouri beat Kansas, as they usually did.

When I was in the seventh grade, I got my first regular job, cleaning up the lobby and toilets of an old hotel near the school I attended. I kept the mirrors and spittoons shined and the halls scrubbed. I was paid fifty cents a week, with which I went to see Mary Pickford and Charlie Chaplin and Theda Bara on the screen. Also Pearl White in *The Clutching Claw,* until the theater (belonging to a lady named Mrs. Pattee) put up a sign: NO COLORED ADMITTED. Then I went to see road shows like *The Firefly* and *The Pink Lady* and Sothern and Marlowe when they came to town, sitting up in the gallery of the Opera House all by myself, thrilled at the world across the footlights.

But there was a glamour in the real world, too. For a while there had been a poet in Lawrence who had left his mark on the town. I remember my mother, when I was a small child, pointing him out to me on the street. His name was Harry Kemp, but I don't remember clearly how he looked.

The great Negro actor, Nash Walker, of "Bon Bon

Buddy, the Chocolate Drop" fame, had lived in Lawrence, too. And my Uncle Nat (before he died) had taught him music, long before I was born. I saw Nash Walker only once, because he was off in the East with the great Williams and Walker shows, since he was a partner of Bert Williams, but I often heard the local people speak of him. And I vaguely remember that he brought to Lawrence the first phonograph I had ever seen, when he came back ill to his mother at the end. He gave a concert at my aunt's church on the phonograph, playing records for the benefit of the church mortgage fund one night. I remember my mother said she had had dinner with Nash Walker and his mother, while he was ill, and that they ate from plates with gold edging. Then Nash (George Walker, as he was known in the theater) died and there was a big funeral for him and I got my hand slapped for pointing at the flowers, because it was not polite for a child to point.

When I went to live with Auntie Reed, whose house was near the depot, I used to walk down to the Santa Fe station and stare at the railroad tracks, because the railroad tracks ran to Chicago, and Chicago was the biggest town in the world to me, much talked of by the people in Kansas. I was glad when my mother sent for me to come to Lincoln, Illinois, where she was then living, not far from Chicago. I was going on fourteen. And the papers said the Great War had begun in Europe.

My mother had married again. She had married a chef cook named Homer Clark. But like so many cooks, as he got older he couldn't stand the heat of the kitchen, so he went to work at other things. Odd jobs, the steel mills, the coal mines. By now I had a little brother. I liked my step-father a great deal, and my baby brother, also; for

I had been very lonesome growing up all by myself, the only child, with no father and no mother around.

But ever so often, my step-father would leave my mother and go away looking for a better job. The day I graduated from grammar school in Lincoln, Illinois, he had left my mother, and was not there to see me graduate.

I was the Class Poet. It happened like this. They had elected all the class officers, but there was no one in our class who looked like a poet, or had ever written a poem. There were two Negro children in the class, myself and a girl. In America most white people think, of course, that *all* Negroes can sing and dance, and have a sense of rhythm. So my classmates, knowing that a poem had to have rhythm, elected me unanimously—thinking, no doubt, that I had some, being a Negro.

The day I was elected, I went home and wondered what I should write. Since we had eight teachers in our school, I thought there should be one verse for each teacher, with an especially good one for my favorite teacher, Miss Ethel Welsh. And since the teachers were to have eight verses, I felt the class should have eight, too. So my first poem was about the longest poem I ever wrote—sixteen verses, which were later cut down. In the first half of the poem, I said that our school had the finest teachers there ever were. And in the latter half, I said our class was the greatest class ever graduated. So at graduation, when I read the poem, naturally everybody applauded loudly.

That was the way I began to write poetry.

It had never occurred to me to be a poet before, or indeed a writer of any kind. But my mother had often read papers at the Inter-State Literary Society, founded by my grandfather in Kansas. And occasionally she wrote original poems, too, that she gave at the Inter-State. But more often, she recited long recitations like "Lasca" and "The Mother of the Gracchi," in costume. As Lasca she dressed as a cowgirl. And as Cornelia, the mother of the Gracchi, she wore a sheet like a Roman matron.

On one such occasion, she had me and another little boy dressed in half-sheets as her sons—jewels, about to be torn away from her by a cruel Spartan fate. My mother was the star of the program and the church in Lawrence was crowded. The audience hung on her words; but I did not like the poem at all, so in the very middle of it I began to roll my eyes from side to side, round and round in my head, as though in great distress. The audience tittered. My mother intensified her efforts, I, my mock agony. Wilder and wilder I mugged, as the poem mounted, batted and rolled my eyes, until the entire assemblage burst into uncontrollable laughter.

My mother, poor soul, couldn't imagine what was wrong. More fervently than ever, she poured forth her lines, grasped us to her breast, and begged heaven for mercy. But the audience by then couldn't stop giggling, and with the applause at the end, she was greeted by a mighty roar of laughter. When the program was over and my mother found out what had happened, I got the worst whipping I ever had in my life. Then and there I learned to respect other people's art.

Nevertheless, the following spring, at a Children's Day program at my aunt's church, I, deliberately and with malice aforethought, forgot a poem I knew very well, having been forced against my will to learn it. I mounted the platform, said a few lines, and then stood there—much to the embarrassment of my mother, who had come all the way from Kansas City to hear me recite. My aunt tried to prompt me, but I pretended I couldn't hear a word. Finally

I came down to my seat in dead silence—and I never had to recite a poem in church again.

The only poems I liked as a child were Paul Lawrence Dunbar's. And *Hiawatha*. But I liked any kind of stories. I read all of my mother's novels from the library: *The Rosary, The Mistress of Shenstone, Freckles,* Edna Ferber, all of Harold Bell Wright, and all of Zane Grey. I thought *Riders of the Purple Sage* a wonderful book and still think so, as I remember it.

In Topeka, as a small child, my mother took me with her to the little vine-covered library on the grounds of the Capitol. There I first fell in love with librarians, and I have been in love with them ever since—those very nice women who help you find wonderful books! The silence inside the library, the big chairs, and long tables, and the fact that the library was always there and didn't seem to have a mortgage on it, or any sort of insecurity about it— all of that made me love it. And right then, even before I was six, books began to happen to me, so that after a while, there came a time when I believed in books more than in people—which, of course, was wrong. That was why, when I went to Africa, I threw all the books into the sea.

CENTRAL HIGH

I had no sooner graduated from grammar school in Lincoln than we moved from Illinois to Cleveland. My stepfather sent for us. He was working in a steel mill during the war, and making lots of money. But it was hard work, and he never looked the same afterwards. Every day he worked several hours overtime, because they paid well for overtime. But after a while, he couldn't stand the heat of the furnaces, so he got a job as caretaker of a theater building, and after that as janitor of an apartment house.

Rents were very high for colored people in Cleveland, and the Negro district was extremely crowded, because of the great migration. It was difficult to find a place to live. We always lived, during my high school years, either in an attic or a basement, and paid quite a lot for such inconvenient quarters. White people on the east side of the city were moving out of their frame houses and renting them to Negroes at double and triple the rents they could receive from others. An eight-room house with one bath would be cut up into apartments and five or six families crowded into it, each two-room kitchenette apartment renting for what the whole house had rented for before.

But Negroes were coming in in a great dark tide from the South, and they had to have some place to live. Sheds and garages and store fronts were turned into living quarters. As always, the white neighborhoods resented Negroes moving closer and closer—but when the whites did give way, they gave way at very profitable rentals. So most of the colored people's wages went for rent. The landlords and the banks made it difficult for them to buy houses, so they had to pay the exorbitant rents required. When my step-father quit the steel mill job, my mother went out to work in service to help him meet expenses. She paid a woman four dollars a week to take care of my little brother while she worked as a maid.

I went to Central High School in Cleveland. We had a magazine called the *Belfry Owl*. I wrote poems for the

Belfry Owl. We had some wise and very good teachers, Miss Roberts and Miss Weimer in English, Miss Chesnutt, who was the daughter of the famous colored writer, Charles W. Chesnutt, and Mr. Hitchcock, who taught geometry with humor, and Mr. Ozanne, who spread the whole world before us in his history classes. Also Clara Dieke, who painted beautiful pictures and who taught us a great deal about many things that are useful to know—about law and order in art and life, and about sticking to a thing until it is done.

Ethel Weimer discovered Carl Sandburg for me. Although I had read of Carl Sandburg before—in an article, I think, in the *Kansas City Star* about how bad free verse was—I didn't really know him until Miss Weimer in second-year English brought him, as well as Amy Lowell, Vachel Lindsay, and Edgar Lee Masters, to us. Then I began to try to write like Carl Sandburg.

Little Negro dialect poems like Paul Lawrence Dunbar's and poems without rhyme like Sandburg's were the first real poems I tried to write. I wrote about love, about the steel mills where my step-father worked, the slums where we lived, and the brown girls from the South, prancing up and down Central Avenue on a spring day.

One of the first of my high school poems went like this:

> *Just because I loves you—*
> *That's de reason why*
> *My soul is full of color*
> *Like de wings of a butterfly.*

> *Just because I loves you*
> *That's de reason why*
> *My heart's a fluttering aspen leaf*
> *When you pass by.*

I was fourteen then. And another of the poems was this about the mills:

> *The mills*
> *That grind and grind,*
> *That grind out steel*
> *And grind away the lives*
> *Of men—*
> *In the sunset their stacks*
> *Are great black silhouettes*
> *Against the sky.*
> *In the dawn*
> *They belch red fire.*
> *The mills—*
> *Grinding new steel,*
> *Old men.*

And about Carl Sandburg, my guiding star, I wrote:

> *Carl Sandburg's poems*
> *Fall on the white pages of his books*
> *Like blood-clots of song*
> *From the wounds of humanity.*
> *I know a lover of life sings*
> *When Carl Sandburg sings.*
> *I know a lover of all the living*
> *Sings then.*

Central was the high school of students of foreign-born parents—until the Negroes came. It is an old high school with many famous graduates. It used to be long ago the high school of the aristocrats, until the aristocrats moved farther out. Then poor whites and foreign-born took over the district. Then during the war, the Negroes came. Now

Central is almost entirely a Negro school in the heart of Cleveland's vast Negro quarter.

When I was there, it was very nearly entirely a foreign-born school, with a few native white and colored American students mixed in. By foreign, I mean children of foreign-born parents. Although some of the students themselves had been born in Poland or Russia, Hungary or Italy. And most were Catholic or Jewish.

Although we got on very well, whenever class elections would come up, there was a distinct Jewish-Gentile division among my classmates. That was perhaps why I held many class and club offices in high school, because often when there was a religious deadlock, a Negro student would win the election. They would compromise on a Negro, feeling, I suppose, that a Negro was neither Jew nor Gentile!

I wore a sweater covered with club pins most of the time. I was on the track team, and for two seasons, my relay team won the city-wide championships. I was a lieutenant in the military training corps. Once or twice I was on the monthly honor roll for scholarship. And when we were graduated, Class of '20, I edited the Year Book.

My best pal in high school was a Polish boy named Sartur Andrzejewski. His parents lived in the steel mill district. His mother cooked wonderful cabbage in sweetened vinegar. His rosy-cheeked sisters were named Regina and Sabina. And the whole family had about them a quaint and kindly foreign air, bubbling with hospitality. They were devout Catholics, who lived well and were very jolly.

I had lots of Jewish friends, too, boys named Nathan and Sidney and Herman, and girls named Sonya and Bess and Leah. I went to my first symphony concert with a Jewish girl—for these children of foreign-born parents were more democratic than native white Americans, and less anti-Negro. They lent me *The Gadfly* and *Jean-Christophe* to read, and copies of the *Liberator* and the *Socialist Call.* They were almost all interested in more than basketball and the glee club. They took me to hear Eugene Debs. And when the Russian Revolution broke out, our school almost held a celebration.

Since it was during the war, and Americanism was being stressed, many of our students, including myself, were then called down to the principal's office and questioned about our belief in Americanism. Police went to some of the parents' homes and took all their books away. After that, the principal organized an Americanism Club in our school, and, I reckon, because of the customary split between Jews and Gentiles, I was elected president. But the club didn't last long, because we were never quite clear about what we were supposed to do. Or why. Except that none of us wanted Eugene Debs locked up. But the principal didn't seem to feel that Debs fell within the scope of our club. So the faculty let the club die.

Four years at Central High School taught me many invaluable things. From Miss Dieke, who instructed in painting and lettering and ceramics, I learnt that the only way to get a thing done is to start to do it, then keep on doing it, and finally you'll finish it, even if in the beginning you think you can't do it at all. From Miss Weimer I learnt that there are ways of saying or doing things, which may not be the currently approved ways, yet that can be very true and beautiful ways, that people will come to recognize as such in due time. In 1916, the critics said Carl Sandburg was no good as a poet, and free verse was no good. Nobody says that today—yet 1916 is not a lifetime ago.

From the students I learnt that Europe was not so far away, and that when Lenin took power in Russia, something happened in the slums of Woodlawn Avenue that the teachers couldn't tell us about, and that our principal didn't want us to know. From the students I learnt, too, that lots of painful words can be flung at people that aren't *nigger*. *Kike* was one; *spick*, and *hunky*, others.

But I soon realized that the kikes and the spicks and the hunkies—scorned though they might be by the pure Americans—all had it on the niggers in one thing. Summer time came and they could get jobs quickly. For even during the war, when help was badly needed, lots of employers would *not* hire Negroes. A colored boy had to search and search for a job.

My first summer vacation from high school, I ran a dumb-waiter at Halle's, a big department store. The dumb-waiter carried stock from the stock room to the various departments of the store. I was continually amazed at trays of perfume that cost fifty dollars a bottle, ladies' lace collars at twenty-five, and useless little gadgets like gold cigarette lighters that were worth more than six months' rent on the house where we lived. Yet some people could afford to buy such things without a thought. And did buy them.

The second summer vacation I went to join my mother in Chicago. Dad and my mother were separated again, and she was working as cook for a lady who owned a millinery shop in the Loop, a very fashionable shop where society leaders came by appointment and hats were designed to order. I became a delivery boy for that shop.

It was a terrifically hot summer, and we lived on the crowded Chicago South Side in a house next to the elevated. The thunder of the trains kept us awake at night. We could afford only one small room for my mother, my little brother, and me.

South State Street was in its glory then, a teeming Negro street with crowded theaters, restaurants, and cabarets. And excitement from noon to noon. Midnight was like day. The street was full of workers and gamblers, prostitutes and pimps, church folks and sinners. The tenements on either side were very congested. For neither love nor money could you find a decent place to live. Profiteers, thugs, and gangsters were coming into their own. The first Sunday I was in town, I went out walking alone to see what the city looked like. I wandered too far outside the Negro district, over beyond Wentworth, and was set upon and beaten by a group of white boys, who said they didn't allow niggers in that neighborhood. I came home with both eyes blacked and a swollen jaw. That was the summer before the Chicago riots.

I managed to save a little money, so I went back to high school in Cleveland, leaving my mother in Chicago. I couldn't afford to eat in a restaurant, and the only thing I knew how to cook myself in the kitchen of the house where I roomed was rice, which I boiled to a paste. Rice and hot dogs, rice and hot dogs, every night for dinner. Then I read myself to sleep.

I was reading Schopenhauer and Nietzsche, and Edna Ferber and Dreiser, and de Maupassant in French. I never will forget the thrill of first understanding the French of de Maupassant. The soft snow was falling through one of his stories in the little book we used in school, and that I had worked over so long, before I really felt the snow falling there. Then all of a sudden one night the beauty and the meaning of the words in which he made the snow fall, came to me. I think it was de Maupassant who made me really want to be a writer and write stories about Negroes, so true that people in far-away lands would read them—even after I was dead.

But I did not dare write stories yet, although poems came to me now spontaneously, from somewhere inside. But there were no stories in my mind. I put the poems down quickly on anything I had at hand when they came into my head, and later I copied them in a notebook. But I began to be afraid to show my poems to anybody, because they had become very serious and very much a part of me. And I was afraid other people might not like them or understand them.

However, I sent some away to a big magazine in New York, where nobody knew me. And the big magazine sent them right back with a printed rejection slip. Then I sent them to one magazine after another—and they always came back promptly. But once Floyd Dell wrote an encouraging word across one of the rejection slips from the *Liberator*.

ABRUPT ENCOUNTER

Eleven years had gone by and I had not seen my father. Suddenly, one day in the spring of 1919, a letter came from Mexico saying:

My Dear Langston:

I am going to New York for a few days on a business trip in June. On the way back I will send you a wire to be ready to meet me as the train comes through Cleveland. You are to accompany me to Mexico for the summer.

Affectionately,

your father,
James N. Hughes.

This letter made my mother very angry. She said it was just like my devilish, evil father—when I got big enough to work and help her earn a living, he wanted to come and take me off to Mexico. Then she began to cry. She said after all she had done for me, if I wanted to go away and leave her, to go ahead, go ahead!

I said I wanted to go to Mexico for the summer to see what the country was like—and my father. Then I would be back in the fall.

My mother was a waitress in a restaurant on Central Avenue, and she and my step-father were back together. My mother wouldn't be alone if I went to Mexico, so I began to get ready to go. My step-father thought it would be a good thing and said: "Sure, go on."

That spring I had got my track letter for the high-jump and the 440-relays, but I didn't have the money to buy a new sweater, so I packed the track letter away in my suitcase to show to my father.

James N. Hughes, my father! I vaguely remembered him carrying me in his arms the night of the big earthquake in Mexico City, when I was six years old. Since then he had always been in Mexico and I had been in the States growing up while my grandmother died and the house went to the mortgage man, my mother traveled about the country looking for my step-father or for a better job, always moving from one house to another, where the rent was cheaper or there was at least a bath-room or a backyard to hang out clothes. And me growing up living with my grandmother, with aunts who were really no relation, with my mother in rented rooms, or alone trying to get through high school—always some kind of crisis in our lives. My father, permanently in Mexico during all those turbulent years, represented for me the one stable factor in my life. He at least stayed put.

"Your father is a devil on wheels," my mother said. "As mean and evil a Negro as ever lived!"

And when I displeased her, she declared I was just like my father.

I didn't believe her. In my mind I pictured my father as a kind of strong, bronze cowboy, in a big Mexican hat, going back and forth from his business in the city to his ranch in the mountains, free—in a land where there were no white folks to draw the color line, and no tenements with rent always due—just mountains and sun and cacti: Mexico!

That spring, I was anxious to see my father.

Then an unfortunate thing happened in Cleveland. We moved on the first of June. But I left word with the landlady, that, should any messages come for me, she should send them directly to the new place where we lived. And every morning, to make sure, I went out to our old lodgings to see if there was any word from my father, now in New York.

But his telegram came late one afternoon, when our former landlady was not at home, so the delivery boy simply stuck it in the mail box, and the woman did not notice it there until the next morning.

The telegram said: "PASSING THROUGH TEN-FIFTY TONIGHT

BE READY BOARD TRAIN AT STATION JAMES N. HUGHES"

That was the night before! The landlady found the wire, when I went out there the following morning. My heart stopped beating. Had my father gone on to Mexico without me, when he did not find me on the station platform? There was no further message from him. Had he, maybe, got off the train and stayed the night in Cleveland? Then where would he be?

I went to the telephone and called up the various colored hotels. The second one I called said, yes, there was a James Hughes stopping there, but that he had gone out to breakfast. I told them to tell him when he came back that his son would be right down.

The hotel was on Central Avenue, a block and a half from the restaurant where my mother worked as a waitress. I began to walk down Central Avenue as fast as I could. When I was about three blocks above the hotel, I saw a little, bronze man with a moustache, coming rapidly up the street toward me. We looked closely at each other as we passed. Then we turned and looked back.

The man said: "Are you Langston?"

I said: "Yes. Are you my father?"

"Why weren't you at the train last night?" he asked.

"We moved, and I didn't get your wire till this morning."

"Just like niggers," he spat out. "Always moving! Are you ready to go?"

"Soon as I tell my mother good-bye."

"I just saw your mother," he said, "waiting table in a restaurant. If she'd stayed with me, she'd have been wearing diamonds."

I didn't know what to say about that, so I just stood there.

"I'm going to a barber shop," my father said. "Meet me at the hotel in half an hour. We'll leave on the noon train."

He turned and went up the street. He never said a word about being glad to see me.

That morning, by accident, he had been for breakfast to the very restaurant where my mother was working. When they recognized each other, he said: "How are you?"

All my mother said was: "What's your order?"

She served him ham and eggs and he left her a dime tip. She told the woman who ran the restaurant to throw the dime in the street.

When I came in, my mother was very angry as she told me this. "But go on if you want to! Go on! Go to Mexico if you want to go."

"Gee, ma! Don't be mad at me," I said. "I didn't pick him out for a father."

"Go with him!" she cried over the counter. "Go on— and leave me! Go ahead!"

"I might as well go," I said. "I haven't got any job in Cleveland."

"Sure, go on!" she said. "Hard as I've worked and as little as you care about me!"

By now, some customers came in and my mother had to wait on them. I sat on a stool at the counter a long time, but she kept walking by me silently to the coffee urns, the steam table, or to the kitchen. I wanted her to say something to me. But finally it was time to go. So I went.

FATHER
~~~~~~~~~~~~~~~~~~~

That summer in Mexico was the most miserable I have ever known. I did not hear from my mother for several weeks. I did not like my father. And I did not know what to do about either of them.

My father was what the Mexicans called *muy americano,* a typical American. He was different from anybody I had ever known. He was interested only in making money.

My mother and step-father were interested in making money, too, so they were always moving about from job to job and from town to town, wherever they heard times were better. But they were interested in making money to *spend.* And for fun. They were always buying victrolas and radios and watches and rings, and going to shows and drinking beer and playing cards, and trying to have a good time after working hours.

But my father was interested in making money to *keep.*

Because it is very hard for a Negro to make money in the United States, since so many jobs are denied him, so many unions and professional associations are barred to him, so many banks will not advance him loans, and so many insurance companies will not insure his business, my father went to Cuba and Mexico, where he could make money quicker. He had had legal training in the South, but could not be admitted to the bar there. In Mexico he was admitted to the bar and practised law. He acquired property in Mexico City and a big ranch in the hills. He lent money and foreclosed on mortgages.

During the revolutions, when all the white Americans

had to flee from the Toluca district of Mexico, because
of the rising nationalism, my father became the general
manager of an electric light company belonging to an
American firm in New York. Because he was brown, the
Mexicans could not tell at sight that he was a Yankee,
and even after they knew it, they did not believe he was
like the white Yankees. So the followers of Zapata and
Villa did not run him away as they did the whites. In
fact, in Toluca, the Mexicans always called my father
el americano, and not the less polite *el gringo,* which is a
term that carries with it distrust and hatred.

But my father was certainly just like the other German
and English and American business men with whom he as-
sociated in Mexico. He spoke just as badly about the
Mexicans. He said they were ignorant and backward and
lazy. He said they were exactly like the Negroes in the
United States, perhaps worse. And he said they were very
bad at making money.

My father hated Negroes. I think he hated himself, too,
for being a Negro. He disliked all of his family because
they were Negroes and remained in the United States,
where none of them had a chance to be much of anything
but servants—like my mother, who started out with a good
education at the University of Kansas, he said, but had
sunk to working in a restaurant, waiting on niggers, when
she wasn't in some white woman's kitchen. My father said
he wanted me to leave the United States as soon as I finished high school, and never return—unless I wanted to be
a porter or a red cap all my life.

The second day out from Cleveland, the train we were
on rolled across Arkansas. As we passed through a dismal
village in the cotton fields, my father peered from the
window of our Pullman at a cluster of black peons on the

main street, and said contemptuously: "Look at the niggers."

When we crossed into Mexico at Laredo, and started south over the sun-baked plains, he pointed out to me a cluster of brown peons watching the train slow down at an adobe station. He said: "Look at the Mexicans!"

My father had a great contempt for all poor people. He thought it was their own fault that they were poor.

In Mexico City we went to the Grand Hotel. Then my father took me to call on three charming middle-aged Mexican ladies who were his friends—three unmarried sisters, one of whom took care of his rents in the city. They were very Latin and very Catholic, lived in a house with a charming courtyard, and served the most marvelous dishes at table—roast duck stuffed with pears and turkey with *mole* sauce, a sauce that takes several days to prepare, so complex is its making. And always there were a pile of steaming-hot tortillas, wrapped in a napkin, at one corner of the table.

In their youth, they were very lovely ladies to look at, I vaguely remembered from my trip there as a child. And they still wore their shawls of black lace with dignity and grace. They were all three the color of parchment, a soft, ivory-yellow—the blood of Spain overcast just a little by the blood of Mexico—for they were not Indians. And they were not revolutionists. They had adored the former dictator-president, Porfirio Diaz, and when they wanted to speak of some one as uncouth, they said: *"Muy indio."* Very Indian!

These three aging ladies were, I think, the only people in the whole world who really ever liked my father. Perhaps that was because his property helped to provide them with an income. And perhaps also because they shared many of his aristocratic ideas regarding the peons.

Their only worry about my father concerned his soul. He was not Catholic and never went to mass. The first thing they gave me as a present was a little amulet of the Virgin of Guadalupe. But my father laughed when we got back to the hotel and said he hoped I did not believe in that foolishness. He said greasers and niggers would never get anywhere because they were too religious, always praying.

The following morning, we left for Toluca. I wanted to see my father's tenement houses in Mexico City, but he said I could see them some other time. He was anxious to get back to the plant in Toluca.

Off the big trunk line between the capital and the border, railroad travel in Mexico then was slow and uncomfortable. Many of the coaches had been burned or bullet-ridden in the revolts, so the trains were very crowded. They had a parlor car coach between Mexico City and Toluca, in which one could reserve a seat, but my father was too frugal with money to use this service. So we rode in a crowded second-class coach, with people standing in the aisles, and all over one's feet, and bundles and baskets hanging from everywhere. My father said: "Be careful of pickpockets and thieves. Mexicans steal."

The train wound up and up into the mountains, and finally came down into one of the most beautiful valleys in the world, all lush, green fields and lakes, where water lilies floated, with a snow-capped volcano in the distance, La Nevada de Toluca. We were in the highest inhabitable valley in Mexico. The air was very cool and sweet and the sky a brilliant blue.

We reached Toluca in time for luncheon. My father's *mozo* met us at the station. He was an Indian boy named

Maximiliano, with a broad, brown face and black hair that fell into his eyes. He wore the common white trousers and shirt you see all over Mexico, and *huaraches* on his feet. He put all our baggage on his back and secured it in a sort of leather thong about his neck, and trotted on ahead of us toward the house.

My father's house faced a small park near the station. It was a low, blue-white house of one story, all spread out and surrounded by a blue-white wall. As you approached the house, you could see only high adobe walls, rimmed with dull red tile at the top. At one end of the wall, there was a big double door for the horses. At the other end, a small door that led into the patio and the house.

The patio would have been nice, had my father bothered to keep the grass and flowers tended. But he took much better care of the corral at the back of the house, where the horses and chickens were, and the cow.

He had recently foreclosed on the cow. But some shrewd Mexicans must have got the best of him that time, because the cow was ill. She had something hard in her udders; she gave bitter milk, and finally stopped giving milk altogether, as her udders began to petrify. A few weeks after I arrived, she was dead.

But there were two beautiful horses in the corral, and about a hundred large, healthy American chickens, not at all like the scrawny Mexican chickens other people had. My father said he could trade a pair of his chickens any day for a calf or a sheep, and it was true.

My father's housekeeper was a tall Mexican woman with a kind tan-brown face, and two children approaching their teens, whom my father would not permit to eat at our house. But she used to take food home to them at night. My father lived on a rather meagre diet of beef and beans.

But the cook and I soon teamed up against him, and when he was away at the ranch, we would order all kinds of good things to eat from the shops where he traded, and put them on his bill. I would take the blame. My father stormed and said I was just like my mother, always wasting money. So he would usually make a scene whenever he came home from the country, sending the cook flying from the kitchen in tears. But, nevertheless, he would always eat whatever good things were set before him.

Maximiliano, the *mozo,* took care of the horses and the chickens, swept the patio and the corral, and saddled the horses for me or my father. He was a silent boy who spoke but little Spanish, his being an Indian language from the hills. He slept on a pile of sacks in the tool shed, so I asked my father why he didn't give Maximiliano a bed, since there were several old beds around.

He said: "Never give an Indian anything. He doesn't appreciate it."

But he was wrong about that. I gave Maximiliano my spare centavos and cigarettes, and we became very good friends. He taught me to ride a horse without saddle or stirrups, how to tell a badly woven serape from a good one, and various other things that are useful to know in that high valley beneath the white volcanos.

My father paid Maximiliano and the cook almost nothing, but he gave me ten pesos a week allowance, which I used to share with the two servants. There was nothing much to spend money for in Toluca. At least, not knowing any one and not yet being able to speak Spanish, I found nothing to spend money for, except the movies once a week, on Sundays.

The weekly movie show was a galà occasion for the whole town. Society and its pretty daughters attended and sat in the horseshoe of circular boxes, running from one side of the stage to the other around the ancient auditorium. The young blades and unmarried males of the better families sat in the orchestra proper, and between each reel of bad Hollywood movies, or arty German ones, practically all the males would rise and sweep the circle of boxes with their eyes until they found the girl each liked. Then they would stare at her until the house went dark again. The shows commenced at four o'clock and lasted an ungodly long time, because they had only one projector and had to show each picture reel by reel. When the sun went down, it got very cold in Toluca, and the old theater had no heat, but you gathered your coat about you and stuck it out until the last cowboy had killed the last redskin and smothered the heroine in a kiss. Then you came home through the badly lighted streets, where the meek Indian policemen, huddled in blankets to the eyebrows, slept leaning against adobe corners, a lantern on the ground at their feet.

I began to get very tired of Toluca. My father did not take me to the ranch with him, because he said the roads were infested with bandits, and I could not yet ride well enough. Instead of letting me go about with him to the country or to Mexico City, he put me to learning bookkeeping. I was never very good at figures, and I got hopelessly tangled up in the problems he gave me. My stupidity disgusted him immeasurably, and he would rail at me about the need of acquiring a good business head. "Seventeen and you can't add yet!" he'd cry. Then he would bend over the ledger and show me all over again how to balance the spoiled page, and say: "Now, hurry up and do it! Hurry up! Hurry up!"

"Hurry up!" was his favorite expression, in Spanish or

in English. He was always telling the employees under him at the electric light company, the cook at home, or Maximiliano, or me, to hurry up, hurry up and do whatever we were doing—so that we could get through and do something else he always had ready to be done.

Hurry up! My father had tremendous energy. He always walked fast and rode hard. He was small and tough, like a jockey. He got up at five in the morning and worked at his accounts or his mail or his law books until time to go to the office. Then until ten or eleven o'clock at night he would be busy at various tasks, stopping only to eat. Then, on the days he made the long trek to the ranch, he rose at three-thirty or four, in order to get out there early and see what his workers were doing. Every one else worked too slowly for him, so it was always, "Hurry up!"

As the weeks went by, I could think of less and less to say to my father. His whole way of living was so different from mine, his attitude toward life and people so amazing, that I fell silent and couldn't open my mouth when he was in the house. Not even when he barked: "Hurry up!"

I hadn't heard from my mother, even by July. I knew she was angry with me because I had gone to Mexico. I understood then, though, why she had been unable to live with my father, and I didn't blame her. But why had she married him in the first place, I wondered. And why had they had me? Now, at seventeen, I began to be very sorry for myself, in a strange land in a mountain town, where there wasn't a person who spoke English. It was very cold at night and quiet, and I had no money to get away, and I was lonesome. I began to wish I had never been born— not under such circumstances.

I took long rides on a black horse named Tito to little villages of adobe huts, nestled in green fields of corn and alfalfa, little villages, each with a big church with a beautiful tower built a hundred years ago, a white Spanish tower with great bells swinging in the turret.

I began to learn to read Spanish. I struggled with bookkeeping. I took one of the old pistols from my father's desk and fired away in the afternoon at a target Maximiliano had put up in the corral. But most of the time I was depressed and unhappy and bored. One day, when there was no one in the house but me, I put the pistol to my head and held it there, loaded, a long time, and wondered if I would be any happier if I were to pull the trigger. But then, I began to think, if I do, I might miss something. I haven't been to the ranch yet, nor to the top of the volcano, nor to the bullfights in Mexico, nor graduated from high school, nor got married. So I put the pistol down and went back to my bookkeeping.

My father was very seldom at home, but when he was, he must have noticed my silence and my gloomy face, because if I looked the way I felt, I looked woebegone, indeed. One day in August, he told me he was going to Mexico City for a week, and would take me with him for the trip. He said I could see the summer bullfights and Xochimilco. The trip was ten days off, but I began to dream about it, and to press my clothes and get ready.

It seemed that my father couldn't resist saying, "Hurry up," more and more during those ten days, and giving me harder and harder bookkeeping problems to have worked out by the time he got home from the office. Besides, he was teaching me to typewrite, and gave me several exercises to master each evening. "Hurry up and type that a hundred times before you go to bed. Hurry up and get that page of figures done so I can check on it. Hurry up and learn the verb, *estar*."

Hurry up . . . hurry up . . . hurry up . . . hurry up, began to ring in my ears like an obsession.

The morning came for us to go to Mexico City. The train left at seven, but unless you reserved parlor-car seats, you had to be in line at the station before dawn to be sure of getting on the train, for the coaches were crowded to capacity. My father did not wish to spend the extra money for parlor-car seats, so he woke me up at four-thirty. It was still dark.

"Hurry up and get dressed," he said through the dark.

At that hour of the morning it is bitter cold in Toluca's high mountain valley. From the well Maximiliano brought us water for washing that was like ice. The cook began to prepare breakfast. We sat down to eat. At the table my father gulped his food quickly, looked across at me, and barked for no reason at all: "Hurry up!"

Suddenly my stomach began to turn over and over. And I could not swallow another mouthful. Waves of heat engulfed me. My eyes burned. My body shook. I wanted more than anything on earth to hit my father, but instead I got up from the table and went back to bed. The bed went round and round and the room turned dark. Anger clotted in every vein, and my tongue tasted like dry blood.

My father stuck his head in the bedroom door and asked me what was the matter.

I said: "Nothing."

He said: "Don't you want to go to Mexico City?"

I said: "No, I don't want to go."

I don't know what else he said, but after a while I heard him telling Maximiliano in Spanish to hurry up with his bags. Then the outside door closed, and he was gone to the train.

The housekeeper came in and asked me what I wanted.

I said: "Nothing."

Maximiliano came back from the station and sat down silently on the tile floor just inside my door, his blanket about him. At noon the cook brought me a big bowl of warm soup, but I couldn't drink it. My stomach kept turning round and round inside me. And when I thought of my father, I got sicker and sicker. I hated my father.

They sent for the doctor. He came and gave me a prescription. The housekeeper took it herself and had it filled, not trusting the *mozo*. But when my father came back after four days in the city, I still hadn't eaten anything. I had a high fever. He sent for the doctor again, and the doctor said I'd better go to the hospital.

This time my father engaged seats in the parlor car and took me to the American Hospital in Mexico City. There, after numberless examinations, they decided I had better remain several weeks, since they thought I had a stomach infection.

The three middle-aged Mexican sisters came to see me and brought a gift of guava jelly. They asked what on earth could have happened to make me so ill. I must have had a great shock, they said, because my eyes were a deep yellow. But I never told them or the doctors that I was sick because I hated my father.

For two or three weeks I got pushed around in a wheel chair in the charming gardens of the American Hospital. When I learned that it was costing my father twenty dollars a day to keep me there, I made no effort to get better. It pleased me immensely to have him spending twenty dollars a day. In September, I went back to Cleveland without having seen Xochimilco, or a bullfight.

BACK HOME

On the way back to Cleveland an amusing thing happened. During the trip to the border, several American whites on the train mistook me for a Mexican, and some of them even spoke to me in Spanish, since I am of a copper-brown complexion, with black hair that can be made quite slick and shiny if it has enough pomade on it in the Mexican fashion. But I made no pretense of passing for a Mexican, or anything else, since there was no need for it—except in changing trains at San Antonio in Texas, where colored people had to use Jim Crow waiting rooms, and could not purchase a Pullman berth. There, I simply went in the main waiting room, as any Mexican would do, and made my sleeping-car reservations in Spanish.

But that evening, crossing Texas, I was sitting alone at a small table in the diner, when a white man came in and took the seat just across the table from mine. Shortly, I noticed him staring at me intently, as if trying to puzzle out something. He stared at me a long time. Then, suddenly, with a loud cry, the white man jumped up and shouted: "You're a nigger, ain't you?" And rushed out of the car as if pursued by a plague.

I grinned. I had heard before that white Southerners never sat down to table with a Negro, but I didn't know until then that we frightened them that badly.

Something rather less amusing happened at St. Louis. The train pulled into the station on a blazing-hot September afternoon, after a sticky, dusty trip, for there were no air-cooled coaches in those days. I had a short wait between trains. In the center of the station platform there was a news stand and soda fountain where cool drinks were being served. I went up to the counter and asked for an ice cream soda.

The clerk said: "Are you a Mexican or a Negro?"

I said: "Why?"

"Because if you're a Mexican, I'll serve you," he said. "If you're colored, I won't."

"I'm colored," I replied. The clerk turned to wait on some one else. I knew I was home in the U.S.A.

I'VE KNOWN RIVERS

That November the First World War ended. In Cleveland, everybody poured into the streets to celebrate the Armistice. Negroes, too, although Negroes were increasingly beginning to wonder where, for them, was that democracy they had fought to preserve. In Cleveland, a liberal city, the color line began to be drawn tighter and tighter. Theaters and restaurants in the downtown area began to refuse to accommodate colored people. Landlords doubled and tripled the rents at the approach of a dark tenant. And when the white soldiers came back from the war, Negroes were often discharged from their jobs and white men hired in their places.

The end of the war! But many of the students at Central kept talking, not about the end of the war, but about Russia, where Lenin had taken power in the name of the workers, who made everything, and who would now own everything they made. "No more pogroms," the Jews said, "no more race hatred, no more landlords." John Reed's *Ten Days That Shook the World* shook Central High School, too.

The daily papers pictured the Bolsheviki as the greatest devils on earth, but I didn't see how they could be that bad if they had done away with race hatred and landlords —two evils that I knew well at first hand.

My father raised my allowance that year, so I was able to help my mother with the expenses of our household. It was a pleasant year for me, for I was a senior. I was elected Class Poet and Editor of our Year Book. As an officer in the drill corps, I wore a khaki uniform and leather puttees, and gave orders. I went calling on a little brownskin girl, who was as old as I was—seventeen—but only in junior high school, because she had just come up from the poor schools of the South. I met her at a dance at the Longwood Gym. She had big eyes and skin like rich chocolate. Sometimes she wore a red dress that was very becoming to her, so I wrote a poem about her that declared:

> *When Susanna Jones wears red*
> *Her face is like an ancient cameo*
> *Turned brown by the ages.*
>
> *Come with a blast of trumpets,*
> *Jesus!*
>
> *When Susanna Jones wears red*
> *A queen from some time-dead Egyptian night*
> *Walks once again.*
>
> *Blow trumpets, Jesus!*

And the beauty of Susanna Jones in red
Burns in my heart a love-fire sharp like pain.

Sweet silver trumpets,
Jesus!

I had a whole notebook full of poems by now, and another one full of verses and jingles. I always tried to keep verses and poems apart, although I saw no harm in writing verses if you felt like it, and poetry if you could.

June came. And graduation. Like most graduations, it made you feel both sorry and glad: sorry to be leaving and glad to be going. Some students were planning to enter college, but not many, because there was no money for college in most of Central's families.

My father had written me to come to Mexico again to discuss with him my future plans. He hinted that he would send me to college if I intended to go, and he thought I had better go.

I didn't want to return to Mexico, but I had a feeling I'd never get any further education if I didn't, since my mother wanted me to go to work and be, as she put it, "of some use to her." She demanded to know how I would look going off to college and she there working like a dog!

I said I thought I could be of more help to her once I got an education than I could if I went to work fresh out of high school, because nobody could do much on the salary of a porter or a bus boy. And such jobs offered no advancement for a Negro.

But about my going to join my father, my mother acted much as she had done the year before. I guess it is the old story of divorced parents who don't like each other, and take their grievances out on the offspring. I got the feeling then that I'd like to get away from home altogether, both homes, and that maybe if I went to Mexico one more time, I could go to college somewhere in some new place, and be on my own.

So I went back to Toluca.

My mother let me go to the station alone, and I felt pretty bad when I got on the train. I felt bad for the next three or four years, to tell the truth, and those were the years when I wrote most of my poetry. (For my best poems were all written when I felt the worst. When I was happy, I didn't write anything.)

The one of my poems that has perhaps been most often reprinted in anthologies, was written on the train during this trip to Mexico when I was feeling very bad. It's called "The Negro Speaks of Rivers" and was written just outside St. Louis, as the train rolled toward Texas.

It came about in this way. All day on the train I had been thinking about my father and his strange dislike of his own people. I didn't understand it, because I was a Negro, and I liked Negroes very much. One of the happiest jobs I had ever had was during my freshman year in high school, when I worked behind the soda fountain for a Mrs. Kitzmiller, who ran a refreshment parlor on Central Avenue in the heart of the colored neighborhood. People just up from the South used to come in for ice cream and sodas and watermelon. And I never tired of hearing them talk, listening to the thunderclaps of their laughter, to their troubles, to their discussions of the war and the men who had gone to Europe from the Jim Crow South, their complaints over the high rent and the long overtime hours that brought what seemed like big checks, until the weekly bills were paid. They seemed to me like the gayest and the bravest people possible—these Negroes from the Southern ghettos—facing tremendous odds, working and laughing and trying to get somewhere in the world.

I had been in to dinner early that afternoon on the train. Now it was just sunset, and we crossed the Mississippi, slowly, over a long bridge. I looked out the window of the Pullman at the great muddy river flowing down toward the heart of the South, and I began to think what that river, the old Mississippi, had meant to Negroes in the past—how to be sold down the river was the worst fate that could overtake a slave in times of bondage. Then I remembered reading how Abraham Lincoln had made a trip down the Mississippi on a raft to New Orleans, and how he had seen slavery at its worst, and had decided within himself that it should be removed from American life. Then I began to think about other rivers in our past —the Congo, and the Niger, and the Nile in Africa—and the thought came to me: "I've known rivers," and I put it down on the back of an envelope I had in my pocket, and within the space of ten or fifteen minutes, as the train gathered speed in the dusk, I had written this poem, which I called "The Negro Speaks of Rivers":

I've known rivers:
I've known rivers ancient as the world and older than the
*   flow of human blood in human veins.*

My soul has grown deep like the rivers.

I bathed in the Euphrates when dawns were young.
I built my hut near the Congo and it lulled me to sleep.
I looked upon the Nile and raised the pyramids above it.
I heard the singing of the Mississippi when Abe Lincoln
*   went down to New Orleans, and I've seen its muddy*
*   bosom turn all golden in the sunset.*

I've known rivers:
Ancient, dusky rivers.

My soul has grown deep like the rivers.

No doubt I changed a few words the next day, or maybe crossed out a line or two. But there are seldom many changes in my poems, once they're down. Generally, the first two or three lines come to me from something I'm thinking about, or looking at, or doing, and the rest of the poem (if there is to be a poem) flows from those first few lines, usually right away. If there is a chance to put the poem down then, I write it down. If not, I try to remember it until I get to a pencil and paper; for poems are like rainbows: they escape you quickly.

MEXICO AGAIN

That summer in Mexico, I wrote a great many poems, because I was very unhappy, in spite of the fact that it was a much more varied summer than the previous one. Even my father seemed kinder and less difficult. He had a new housekeeper now, a German woman named Frau Schultz, whom he later married. She helped to make the house much pleasanter.

Frau Schultz had just come from Germany, where she said people were starving. She was a widow with several children, the youngest of whom, Lotte, a child of ten, she had brought with her. She came with a big boatload of other Germans voyaging to the new world, to Cuba, Mexico, and South America, to start all over again. Her husband had been killed in the war, and when you mentioned war to her, she would say: *"Mensch!"* and spit.

She was a portly, kindly woman, with dull blue eyes and chestnut hair. Her little girl was very lively and very German-looking. What German I know I learned from Frau Schultz and Lotte, for they could speak neither English nor Spanish then, and I had to learn German to say anything at all to them. It was because my father had studied German for years, and was a great admirer of the German people, that he had employed her as his housekeeper. And Frau Schultz was happy to have work, because she had arrived in Mexico with only a few pesos, and had had to depend on the kindness of fellow-countrymen to whom she had letters.

Since Frau Schultz did not know a word of Spanish in which to give orders, she was unable to keep our Mexican cook, so she did all the cooking herself. And good it was, too, for a while—until my father felt that the butcher's bills were too high. Then for weeks at a time, we would revert to Mexican beans, except on days when he was at the ranch. Then Frau Schultz and I would often kill one of his prize American hens and she would stew the hen with dumplings and we would have a grand meal. Or else I would take the responsibility for running the grocery bills up, and would go to the store with Maximiliano and a gunny sack, and come back with all sorts of cheeses and sausages and good imported German things that Frau Schultz liked, and several cans of sardines, salmon, fruit, and American corn.

Once I came back with a delicious kind of white meat in a can with a Spanish label that neither of us could read. The meat was so good that I went back to the store and bought three or four cans more, and Frau Schultz made sandwiches of it at coffee time in the afternoons. Finally, one day it occurred to me to look up the delicacy's name in my Spanish-English dictionary. It turned out to be eel. I didn't mind, since I have no prejudice against eels. But when, in the English-German dictionary, Frau Schultz saw the frightful word in her own tongue, she almost died, declaring she'd as soon have eaten a snake! But by then we had both consumed several pounds of eel.

My father was away at the ranch a great deal of the summer. But when he was at home in town, he spoke German all the time at the table. And Spanish all the time elsewhere. So I began to learn Spanish fairly well, at least well enough to get about and meet people, and to read the novels of Blasco Ibáñez, whose *Cuentos Valencianos* I liked very much. And the terrific realism of *Caños y Barro* still sticks in my head.

I didn't do much that summer but read books, ride my horse, Tito, eat Frau Schultz's apple cake, feel lonesome, and write poems when I felt most lonesome. I began to wish for some Negro friends to pal around with. With my bad Spanish, I was still shy about making friends with the Mexicans. And I was worried about the days to come. My father hadn't yet got around to having a talk with me about college, and it was now already late July.

That summer my father was doubly busy, because the electric light company was in process of liquidation. Its main plant in the mountains had been destroyed by the revolutionists, who hated gringoes for the airs they put on, and the low wages they paid. The revolutionists had also taken off all the cattle and sheep on my father's ranch, and left it bare. The road to the ranch was infested with bandits, and since they had twice robbed my father, stopping him on the road and taking everything, from his boots to his horse, and leaving him standing in a pine forest in nothing but his underwear—since then my father never went to the ranch alone, but always with a party of other ranchers, or else German mining investors who were then making frequent trips to the silver mines in that region.

My father's ranch was most valuable for timber, he said. Now the mines were flooded, but should they ever open again, he would make thousands of dollars from his timber lands, since the mines would all have to be reshafted, and new barracks and houses built for the men.

When my father felt that I could ride rapidly enough and shoot straight enough to take care of myself in case of danger, he let me go with him to the ranch one weekend, in company with a party of German mine owners and Mexican rancheros. We started out at dawn. It was a good day's ride over rocky roads and mountain trails, through majestic scenery. The way was temporarily safe, since the Federal troops had recently been over the road and, appropriately enough, on a high pass called *Las Cruces* (the Crosses) they had hanged three bandits, and left them hanging there as examples to others. They were still there the day we passed, three poor Indian bandits with bare feet, strung from scrubby pine trees near the road, their thin dirty-white trousers flapping in the cold mountain wind. One had long black hair that lashed across his face. Their bodies swayed slowly in the high wind at the top of the pass, like puppets stiff against the sky.

That afternoon we passed through a large ruined village, destroyed, my father said, several years before by the Zapatistas. Now wild grass grew between the cobblestones of the main street, and nobody lived in the tumbled-down houses. The church stood roofless, with its tall bell-tower of carved stone lording it above the desolation of what had once been a town.

"The Zapatistas were bandits," my father said. "They loved to destroy property."

"I read somewhere that Zapata was a poor shoemaker, who wanted to get the land back for the peons," I answered.

"Lies!" my father cried. "Zapata, Villa, all of 'em dirty bandits!"

We got to the ranch at sundown. We had been delayed on the road because Tito, the horse I was riding, became enamoured of a mare belonging to the Germans. In a sudden burst of affection, Tito made a flying leap for the mare. The mare bolted, broke her bridle and threw her German rider to the ground, then dashed off down the road. It was all I could do to hold Tito, who acted like a bronco in a rodeo, as all the horses began to wheel and whinny and neigh.

Several of the men galloped off in pursuit of the mare. The rest of us went to the aid of the deposed German, who had landed in a rocky gulley, six feet below the road. He was somewhat shaken up, but when he got himself together, he seemed none the worse for his fall, except a few stone bruises, and a tear in his trousers.

We were in a wild and lonesome-looking country as the shadows grew long in the late afternoon, and the mountains hid the sun. The party began to break up, some going to the abandoned mines, others to a ranch farther on. Those who were returning to Toluca shortly agreed to meet at dawn two days later to make the trip together.

My father's ranch seemed to take in a whole mountain side and on over the rim beyond that. Little fires were glowing on his mountain, as we rode upward in the dusk toward a cluster of peasant huts, half-hidden in the foliage at the far edge of a broad, slanting field. It was cold and the peons had lighted bonfires outside their doors, and were sitting about the fires, wrapped in blankets. A withered old woman fixed us a meal of tortillas and red beans that were very good. Then we slept on the floor inside one of the mud huts.

The next day I went with my father to a flooded mine shaft nearby. The German, who had fallen off the horse the day before, was there. He and my father did a great deal of talking and figuring, while Tito and the mare champed and neighed and rolled their eyes at each other from the respective trees where they were tied, yards apart.

On the way back to the ranch, my father suddenly announced that he had made up his mind to have me study mining engineering.

"In another five or six years," he said, "these mines will be open and there will be plenty of work for you here, near the ranch."

"But I can't be a mining engineer, I'm no good at mathematics," I said, as we walked the horses.

"You can learn anything you put your mind to," my father said. "And engineering is something that will make you some money. What do you want to do, live like a nigger all your life? Look at your mother, waiting table in a restaurant! Don't you want to get anywhere?"

"Sure," I said. "But I don't want to be a mining engineer."

"What do you want to be?"

"I don't know. But I think a writer."

"A writer?" my father said. "A writer? Do they make any money?"

"Some of them do, I guess."

"I never heard of a colored one that did," said my father.

"Alexandre Dumas," I answered.

"Yes, but he was in Paris, where they don't care about color. That's what I want you to do, Langston. Learn something you can make a living from anywhere in the world, in Europe or South America, and don't stay in the States, where you have to live like a nigger with niggers."

"But I like Negroes," I said. "We have plenty of fun."

"Fun!" my father shouted. "How can you have fun with the color line staring you in the face? I never could."

We were riding in a bowl of pine trees, with the distant rim of the mountains all around and the sky very blue. For once, my father did not seem to be in a hurry. He let his horse mosey along, biting at the wayside grass. As we rode, my father outlined a plan he had made up in his mind for me, a plan that I had never dreamed of before. He wanted me to go to Switzerland to college, perhaps to Basle, or one of the cantons where one could learn three languages at once, French, German, and Italian, directly from the people. Then he wanted me to go to a German engineering school. Then come back to live in Mexico.

The thought of trigonometry, physics, and chemistry in a *foreign* language was more than I could bear. In English, they were difficult enough. But as a compromise to Switzerland and Germany, I suggested Columbia in New York—mainly because I wanted to see Harlem.

My father wouldn't hear of it. But the more I thought of it, the better I liked the idea myself. I had an overwhelming desire to see Harlem. More than Paris, or the Shakespeare country, or Berlin, or the Alps, I wanted to see Harlem, the greatest Negro city in the world. *Shuffle Along* had just burst into being, and I wanted to hear

Florence Mills sing. So I told my father I'd rather go to Columbia than to Switzerland.

My father shut up. I shut up. Our horses went on down the mountain into the blue shadows. We didn't talk much for days. At home he gave me several involved problems in bookkeeping to do and told me to stop spending so much time with the Mexicans, promenading in the Portales in the evening. But his advice went in one ear and out the other. I liked the Portales, but I didn't like bookkeeping.

PROMENADE

In Toluca, the evening promenade was an established institution for the young people of the town and, on band concert nights, for the older people, too. Toluca's business district consisted largely of three sides of a square, with a cloistered walk running around the three sides. An enormous and very old church formed the fourth side of the square. The covered walkway had tall arched portals open to the cobblestoned street, hence its name, *Los Portales*.

The leading shops were along the Portales. The post office was there as well. And the biggest hotel. And a very appetizing chocolate and sweet shop, displaying enormous layer cakes, dripping with syrupy icings and candied fruits. Once a week, the town band gave a concert in the Portales. But every evening, concert or no concert, the young people of the town, between six and seven o'clock, took their evening stroll there.

I had become acquainted with Tomas, son of a dry goods

merchant who had business dealings with my father, and
Tomas took me to walk with the other young men of the
town in the Portales, at the hour when all the girls were
out walking, too. But not walking with young men. Oh,
no! Not at all. That was unheard of in Toluca. The girls
of the better Mexican families merely strolled slowly up
and down with their mothers or married sisters, or old
aunts, or the family servant, but never unchaperoned or
alone.

The boys promenaded in groups of three or four, usually, slowing down when you passed a particular girl you
wanted to make an impression on. The girls would always
pretend not to notice any of the boys, turning their heads
away and giggling and looking in the shop windows. It
was not considered polite for a nice girl really to notice
boys, although it was all right for the boys to turn and
stare at the girls as they went by. So the boys would pause
and look and then walk on, turning at the end of the walk
to retrace their steps until they had covered the three-sided
promenade of the Portales perhaps fifteen or twenty times
an evening. Then suddenly, it would be supper time, and
the sidewalks would be deserted. The shops would begin
to pull down their zinc shutters, and everybody would go
home through the cool mountain darkness to a hot *meri-
enda* of steaming chocolate, tamales, goat's cheese, and
buns. And maybe some of the sticky and very sweet cake
you had seen in the shop window on the Portales.

In Toluca, if a boy fell in love with a girl, he could not
visit the young lady in her home until he had become
engaged to her. He could only go to call on her outside the
iron grilles of her front window, for all the houses in
Toluca had iron grilles at the windows to keep lovers and
bandits out. Within the living room, back in the shadows

somewhere, the chaperon sat, and the lovers would have
to speak very low indeed for that attentive female not to
hear every word. The boy could hold the girl's hand, and
maybe kiss her finger tips, but not very often would he be
tall enough to steal a kiss from her lips, for most of the
windows had a fairly high sill. And even if the girl sat on
the floor, it is not easy to achieve a real kiss through
grilled bars and with a vigilant chaperon in the offing.

Good girls in Toluca, as is the custom in very Catholic
and very Latin countries, were kept sheltered indeed, both
before and after marriage. They did not go into the street
alone. They did not come near a man unchaperoned.
Girls who worked, servants, typists, and waitresses, and
others who ran the streets free, were considered fair game
for any man who could make them. But good girls—between them and the world stood the tall iron bars of
la reja, those formidable grilled windows of the Latin
countries. Sometimes groups of boys in love got together
with guitars and went from house to house serenading
their sweethearts. And lots of boys wrote poems to their
girls and handed the poems, in carefully folded little notes,
through the grilles for the beloved to read at night in
her bed.

But when the mother, or the old aunt, or the family
servant decided it was time to close the shutters of *la reja,*
the suitor would move on up the street in the dusk, for
the shutters were usually closed early. Perhaps he would
go home, or perhaps he would play a game of *carambola*
in the town's one billiard hall. Or perhaps, if he could
afford it, he would go to Natcha's house. There were in
Toluca, two houses of love—one for gentlemen and army
officers, the other for laborers and common soldiers.
Natcha's house was for gentlemen and officers.

MEANS OF ESCAPE

September approached and still I had made no head-way with my father about going to college. He said Europe. I said New York. He said he wouldn't spend a penny to educate me in the United States. I asked him how long I had to stay in Mexico. He said until I decided to act wisely. Not caring what that meant, I made up my mind to see about getting away myself.

I had no money, but Tomas' father had asked me if I would teach his son English, so I accepted, receiving a modest fee. Probably because Tomas proved an apt pupil (and we pal'd around together quite a little, too), others heard of his rapid progress in speaking *at* English, and I soon found myself with more applicants for classes than I could accept. I raised my fee. When the schools opened, I was offered two positions as an English instructor—one in Señor Luis Tovar's business college, another in Señorita Padilla's private finishing school for girls. I was able to take them both, since Señorita Padilla's classes were in the mornings and Señor Tovar's in the afternoon and early evening.

I used the Berlitz method, all instruction entirely in English, and I found that it worked very well. My students really did learn something, and we had lots of fun together, besides. Very shortly, the mayor of the town sent for me and asked if I would give private lessons to his son and daughter at home.

The daughter was about sixteen and very beautiful, but the son was as bad a fifteen-year-old youngster as ever de-

cided *not* to learn a word of anything. Result, neither girl
nor boy got much beyond the words *door* and *chair* that
winter, and I don't think they cared. They were rather
spoiled, cream-colored children, who played tennis with a
doctor's family, browner and more Indian-looking—one of
the few Indian families considered "aristocracy" in Toluca, where Spanish blood still prevailed in the best circles
and the exaltation of things Indian had not yet triumphed
—for Diego Rivera was still in Paris.

As a teacher of English to the "best" families, I met a
great many interesting people and my funds for escape
grew apace. For the first time in my life, I had my own
money to spend in decent amounts, to send my mother,
and to save. All that winter I did not ask my father for a
penny. And I knew by summer I would have enough to
go to New York, so I began to plan my trip long before
the winter was over. I dreamt about Harlem.

CARD FROM CUERNAVACA

Six months anywhere is enough to begin to complicate
life. By that time, if you stay in one place, you are bound
to know people too well for things to be any longer simple.
Well, that winter one of my pupils fell in love with me.
She was a woman in her thirties, to whom I had been giving lessons two afternoons a week. She lived a secluded
life with her old aunt, no doubt on a small income. And
she had never been married because, since childhood, she
had suffered with a heart ailment. She was a very delicate

little woman, ivory-tan in color, with a great mass of heavy black hair and very bright but sad eyes. I always thought perhaps she was something like Emily Dickinson, shut away and strange, eager and lonesome, as Emily must have been.

But I had no way of knowing she was going to fall in love with me. She read and spoke a little English, but she wanted to be able to read big novels like Scott's and Dickens's. Yet she didn't pay much attention to her lessons. When I read aloud, she would look at me, until I looked at her. Then her eyes would fall. After several weeks of classes, shyly, in a funny little sentence of awkward English, she finally made me realize she must be in love.

She began to say things like: "Dear Mister, I cannot wait you to come back so long off Friday."

"But you have to learn your verbs," I'd say. "And it will take until Friday."

"The verbs is not much difficult. It's you I am think about, Mister."

She seemed almost elderly to me then, at eighteen. I was confused and didn't know what to say. After a few such sentences in English, she'd blush deeply and take refuge in Spanish. And all I could think of to tell her was that she mustn't fall in love with me, because I was going to New York as soon as I had saved the fare.

The little lady's eyes widened and her face went white when I said it. I thought for a moment she was surely going to faint. And one day she did faint, but it was not, I suppose, for love. It was while we were going over conditionals, sentences like, "I would write if I could," when she simply keeled over in her chair.

Her old aunt and the servants had told me that that might happen almost any time. Strains and excitement upset her. So after that I was never sure as to the safe thing to do when I found her looking at me. She might faint if I held her hand—or she might faint if I didn't.

But all things end in time. When I came to her house one afternoon at the class hour, I was very sorry (and ashamed at my feeling of relief) to learn that she was quite ill with a heavy cold. She remained in bed several days. I took her flowers and sat with her, surrounded by little bottles and boxes of pills. When she was better, her aunt carried her away to a lower and warmer climate to convalesce. I never saw her any more. But she wrote me a card once from Cuernavaca, and signed it just, "Maria."

BULLFIGHTS

Almost every week-end that winter, now that I was earning my own money, I went to the bullfights in Mexico City. Rudolfo Gaona was the famous Mexican matador of the day, a stocky Indian of great art and bravery. Sanchez Mejias was there from Spain that season, greatly acclaimed, as well as Juan Silveti, and a younger fighter called Juan Luis de la Rosa, who did not win much favor with the crowd. One afternoon, in the sunset, at the end of a six-bull corrida, (bulls from the Duque de Veragua) I saw de la Rosa trying to kill his final bull amidst a shower of cushions, canes, paper bags, and anything else throwable that an irate crowd could hurl at him. But he stuck it out, and finally the enormous animal slid to his knees, bleeding on the sand. But the matador was soundly hissed as he left the ring.

At the annual festival bullfight for the charities of la Cavadonga, when the belles of Mexico City, in their lace mantillas, drove about the arena in open carriages preceding the fight, and the National Band played, and the *Presidente de la Republica* was there, and Sanchez Mejias made the hair stand on your head and cold chills run down your back with the daring and beauty of his *veronicas,* after the fight there was a great rush into the ring on the part of many of the young men in the crowd, to lift the famous fighters on their shoulders or to carry off a pair of golden banderillas as a souvenir, with the warm blood still on them. I dived for the ring, too, the moment the fight was over. In leaping the *barrera,* I tore my only good trousers from knee to ankle—but I got my banderillas.

After the fights, I would usually have supper with the three charming and aging Mexican sisters, the Patiños, friends of my father's, who lived near the Zocalo, just back of the cathedral, and who always invited me to vespers. To please them, I would go to vespers, and I began to love the great, dusky, candle-lighted interiors of the vast Mexican churches, smoky with incense and filled with sad virgins and gruesome crucifixes with real thorns on the Christ-head, and what seemed to be real blood gushing forth from His side, thick and red as the blood of the bulls I had seen killed in the afternoon. In the evenings I might go to see Margarita Xirgu, or Virginia Fabregas in some bad Spanish play, over-acted and sticky like the cakes in our Toluca sweet shop.

Meanwhile, ambitiously, I began to try to write prose. I tried to write about a bullfight, but could never capture it on paper. Bullfights are very hard things to put down on paper—like trying to describe the ballet.

Bullfights must be seen in all their strength of vigorous and graceful movement and glitter of sun on sleek hides and silken suits spangled with gold and silver and on the sharp points of the banderillas and on the thin blades of the swords. Bullfights must be heard, the music barbaric and Moorish, the roar of the crowd, the grunt of the bull, the cry of the gored horse, the trumpet signalling to kill, the silence when a man is gored. They must be smelt, dust and tobacco and animals and leather, sweat and blood and the scent of death. Then the cry of glory when a great kill is made and the flutter of thousands of handkerchiefs, with roses thrown at the feet of the triumphant matador, as he is awarded the tail and ears of the bull. Or the hiss of scorn when the fighter has been cowardly or awkward.

Then the crowd pouring out into the sunset, and the fighters covered with sand and spattered with blood, gliding off to their hotels in swift, high-powered cars; the women on the street selling lottery tickets; beggars; and men giving out cards to houses of pleasure; and the police clearing a passage for the big Duesenbergs of the rich; and the naked bulls hanging beneath the arena, skinned, ready for the market.

A bullfight is like a very moving play—except that the fight is real, unrehearsed, and no two *corridas* are ever the same. Of course, the bull gets killed. But sometimes, the man dies first. It is not a game or a sport. It's life playing deliberately with death. Except that death is alive, too, taking an active part.

TRAGEDY IN TOLUCA

I could not put the bullfights down, so, wanting to write prose, I wrote instead an article about Toluca, and another about the Virgin of Guadalupe, and a little play for children called, *The Gold Piece*. I sent them to the *Brownie's Book*, a magazine for Negro children, just begun in New York by Dr. DuBois and the *Crisis* staff. These pieces of mine were accepted, and encouraging letters came back from Jessie Fauset, who was managing editor there. So I sent her my poem written on the train, "The Negro Speaks of Rivers." And in June, 1921, it appeared in the *Crisis*, the first of my poems to be published outside Central High School.

My father reacted to my published work with two questions: "How long did it take you to write that?" And next: "Did they pay you anything?"

Neither the *Crisis* nor the *Brownie's Book* paid anything, but I was delighted to be published. For the next few years my poems appeared often (and solely) in the *Crisis*. And to that magazine, certainly, I owe my literary beginnings—insofar as publication is concerned.

Finally my father gave in and said, yes, he would send me to Columbia. So I wrote for registration and dormitory space. I was admitted, and planned to leave for New York late in the summer. But that spring the block which our house occupied, facing the little park, was the scene of several weird and depressing happenings. I began to wish I had gone away sooner.

It began with my seeing an Indian at our corner get both his legs cut off by the bouncing little street car (on a Ford chassis) that wound from the center of the town to the station. Shortly after that, one early morning, I opened the big doors in the wall of the corral to let my father through, bound for the ranch. His horse dashed out, but suddenly balked for no reason in the middle of the road and threw him head-over-heels in the dust. My father got up, rubbed his head, grabbed the horse, and went on to the ranch. But Maximiliano declared the horse had seen the poor Indian's ghost walking through our park in the sunrise, with no legs.

A week or two later, one Sunday morning, leaving the house early to catch the seven o'clock train for Mexico City, I noticed a small crowd of Indians in their serapes, standing around the shallow basin of the fountain in the center of the park. As I passed, I looked down and there in scarcely three feet of water, lay the body of a young woman, curled about the base of the fountain. She was nicely dressed, and obviously of a decent family. The police found a suicide note. She was one of the good girls whose grilled *rejas* had not protected her from the step that in Mexico brings ruin and disgrace. But *what* will power it must have taken—to drown one's self in a shallow fountain of water hardly as deep as your knees!

In Mexico City, I told the three kind maiden ladies of the strange happenings on our plaza in Toluca, and they looked distressed and worried. They said they would pray that nothing happened to my father or me. And they begged me to go to mass with them. Perhaps their prayers worked. For, although tragedy soon descended in a most unexpected manner upon our house itself, neither my father nor I was home when that strange explosion of passion and of violence took place.

Our German housekeeper, Frau Schultz, had an old

friend from Berlin in Mexico City, whose husband was not well and whose income was therefore reduced. This friend had several children, the oldest, a daughter of seventeen or eighteen in need of work.

That winter in Toluca, the wife of the German brewery-master died, and so he began looking about for a house-keeper. The brewery-master was sixty-five years old, and merely wanted someone to manage his Mexican servants and see that he got something to eat, German-style, once in a while. Frau Schultz immediately thought of her friend's daughter for the job. Although a young girl, she was nevertheless sober and industrious in her habits, and a very good cook, to boot.

She sent for the girl. Her name was Gerta Kraus. She was a very plain girl, awkward, shy and silent, with stringy ashen hair and a long face. She spoke no Spanish beyond *Buenos Dias,* so that was all we ever said to each other as long as I knew her. The old German gave her the job as his housekeeper. And as the winter went on, Frau Schultz reported that the girl was doing very well, that she kept the brewery-master's home spotless, and sent her wages to her parents in Mexico City.

Perhaps twice a week, Gerta would come down to our house and spend a few hours in the afternoon with Frau Schultz. Occasionally, I would come home from my various English classes and find them chattering away in German at a great rate, over a big pot of coffee and a platter of cakes. But I seldom joined them. My pupils' parents gave me chocolate, or sweetmeats, or something to eat or drink almost every time I taught a class, so I was seldom hungry until dinner time.

In the spring, Frau Kraus came up from Mexico City to spend a week with Frau Schultz and see her daughter, whom she hadn't seen all winter. That week the outdoor brick oven in our corral was always full of long loaves of bread and yellow cakes. All the German friends of Frau Schultz in Toluca came to call on Frau Kraus from Mexico City—that is all the Germans in *their* circle—for the wealthier Germans, like the brewery-master, did not move in such poor society.

My father had gone to the ranch, so the women had the house to themselves. Because I found Frau Schultz very kind and amiable, I was glad she was having a holiday week with her friends. Every day, Gerta came down to our house to be with her mother, and things were very lively and the patio was filled with feminine voices speaking German. Most of the time, I kept out of the way, since we couldn't understand one another, the Germans and I.

Then Friday came. The week was almost over and Frau Kraus would return to Mexico City on Sunday. But on Friday the terrible thing happened. Fortunately, there were no guests in the house that afternoon. Only Frau Schultz and her little girl, Lotte, Frau Kraus and her daughter, Gerta. It was a chilly, dismal afternoon, so they were all seated at the table in the dining room just off the warm kitchen. The coffee was hot, and the apple-cakes almost like the cakes at home in Germany, where the ovens were not built of adobe brick in dusty corrals. They were having a good time, the two women talking of days before the war in their suburb of Berlin, and of their children, and how ten-year-old Lotte was learning Spanish and becoming Catholic already in that Catholic school, and of how well Gerta had done with her job under the tall, cranky old brewery-master.

Just then someone knocked commandingly at the street

entrance. Ten-year-old Lotte went down the corridor and across the patio to answer the door. There stood the brewery-master, tall with iron-white hair and a big white mustache. He did not say a word to Lotte. He came in and strode slowly along the corridor that skirted the patio, looking into each room as he passed. He came to the dining-room, which was at the end of the corridor. Hearing voices, he pushed open the door and walked in.

No one had time to say a word, to rise to greet him, or to offer him a chair. For the brewery-master took a pistol from his pocket and, without warning, began to fire on the women. First he fired on Gerta point-blank, sending a bullet through her head, another through her jaw, another through her shoulder, before she slumped unconscious to the floor beneath the table. In panic, the two women tried to run, but the old man, blocking the door, fired again, striking Frau Schultz in the right arm and breaking it. Then he went all through the patio looking for me, looking, looking, out into the corral and through the stables.

Lotte, wild-eyed, reached the street and called the neighbors. Frau Kraus lay in a dead faint in the kitchen. Frau Schultz crouched, stunned, in a corner against the wall, afraid to move. A crowd of Indians assembled, but were wary of entering the house.

Finally the old German walked past the men on the sidewalk, with his pistol still in hand, and no one stopped him. He went directly to the police station and gave himself up. He had two bullets left in his gun, and he told the police he had intended them for me. He said he thought Gerta had been coming to our house to be with me. He said he was in love with Gerta and he wanted to kill her and to kill me.

When I got home a half-hour after the shooting, the ambulance had just taken every one to the hospital. The police would not let me in until they had completed their inspection. When I finally did get into the house, I found the dining room floor a pool of blood, a chair splintered by a bullet, and the tiles of the corridor spotted with red.

Since my father was at the ranch, I went in search of a German friend of his, a buyer of mines, who saw to it that proper hospitalization was provided for the women. Then we went to visit the jail. The old brewery-master sat in his cell, not saying a word, except that he was glad he had killed the girl. He was glad, he mumbled, glad!

But strangely enough, Gerta did not die! She was unconscious for six weeks, and remained in the hospital almost a year—but she didn't die. She finally got well again, with the marks of three bullets on her face and body. The court gave the old man twenty years in prison.

Had I arrived at home that afternoon a half-hour earlier, I probably would not be here today.

DEPARTURE

In the late summer I began to make ready to leave for Columbia. In Toluca the schools had vacation at odd times, so most of my English classes continued throughout the summer. I hated to leave them, but I told Señorita Padilla and Professor Tovar that they would have to find someone else.

A short time later, Professor Tovar told me he had

learned that a new American couple had come to Toluca, a road engineer and his wife, and that the woman was willing to take over my English classes. I was glad, because the two Mexican teachers of English I had met there had a good knowledge of grammar, but atrocious pronunciation.

While I went for a final trip to the ranch with my father, Professor Tovar and Señorita Padilla called on the American woman and made final arrangements with her to take over the girls' school and business school classes. They set a day for her to come to the business school in the Portales to go over the lessons with me, and to visit the commercial classes.

Professor Tovar had neglected to tell the new teacher that I was an *americano de color,* brown as a Mexican, and nineteen years old. So when she walked into the room with him, she kept looking around for the American teacher. No doubt she thought I was one of the students, chalk in hand, standing at the board. But when she was introduced to me, her mouth fell open, and she said: "Why, Ah-Ah thought you was an American."

I said: "I am American!"

She said: "Oh, Ah mean a white American!" Her voice had a southern drawl.

I grinned.

She was a poor-looking lady of the stringy type, who probably had never been away from her home town before. I asked her what part of the States she came from. She said Arkansas—which better explained her immediate interest in color. The next two days, as she sat beside me at the teacher's desk, and I went over with her the different types of courses the students had—the conversation for the girls from Señorita Padilla's school, and the business

English for the pupils of the academy—she kept looking at me out of the corners of her eyes as if she thought maybe I might bite her.

At the end of the first day, she said: "Ah never come across an educated Ne-gre before." (Southerners often make that word a slur between *nigger* and *Negro*.)

I said: "They have a large state college for colored people in Arkansas, so there must be some educated ones there."

She said: "Ah reckon so, but Ah just never saw one before." And she continued to gaze at me as her first example of an educated Negro.

I was a bit loath to leave my students, with whom I had had so much fun, in charge of a woman from one of our more backward states, who probably felt about brown Mexicans much as my father did. But there was no alternative, if they wanted to learn English at all. Then, too, I thought the young ladies from Señorita Padilla's academy might as well meet a real *gringo* for once. Feminine gender: *gringa*.

MANHATTAN ISLAND

I was glad to leave Mexico. My father came with me as far as the capital and when the train pulled out of Buena Vista station for Vera Cruz one day in September, 1921, I said: *"Gracias a dios!"*

The next day for the first time in my life I saw the ocean —the Gulf of Mexico, with its smell of seaweed and salt water, its wharves, and big boats. But Vera Cruz in September was the hottest city I have ever known and the mosquitoes were legion. You sweltered in a bed made airless by double mosquito netting, in a room that hummed like a beehive. And when you got on the boat for New York, you were *mighty* glad.

In Merida there was quarantine. In Havana there was quarantine. Folks were sick. We couldn't go ashore.

But, boy! At last! New York was pretty, rising out of the bay in the sunset—the thrill of those towers of Manhattan with their million golden eyes, growing slowly taller and taller above the green water, until they looked as if they could almost touch the sky! Then Brooklyn Bridge, gigantic in the dusk! Then the necklaces of lights, glowing everywhere around us, as we docked on the Brooklyn side. All this made me feel it was better to come to New York than to any other city in the world.

I didn't know how to get to Harlem or where to stay after I got there, so I went that night with two Mexican friends I'd met on the boat, to a hotel off Times Square. One was a young mechanic, coming to take a course at an automobile school in Detroit and he kept saying, as the taxi carried us up town: "But where are all the poor people? *Caramba!* Every one is dressed up here! Everybody wears shoes!" The other friend was an old man, coming to live with his son's family in Jersey. He kept saying: "Where is the grass? Where will I keep my chickens? *Puta madre!* Is there no grass?" He had brought along a crate of game cocks, which he refused to surrender even to the bell boy in the crowded lobby of the hotel.

It was a gyp-joint hotel, between Broadway and Sixth. The clerk declared all their rooms came in suites, and he rented us a suite at nine dollars a day, each. We didn't want a suite. And we didn't want to pay nine dollars, but we didn't know where else to go that night, so we paid it, and each of us slept in an enormous bed, in an apartment that looked out onto a noisy street off the Great White Way.

Toward morning, the old man's chickens began to crow and woke me up, so we had breakast early, shook hands, promised to write each other, and went our separate ways. I took the subway to Harlem and never saw either of them again.

DORMITORY

Like the bullfights, I can never put on paper the thrill of that underground ride to Harlem. I had never been in a subway before and it fascinated me—the noise, the speed, the green lights ahead. At every station I kept watching for the sign: 135TH STREET. When I saw it, I held my breath. I came out onto the platform with two heavy bags and looked around. It was still early morning and people were going to work. Hundreds of colored people! I wanted to shake hands with them, speak to them. I hadn't seen any colored people for so long—that is, any Negro colored people.

I went up the steps and out into the bright September sunlight. Harlem! I stood there, dropped my bags, took a deep breath and felt happy again. I registered at the Y.

When college opened, I did not want to move into the dormitory at Columbia. I really did not want to go to college at all. I didn't want to do anything but live in

Harlem, get a job and work there. But I had passed the entrance examinations and my father had paid my tuition by draft, so I had to go to college. When I went to get my room in the Hartley Hall dormitory on the campus, the lady at the office looked slightly startled and said: "Oh, there must be some mistake! All the rooms were gone long ago."

I said: "But I reserved mine *long ago*, and paid the required deposit by mail."

She said: "You did? Then let me see."

Of course, she found my reservation, made from Toluca, but she kept looking at me in a puzzled and not very friendly fashion. Then she asked if I were a Mexican. When she discovered I wasn't, she consulted with several other people, papers fluttered, a telephone call was made, but finally they gave me the admittance slip to the dormitory. Having made my reservation early, I had one of the most convenient rooms in Hartley Hall, on the first floor just off the lobby. But they certainly didn't seem any too anxious to give it to me because (no doubt) they realized I was colored.

Of course, later I was to run into much of that sort of thing in my grown-up travels in America, that strange astonishment on the part of so many whites that a Negro should expect any of the common courtesies and conveniences that other Americans enjoy.

COLUMBIA

I didn't like Columbia. It was too big. It was not fun, like being in high school. You didn't get to know anybody, hardly. The buildings looked like factories.

By the end of my first term I got to know Chun, a Chinese boy, pretty well. And a boy named Best, whose father made pencils and who lived on Riverside Drive. And a very rich boy named Craig in my dormitory, who always asked me to help him do his French or write his English themes. The rich boy used to know lots of chorus girls and sometimes, after the Broadway shows were over, he would drive up to the Hartley Hall windows on the Amsterdam Avenue side with a taxi-full of girls, call some of his pals and they would all go out for a ride. He would never call me, of course, but if he saw a light in my window, he might yell in: "See you tomorrow, Lang, third hour, and we'll get on them French verbs. I don't need no verbs tonight."

Like me, Chun, the Chinese boy, didn't like the big University, either. He said white people were much nicer in the missionary school in China from which he came. Here nobody paid any attention to him, and the girls wouldn't dance with him at dances. (I didn't expect them to dance with me, but he did, not being used to American ways.)

Nobody asked him to join a frat and nobody asked me, but I didn't expect anyone to. When I tried out for the *Spectator*, they assigned me to gather frat house and society news, an assignment impossible for a colored boy to fill, as they knew. I remember Corey Ford was on the editorial board. And there was a pleasant young man around named Charles A. Wagner, a poet, who later became Book Editor of the *New York Mirror*. But they were upper classmen and, I suppose, not particularly interested in the relationship of Chinese and Negroes to the rest of the student body, anyhow. It was all a little like my senior year in high school—except more so—when one noticed that the kids began to get a bit grown and girl-conscious and stand-offish and anti-Negro in the American way, that increases when kids take on the accepted social habits.

As for the instructors at Columbia whom I knew, the only one who interested me much was a Mr. Wasson, who read Mencken aloud all the time. In physics, I never understood a thing. And the instructor would never explain. He always said you had to work it out for yourself—which isn't so easy if you haven't got that kind of a mind or anybody to help you. Higher mathematics were like a Chinese puzzle. And French was taught to an enormous class, with the instructor having each one recite by going down the roll with the speed of an express train—evidently so he could get some sort of mark down for everybody before the bell rang.

Living in New York was higher than my father had anticipated, and he asked every month for an accounting of my expenses, penny by penny. Since I had always spent it all, "All gone" seemed to me a sufficient accounting to give, simple and clear. But it did not please my father.

About that time, my mother and step-father had parted again. My mother came to New York to live, so I had to use my allowance to help her until she found a job. My father kept on wondering why I ran out of money so quickly. But I didn't have enough for college, my mother, and me, too.

What an unpleasant winter! I didn't like Columbia, nor the students, nor anything I was studying! So I didn't study. I went to shows, read books, attended lectures at the Rand School under Ludwig Lewisohn and Heywood Broun, missed an important exam in the spring to go to Bert Williams's funeral, sat up in the gallery night after night at *Shuffle Along,* adored Florence Mills, and went to Chinatown with Chun. I even acquired a small Mandarin vocabulary.

Of course, I finished the year without honors. I had no intention of going further at Columbia, anyhow. I felt that I would never turn out to be what my father expected me to be in return for the amount he invested. So I wrote him and told him I was going to quit college and go to work on my own, and that he needn't send me any more money.

He didn't. He didn't even write again.

ON MY OWN

After the finals, I moved out of Hartley Hall at Columbia and down into Harlem, where I began life on my own. I was twenty.

Before June my mother had gone back to Cleveland. So I took a room alone and started to look for work. In those days there was no depression—at least, not much of a one—so there were lots of ads in the morning papers. I bought the papers and began to answer ads regarding jobs I thought I could handle—office boy, clerk, waiter, bus

boy, and other simple occupations. Nine times out of ten
—*ten* times out of ten, to be truthful—the employer would
look at me, shake his head and say, with an air of amazement: "But I didn't advertise for a colored boy."

It was the same in the employment offices. Unless a job
was definitely marked COLORED on the board outside,
there was no use applying, I discovered. And only one
job in a thousand would be marked COLORED. I found it
very hard to get work in New York. Experience was prov-
ing my father right. On many sides, the color line barred
your way to making a living in America.

I finally got work on a truck-garden farm on Staten
Island. The farm belonged to some Greeks, who didn't
care what nationality you were just so you got up at five
in the morning and worked all day until it was too dark to
see the rows in the field. They paid you fifty dollars a
month, with bed and board. The bed was a pile of hay
in the loft of the barn—but it was summer, and the hay
was pleasant. They had two Greek hired hands, a couple
of Italians, a Jewish boy from Brownsville, and me. These
were good-natured people to work with, and the Greek
owners, two brothers and their wives, worked hardest of
all. They woke us up at daybreak, and worked along with
us, or ahead of us, in the fields all day.

We had a breakfast of goat's cheese and coffee. At mid-
day, a big dinner, at four o'clock more cheese and coffee in
the open field. And a late supper after dark, of sandwiches and tea. Healthy food. Plenty of watermelons,
onions, cheese, and tomatoes. We worked hard, ploughing, hoeing, spreading manure, picking weeds, washing let-
tuce, beets, carrots, onions, tying them and packing them
for market, loading the wagons, and standing by lantern
light to watch one of the indefatigable little Greek broth-

ers drive off in the night to the New York market.

The food we had grown went off to market to feed a big city. There was something about such work that made you feel useful and important—sending off onions that *you* had planted and seen grow from a mere speck of green, that *you* had tended and weeded, had pulled up and washed and even loaded on the wagon—seeing them go off to feed the great city of New York. *Your* onions!

It was a pretty good job, and I liked it—that is, all but the mosquitoes in the dawn, that bit your ears off before the sun came out, blazing and strong.

We even worked Sunday mornings. Sunday afternoons we had off. Usually we slept then, dead-tired, among the flies in the heat of the barn, or else lay out under the shade of a lone tree, the only one on the whole farm. Sometimes some of the fellows went into Port Richmond to find girls and wine. Or occasionally to New York, but not often, for most of them were saving money to send back to the old country.

The Brownsville boy and I were the only two native Americans. The Brownsville boy confided to me that he wanted to stay away from Brooklyn until the police forgot about something he did not want to face.

Only once during the whole summer did I go to New York, and that was to see Rudolph Valentino in *Blood and Sand,* because I liked bullfights and I wanted to see if they had a real one in the picture. They didn't have much of a one. I guess the censors cut it out.

After a visit to Harlem, I got back to the farm after midnight. The other men had taken all the loose hay in the loft and were asleep on it, so I had to roll down an unopened bale for my bedding. The heavy bales were packed compactly one on top of another, so I had to climb to the top of the block-like heap and roll down a bale from there, eight or ten feet up. Unfortunately, however, not one but several bales came rolling down, shaking the whole barn, and making a great racket.

The next thing I knew, I was alone in the big loft and all the Greeks and Italians were running for dear life through the barnyard.

Astonished, I went to an opening in the loft and called out: "Hey! What's the matter?"

"*Terremoto!*" they yelled. "*Terremoto!* Come down quick! Come out!"

I began to shake with laughter. They thought it was an earthquake!

When the truck-farming season was over, I went back to New York with enough cash to buy an overcoat and pay a few weeks' rent in advance. I took a room with a kind woman in Harlem named Mrs. Dorsey, who had a son and a daughter about my own age. I wrote a few poems and sent them to the *Crisis*. Then shortly, I found a job delivering flowers for Thorley, but I didn't like the job.

The flowers were terrifically expensive and they usually went to very *comme il faut* people—the Baroness d'Erlanger at the Ritz, Marion Davies on a yacht, the Roosevelts at Oyster Bay, Vivienne Segal at the Empire. Each box I delivered was billed, as a rule, for more than my month's rent—more money for a box of flowers than I could earn in ten days—and those receiving the flowers seldom gave you a tip for bringing them! Butlers and maids usually took the boxes, so you didn't even see the celebrity whose flowers you carried. Sometimes you would catch a glimpse of the great one, though, and then you would feel a little more cheerful, having laid eyes on some famous and successful person. But when you got back to the shop, the boss would always ask why in the hell you took so long to make a delivery.

"Hurry up and get the next order out," would be his command. "Quick now! Hurry!"

My father would have loved his efficiency. He and Mr. Thorley could have been good friends.

On the day following those nights when you worked until nine o'clock, or more, you were entitled to come an hour late the following morning. One night I worked until almost midnight, making a delivery on Long Island. The next morning I came at ten. Mr. Thorley himself happened to be standing at the door, looking down Fifth Avenue. He said: "Don't you know better than to be showing up here at such an hour?"

I started to explain that the night before had been my late night, and that I had worked four or five hours overtime, but he cut me off to order me brusquely to take the whole morning off—because he would take a morning out of my pay, anyhow! He told me to come back after lunch.

I never went back again. But finding another job that fall was not easy. Want ads, employment offices, the Y, the railroad stations, the big hotels, the shoe shine stands. No luck.

But all those months in New York I'd kept remembering the smell of the sea on my first night in Vera Cruz. And it seemed to me now that if I had to work for low wages at dull jobs, I might just as well see the world, so I began to look for work on a ship.

HAUNTED SHIP

After two or three weeks of walking up and down South Street and West Street, haunting the docks and shipping offices, at last I found a job. I was in the office of the United States Shipping Board one morning, when a big stout man, behind a long, shabby desk, called out a job for one mess boy. There were very few fellows there at the time, so I beat all of them to the desk and got the job. I passed the doctor, took my slip of paper, and rushed home to Harlem to pack. I was so excited, I had forgotten to ask the man at the desk where the boat was going.

With my two suitcases, I rushed down to the pier indicated, got into a motor launch, and went out into New York harbor, past the Statue of Liberty and on toward Staten Island. We drew up alongside a rusty old freighter, standing at anchor. I climbed aboard. The first thing I said to a sailor standing near the gangplank was: "Where are we going?"

The sailor looked at me a long time. Finally he said: "Nowhere."

I couldn't believe my ears.

"This boat ain't going nowhere," he repeated. "What's the matter with you?"

I felt sick.

"Nowhere?" I said.

"Don't you know we gonna be tied up?" he asked.

"Then why are they hiring people?"

"Because this tub here is gonna be a mother ship," he said, and walked away.

I found the steward, a tall, lanky, white fellow with red hair and freckles, slightly drunk, but very cordial. He was glad to have me, he said, and he hoped I would stay, because, so far, he couldn't keep any mess boys on a ship like this, going nowhere.

From him I learned that the boat was one of the hundreds built for the government during the First World War, many of them built very badly—so badly that they were now unseaworthy and had to be laid up. (Some shipping contractors must have made a lot of money on them in the rush of war-time building.) This rusty tub was towed up the Hudson to Jones Point a few days after I boarded her and put at anchor with eighty or more other dead ships of a similar nature, and there we stayed all winter.

Every twentieth ship or so in the line was a mother ship, housing a skeleton crew to keep the machinery oiled in the other boats and the cables in place so that none of them floated away. We were the last mother ship in the fleet. To reach us from Jones Point, you came out in a rowboat, boarded the first ship in the fleet, at the head of a long line of boats anchored in the river, then walked the whole length of the entire fleet, sometimes across planks connecting boats with no sign of a railing or rope, and finally you reached our mother ship at the far end.

We were good and isolated, all right, way out in a wide bend of the Hudson. When the river froze but the ice was unsure for walking, sometimes for days you could not get ashore. And there was nothing ashore but a way station for the trains, anyway. Newburgh was the nearest town. All winter long, I went ashore but twice, so I had plenty of time to write, since the work was very easy.

I was the only Negro in the whole fleet. The others were

mostly Swedes and Spaniards. Paydays there were big poker and blackjack games. The rest of the time, the fellows just slept.

There was one college boy on our boat, a boy named Keys, intending to be a ship's engineer. He had an aunt who sang at the Metropolitan. And he had read lots of books, so we used to talk about books. But mostly I was interested in talking with sailors, who had been everywhere and had marvellous tales to tell about far-off parts of the world, strange boats they had worked on, women they had loved, and fights they had had.

There was a Spanish sailor from Seville named Pedro, who told me about Triana and the gypsies. This Spaniard and a short, stocky, albino Scot were my best pals. The Scot was seventeen or eighteen and spoke with the thickest of brogues. I never got tired of hearing the amusing way he talked. No other brogue intrigued me quite as much except that of the British West Indians I met later.

When spring came, Scotty and I used to spend our Sundays hiking to Bear Mountain, and he would talk most of the way up and back. Sometimes I would have to stop dead to puzzle out what he was saying.

That winter I wrote a poem called "The Weary Blues," about a piano-player I heard in Harlem, but I didn't send it anywhere because I wasn't satisfied with it. Every so often I would take it out of the suitcase and do something about the ending. I could not achieve an ending I liked, although I worked and worked on it—something that seldom happens to any of my poems.

Meanwhile, there came to me at the fleet, a letter from a gentleman in Washington named Alain Locke. Written in a very small hand, it commented upon what he felt to be the merits of my poems he had seen in the *Crisis,* and he asked if he might come to Jones Point to see me—evidently thinking I lived in the village. I couldn't picture a distinguished professor from Howard, a Ph.D. at that, clambering over the hundred-odd freight boats that made up our fleet, slipping on the wet decks and balancing himself over precarious runways between rocking old vessels. So I wrote back "No."

I didn't want to see him, anyway, being afraid of learned people in those days. I had seen the *Crisis* editors but once or twice during my previous winter at Columbia. And then I had had no intention of seeing them—but when I changed the subscription of my magazine from Toluca to Hartley Hall, the editorial department learned of it and tracked me down. Jessie Fauset, the managing editor, invited me to luncheon at the Civic Club. I was panic-stricken. I pictured the entire staff of the *Crisis* as very learned Negroes and very rich, in nose glasses and big cars. I had a tremendous admiration for Dr. W. E. B. DuBois, whose *Souls of Black Folk* had stirred my youth, but I was flabbergasted at the thought of meeting him. What would I say? What should I do? How could I act—not to appear as dumb as I felt myself to be? So I didn't go near the *Crisis* until Jessie Fauset sent for me. Then I asked if I might bring my mother, for I knew she would do the talking, since my mother loved to talk and meet people.

I remember we had *filet de sole* for luncheon, and it was the first time I had ever eaten *filet de sole*. I think I met Martha Gruening, too. The Civic Club was one of the few clubs in New York admitting both Negro and white members, and the leaders of the National Association for the Advancement of Colored People, the organization that published the *Crisis*, belonged. The club being near their office, they usually lunched there.

I found Jessie Fauset charming—a gracious, tan-brown lady, a little plump, with a fine smile and gentle eyes. I was thrilled when she told me that readers of the *Crisis* had written in to say they liked my poems. I was interested, too, to hear that she was also writing poems and planning a novel. From that moment on I was deceived in writers, because I thought they would all be good-looking and gracious like Miss Fauset—especially those whose books I liked or whose poems were beautiful.

Jessie Fauset introduced me to Mr. Dill, the business manager of the *Crisis,* a short, voluble man of middle-age who, besides running the magazine, was a fine musician on the pipe organ and the *piano forte* (as he always said) as well. He attended the Community Church, where John Haynes Holmes preached, and sometimes played the organ for services there. He told them of my poetry, and that church was, I believe, the first church in which I was invited to read my poems, through the good offices of Augustus Granville Dill, of Harvard and the *Crisis.*

The *Crisis* people, I am sure, did everything they could to put me at ease; still I was afraid to see any more like them. So when Alain Locke wrote me, I was glad the Hudson and a hundred freighters stood between us and the likelihood of meeting. A seaman had already been drowned crossing those narrow planks from one boat to another, so it would be pretty risky for a professional landlubber, even if he should ever reach Jones Point, several hours up the river from New York.

So there were no visitors and I almost never went ashore. Those long winter nights with snow swirling down the Hudson, and the old ships rocking and creaking in the wind, and the ice scraping and crunching against their sides, and the steam hissing in the radiators were ideal

for reading. I read all the ship's library. I found there
Butler's *The Way of All Flesh,* Conrad's *Heart of Darkness*
and d'Annunzio's *The Flame of Life.*

The work was pleasant, the men I served good-natured,
and I was mostly my own boss because our red-headed
steward stayed drunk almost all the time. That was why
he couldn't keep a job on an ocean-going steamer. But he
would always know in advance when he was going to be
drunk, so he would give me his keys to the refrigerator
room and all the supplies, and ask me to look out for
things. Then he would go into his cabin and sometimes
not come out for three or four days. I do not know how
he could stay drunk so long. He was a very good fellow,
though, and everybody liked him, so he didn't get fired.

Among the empty boats of this dead fleet, there was a
haunted ship, aboard which, during the war, there had
been a mutiny somewhere at sea, when a pitched battle
between the officers and the crew took place. There were
bullet holes in the steel plates of the bridge. The Captain
had been killed there. And one of the mates, they said, had
tumbled down the forward steps, mortally wounded. It was
a sinister-looking boat, shabby from lack of paint and filled
with dust and cobwebs. And it had a bad record. At night,
almost everyone agreed, ghosts walked.

One pay day, Sully, an Irish fireman, offered to bet that
nobody would spend a night alone on that haunted boat.
I said I didn't believe in ghosts and that I would. The
Irishman said I was lying, but if I did stay there all night,
ten dollars would be mine.

I said. "O.K. Tomorrow." And I meant it. I wanted
to prove to myself that I wasn't scared. And if there were
ghosts, I wanted to see one. Besides, I could use ten
dollars.

That same night, however, Sully, the fireman, lost all his money in a poker game. But the next day I declared I would sleep there anyway, even if the bet was off, just to prove him wrong about ghosts. So in the afternoon I moved my bedding over to the haunted ship, took along a couple of candles, and picked out a cabin—one with a good lock on the door—so if there were ghosts, they would have to enter through the keyhole in a ghostly fashion. The sailors arranged for the night watchman to come by every so often in the night and see if I was still there. To frighten me, all day they kept on repeating the mutiny story with gruesome variations. They declared I had picked out the very cabin of the slain mate. They said I would turn white by morning from pure fear. They said I had better leave the door unlocked so I could run.

They had all seen Negroes in the motion pictures portrayed so often as superstitious and frightened, that I guess that was another reason for my going. I wanted to prove to them Negroes are no more afraid of ghosts than other people. So about ten o'clock, I went over to the haunted ship, accompanied by Sully, Scotty, and the watchman. They sat around with me for a while, pretending every creak of the cables was the whine of a ghost, and every knock of the wind the footsteps of a dead man.

But when they left, I blew out my candles and went to bed. (Since it was a dead ship, there was no heat, or electric current.) It was pretty windy that night, and the boats rolled and creaked a-plenty. The gale roared in the mastheads. But beyond that, I heard nothing strange. And, having always been a sleepy-head, I soon went to sleep. I remember once, Pug, the watchman, knocked on the door. I woke up enough to yell: "Beat it, Pug, and lemme alone! You're no ghost." And the next thing I heard was the alarm clock at six in the morning. Thus passed my night on the "haunted" ship.

That day I bet Sully, the Irishman, ten dollars he wouldn't do the same thing.

He wouldn't.

TIME TO LEAVE

When spring came, and the banks of the Hudson were a fresh, clean green, and the New York–Albany boats appeared on the river, I thought it was about time to leave the dead ships and find a vessel that was moving. So I quit the fleet and went back to New York, determined now to get on a boat actually going somewhere. It didn't take long. My red-headed steward gave me a splendid recommendation: "Competent, courteous, capable, trust-worthy, and efficient." So I took his letter to a shipping office and that very day was assigned a boat sailing for Africa—providing the Filipino steward didn't mind a Negro in his crew. He didn't, so I got the job.

I'd left a box of books in Harlem in the fall, and before we sailed I went after them. I brought them aboard ship with me. But when I opened them up and looked at them that night off Sandy Hook, they seemed too much like everything I had known in the past, like the attics and basements in Cleveland, like the lonely nights in Toluca, like the dormitory at Columbia, like the furnished room in Harlem, like too much reading all the time when I was a kid, like life isn't, as described in romantic prose; so that night, I took them all out on deck and threw them over-board. It was like throwing a million bricks out of my heart—for it wasn't only the books that I wanted to throw away, but everything unpleasant and miserable out of my past: the memory of my father, the poverty and uncertain-ties of my mother's life, the stupidities of color-prejudice, black in a white world, the fear of not finding a job, the bewilderment of no one to talk to about things that trouble you, the feeling of always being controlled by others—by parents, by employers, by some outer necessity not your own. All those things I wanted to throw away. To be free of. To escape from. I wanted to be a man on my own, control my own life, and go my own way. I was twenty-one. So I threw the books in the sea.

Whiffs of salt spray blew in my face. It was dark. Up on the poop, the wind smelt good, but I was sleepy, so I went down a pair of narrow steps into the cabin with George and Puerto Rico, and we laughed about George's landlady, who didn't know he had left Harlem for Africa that evening.

Then I went to bed.

II

Big Sea

〜〜〜〜〜〜〜〜〜〜

AFRICA

The first day out of New York harbor, the sailors began to clean up the ship. All the filth and garbage that had accumulated in the harbor was dumped into the ocean, and the limpid blue-green of the sea received the garbage and swill, and didn't seem to be dirtied at all. That is one of the many wonders of the sea—that the garbage and bilge water of ten thousand ships is dumped into it every day, and the sea is never dirty.

Soon our ship became bright and shining, the brass all polished, the decks chipped, and the bulkheads painted. And the crew became rested and clean, sleep all caught up after nights ashore in New York. The sun was very bright, a brisk breeze was blowing, the spray salt and cool, the waves foamy-white, and the air like a tonic in the lungs. And nobody was afraid of being hungry or homeless or out of work or not needed in the scheme of things for six months as we headed toward Africa.

The crossing was bright and sunny. We reached the Azores, the Canaries, and finally Africa. A long, sandy coast-line, gleaming in the sun. Palm trees sky-tall. Rivers darkening the sea's edge with the loam of their deltas. People, black and beautiful as the night. The bare, pointed breasts of women in the market places. The rippling muscles of men loading palm oil and cocoa beans and mahogany on ships from the white man's world, for that was why our ship was there—to carry away the treasures of Africa. We brought machinery and tools, canned goods, and Hollywood films. We took away riches out of the earth, loaded by human hands.

We paid very little for the labor. We paid but little more for the things we took away. The white man dominates Africa. He takes produce, and lives, very much as he chooses. The yield of earth for Europe and America. The yield of men for Europe's colonial armies. And the Africans are baffled and humble. They listen to the missionaries and bow down before the Lord, but they bow much lower before the traders, who carry whips and guns and are protected by white laws, made in Europe for the black colonies.

At that time, 1923, the name of Marcus Garvey was known the length and breadth of the West Coast of Africa. And the Africans did not laugh at Marcus Garvey, as so many people laughed in New York. They hoped what they had heard about him was true—that he really would unify the black world, and free and exalt Africa. They did not understand the terrific complications of the Colonial Problem. They only knew the white man was there in Africa, heavy and oppressive on their backs. And they wanted him to go away.

"Our problems in America are very much like yours," I told the Africans, "especially in the South. I am a Negro, too."

But they only laughed at me and shook their heads and

said: "You, white man! You, white man!"

It was the only place in the world where I've ever been called a white man. They looked at my copper-brown skin and straight black hair—like my grandmother's Indian hair, except a little curly—and they said: "You—white man."

One of the Kru men from Liberia, working on our ship, who had seen many American Negroes, of various shades and colors, and knew much of America, explained to me.

"Here," he said, "on the West Coast, there are not many colored people—people of mixed blood—and those foreign colored men who are here come mostly as missionaries, to teach us something, since they think we know nothing. Or they come from the West Indies, as clerks and administrators in the colonial governments, to help carry out the white man's laws. So the Africans call them all *white* men."

"But I am not white," I said.

"You are not black either," the Kru man said simply. "There is a man of my color." And he pointed to George, the pantryman, who protested loudly.

"Don't point at me," George said. "I'm from Lexington, Kentucky, U.S.A. And no African blood, nowhere."

"You black," said the Kru man.

"I can part my hair," said George, "and it ain't nappy."

But to tell the truth, George shaved a part in his hair every other week, since the comb wouldn't work. The Kru man knew this, so they both laughed loudly, for George's face was as African as Africa.

(Yet, dark as he was, George always referred to himself as brownskin, and it was not until years later, when a dark-skinned minister in New Jersey denounced me to his congregation for using the word *black* to describe him in a newspaper article, that I realized that most dark Negroes in America do not like the word *black* at all. They prefer to be referred to as *brownskin,* or at the most as *dark* brownskin—no matter how dark they really are.)

In one of the smaller African ports, I came across a peculiarly poignant tragedy of mixed blood. I do not know if this is typical, but I tell it for what it is worth. (Much later, I wrote a short story derived from it, called "African Morning," that is, I think, one of my best stories.)

We were in a small port, up a river mouth, in an English colony. As our ship dropped anchor, I noticed, in a group of dark-skinned natives on the deck, a mulatto boy of perhaps sixteen or seventeen, whose skin was golden, not brown, or black. He was dressed in European clothing. When I came ashore with some of the other sailors to barter for fruit or parrots, the boy spoke to us and asked if we had any English papers or magazines.

The boy's name was Edward. He spoke very good English, and he liked to come down to the boat often to talk with us during the week we were there. He took me one day to his house, a very modest house, much like the other African huts, and I was introduced to his mother, who did not speak English. She was young and not unbeautiful, in African clothing, a flowered cloth wrapped about her body. She offered me cocoanut juice to drink and the only chair.

Edward's father was an Englishman, I learned, who had been in charge of the bank at this far-flung post of the British Empire. He had lived inside a kind of compound, where the bank and the various government officials' homes were located. Four years ago, Edward had lived inside that compound, too, for a while with his mother, the house servant. But his father had retired and gone back to England. And now Edward and his mother lived outside the compound. His father had left a small allowance for them and occasionally he wrote them a letter from London. But he would not permit the boy or his mother to come to England.

Edward said that it was very lonely for them there. The whites inside the compound naturally would have nothing to do with them, nor would they give him a job, and the Negroes did not like his mother, because she had lived for years with a white man, so Edward had no friends in the village, and almost nobody to talk to. Was our boat going to England? Could we take him away with us? Was it true that in America the black people were friendly to the mulatto people? But the white people were bad to them all? Were the white people generally bad to colored people everywhere? Edward said his own father was not bad, but now his father had gone away to England and left him there alone with his mother. What could he do?

Poor kid! He looked very lonely, as he stood on the dock the day our ship hauled anchor. He had taken my address to write me in America, and once, a year later, I had a letter from him, but only one, because I have a way of not answering letters when I don't know what to say.

SAILOR'S HOLIDAY

African weather was no hotter than a Chicago summer. In fact not so hot, because, almost always, there was a sea breeze blowing. So along the West Coast, life was a picnic for the crew of the S.S. *Malone*. Our supplementary African crew did almost all the work aboard, and I had an African boy to wash my dishes, set the tables, and make up the rooms for me.

Along the West Coast we visited some thirty-two ports, from Dakar in Senegal to Loanda in the South. The Ivory Coast, the Gold Coast, Lagos, the Niger, the Bight of Benin, and the Slave Coast, Calabar, the Kamerun, Boma up the Congo, where we were moored to a gigantic tree, and our last port, San Paolo de Loanda in Portuguese Angola. Singing boatmen on dark rivers, monkeys and bright birds, Capstan cigarettes in tins, hot beers, quarts of Johnny Walker and stone jugs of gin, barefooted black pilots guiding us into reed-hutted ports, ten-year-old wharf rats offering nightly to take the sailors to see "my sister, two shillings," elephantiasis and swollen bodies under palm trees, white men with guns at their belts, inns and taverns with signs up, EUROPEANS ONLY, missionary churches with the Negroes in the back seats and the whites who teach Jesus in the front rows, soft winds, flaming sunsets, the rattle of palm leaves, the distant beat of obea drums in the night, the surf booming restless on a sandy beach, and the ships from the white man's land anchored with lights aglow offshore in the starry darkness. Africa!

One morning at Sekondi there was a heavy white fog, hiding the coast line from our ship at anchor a mile offshore, where we were unloading cargo into enormous rowboats manned by a dozen men. As the boats came and went, the black boatmen at the oars sang and their song came from away off through the fog. About them I wrote this poem, called "African Fog":

> *Singing black boatmen,*
> *An August morning*
> *In the thick white fog at Sekondi;*
> *Coming out to take cargo*

From anchored alien ships—
You do not know the fog
We strange so-civilized ones
Sail in always.

Africa! When the Captain let us draw money, we enjoyed ourselves in what is, I suppose, the fashion of sailors everywhere. We drank licker and went looking for girls. Some of the fellows complained because there were only African girls. But they slept with them just the same. Sometimes, however, there were French girls, who travelled a circuit like theatrical troupers, seventeen days in each port, but they were expensive and catered only to officers and traders.

The African girls were usually very young, small, with bushy hair, and often henna'd nails. Little boys, their couriers, would take you to them and wait for you outside their doors, or if you stayed all night, they would sleep on a mat beside you on the floor. The small black boys always said the girls were their sisters, but perhaps that was because they knew no other English word to describe them.

No women were permitted on the boat, and often we anchored two or three miles offshore, when the surf was high and the harbor shallow. In such cases, the Captain would issue no money. And even if he had issued money, there was no safe way of getting ashore, unless one paid a boatman extra to carry you on his shoulders through the rolling surf, which was deep and dangerous and often overturned the rowboats.

Once we were anchored for more than a week away out in the water, too far to see clearly the port from which our cargo came. We had no money, even to buy fruit from the bum-boats that occasionally drifted out. But one night, very late, two little African girls rowed through the surf in a boat to our vessel, all alone, and stole aboard past the night watchman, hoping to make some money. No doubt the seaman on watch helped them aboard, because someone brought them straight back to the sailors' quarters. The sailors woke up excited and jubilant and went around knocking on everybody's doors, calling: "Women aboard! Women aboard!"

Firemen, messboys, cooks, the bo'sun, Chips, the oilers poured forth from their respective sleeping places. The bo'sun, boss-like, grabbed one of the girls and took her off privately to his cabin. Someone threw the other girl down on the floor on a blanket in the middle of the sailors' quarters and stripped her of her flowered cloth.

She lay there naked and held up her hands. The girl said: "Mon-nee! Mon-nee!" But nobody had any money.

Thirty men crowded around, mostly in their underwear, sat up on bunks to watch, smoked, yelled, and joked, and waited for their turn. Each time a man would rise, the little African girl on the floor would say: "Mon-nee! Mon-nee!" But nobody had a cent, yet they wouldn't let her get up. Finally, I couldn't bear to hear her crying: "Mon-nee!" any more, so I went to bed. But the festival went on all night.

Once before, I had seen the men from our ship take advantage of the people ashore, although in a different way. We had drawn British money in a French colony. The natives would not take the British money. They didn't know what it was. In fact, they thought it wasn't money at all, so we couldn't buy anything. But some bright boy in our crew had saved up a thousand or more United Cigar Store coupons. One day he took a package of them ashore and decided to try them out, since they looked like French francs. The natives thought they were French francs, and we bought up the town. (No doubt it was a good thing our ship pulled out that night, and went away down the coast to another colony before they discovered the deception.)

About this time, the young Irish lad from Brooklyn fell ill. His skin broke out all over, so we left him in a hospital in the Kamerun and went on toward the Congo.

At the equator, those of us who had never crossed it before were baptised in salt water and shaved with crude oil by Father Neptune, who was really Chips, the carpenter, in a wooden crown and a false beard. Then I received my credentials:

This is to certify that the bearer has been duly initiated into the mysteries of the amalgamated Society, "The Sons of Neptune," and is hereafter entitled to officiate at any similar ceremonies on any other ship.

So now I can duck people in salt water at the equator, too.

From then on, in port, life began to be a riot. Our crew gradually became more unruly and drunken. The chief engineer was almost never sober, nor were many of the firemen. They let the oil lines clog up, and several times the oil ran over and flooded the deck with its black, sticky substance. The sailors were kept busy scrubbing it up. A feud developed between the sailors and the black-gang (the men who worked in the engine room), because the sailors did not like to be always scrubbing up the oil that the engineers allowed to flow over the deck, and that the wind blew in a black spray against the white paint of the bulkheads.

One day the Captain drew a gun on the Chief Engineer and they had a terrific brawl in the Captain's cabin, until the Captain ran him out with his pistol. But it didn't do any good. Shortly, the oil ran over again while we were in port. And to cap the climax, the Chief Engineer came aboard drunk that night in a white suit and fell sprawling in his own oil that had made the deck slippery.

The Chief Engineer was an amiable fellow, though. He was the only one of the officers who ever gave a mess boy a tip. When George came aboard in New York with nothing but a shirt and a pair of overalls, it was the Chief who gave George one of his own suits. But George later gave the suit to a woman in Lagos with whom he stayed the night, because, in the morning he had no money to pay her, so she raised hell. Therefore, he gave her the suit.

When the Captain would not let the men draw money, the men would steal loaves of bread from the mess table and take them ashore and trade them for whiskey or for love. Canned goods, also, one could trade at a good rate of exchange in Africa, particularly canned peaches. The Africans seemed to love canned peaches. The Filipino steward was forever kept busy watching the storeroom, to keep the crew from raiding it. Successfully, once or twice, they did raid it. Thus our supplies from New York dwindled considerably—in fact, tragically.

Sometimes the sailors would go ashore in the afternoon and start a baseball game on the bank near the ship. And if the game was a good one, the Captain could blow the ship's whistle as much as he chose, but nobody would budge until the last inning was over. One day the Old Man threatened to declare the whole crew in a state of mutiny if the game was not called at once, because the cargo was all loaded, and he wanted to sail.

But nobody paid the Captain the least mind, not even George, who would often lie abed for days at sea, saying he had the backache, and could not work. One day, however, the Captain got tired of George having the backache, and came aft to our cabin with drawn pistol to make George get up and go to work. George said as soon as he saw the pistol, his back stopped aching *at once*. Certainly, that evening at dinner he was back at his post in the pantry.

S. S. "MALONE"

The poor missionaries on our boat, the passengers, were in a state of continual distress. They declared the ship unsafe, and they were glad, when they came to their respective ports, to get off. Later, we learned, they wrote irate letters back to the New York office, disclosing in full the gaily mutinous state of things aboard the S.S. *Malone*. They said they would never sail on that line again. Some even threatened to sue the company. Others wrote their congressmen.

On the surface, the missionaries seemed to be nice, stout, white folks from places like Iowa and Vermont, but, naturally, they didn't like all the excitement of a drunken crew, oily decks, riotous nights, and a host of naked Africans— our extra helpers—bathing nude beneath a salt-water hose every evening on the afterdeck in plain sight of everybody. The Africans were very polite, however—more so than the Nordics—and, respecting the missionaries, they turned their backs and hid their sex between their legs, evidently not realizing it then stuck out behind.

They were of the Kru tribe, those Africans. And they proved very useful, working, loading, and cleaning all day long. They had one very dangerous job. They had to load the mahogany logs. These logs, some of them weighing tons, were dragged by human beings driven like mules, from the forests to the beaches. There they were floated out to our ship, at anchor offshore. Bouncing and bobbing in the waves, they had to be secured with great iron chains so that the cranes could lift them into the hold of the ship. To chain them was the job!

A dozen black Kru boys would dive into the water, swimming under and about the log until the chains were tight around the great bobbing hulk of wood. If a boy was caught between the floating black logs, or between a log and the ship, death would often result. Or if the sharks came, death would come, too. Watching them, I had somewhat the same feeling I had had in Mexico, watching Sanchez Mejias turning his red cape so gracefully before a bull's horns. It was beautiful and dangerous work, those black boys swimming there in the tossing waves among the iron chains and the great rolling logs, that would perhaps someday be somebody's grand piano or chest of drawers made of wood and life, energy and death out of Africa.

The colored tailor got off at Lagos, a largely Mohammedan city, peopled with Hausas in flowing robes and colored turbans, Lulani, and Yorubas. (Years later, by accident, I ran into that same tailor in Washington and he said he had had no luck at all selling suits to Africans.)

When we got to Loanda, we began to pick up passengers for the return trip. All the way up and down the coast, we carried deck passengers from one port to another, natives. Once, on a windy day when the surf was high off some French African Village, whose name I have forgotten, a rowboat came out for the debarking passengers, but no one landed. The boat went back empty. Our whistle sounded and we continued our voyage.

Two days later, down the coast, when we came to our next port of call, a little family of Africans who had been travelling on deck came to the gangplank to go ashore. But the English inspector found that their papers called for a French colony, not a British one. They should have got off at the last stop. The father said they couldn't have got off there because the surf was too high to go ashore, and he did not wish to risk his family in the rowboat that came out to get them. The African said they would get off here in the British colony and walk back.

The inspector would not let them off. He sent for the Captain, who came fuming down from the bridge, very wroth at all the trouble this barefooted little family of Africans was causing him. Angrily, he raised his cane to strike them, but they ran. The Captain, looking like the father of the Katzenjammer Kids, very fat and German in his white suit, chased them half-way around the deck. But the Africans were so fleet of foot that they did not feel a single blow of his cane, because they ran too fast, man, wife, and offspring, like deer.

It looked very funny—this chase—and I wanted to laugh, but somehow I couldn't laugh, because it is too much like today's Africa, real, beyond humor—the raised club, the commanding white man, and the frightened native.

Somehow, it was arranged with the officials for the little black family to get off in that strange English colony, where the surf was not so high, and to walk back the two or three hundred miles that they had come beyond their destination.

I never had a session with the Captain. In fact, he

never said a word to me the whole trip except, when money was being issued, the customary: "How much?"

And all I ever said to him was: "A pound, sir," each time.

I had had no reason to be called before the Captain, because I never acted any worse than the rest of the crew. And, although it was a pretty tough crew, I got along fine with everybody but the Third Engineer.

The Third Engineer was from Arkansas, the same State, strangely enough, as the lady who had taken my English classes in Mexico. He was tall, sallow of complexion, and very dour. Nobody liked him. The Filipinos hated him. He frequently made unkind remarks about spicks and niggers, but he ate in my mess room, so I had to look at him three times a day, sitting at the table.

In my mess room, I had also to feed the customs inspectors, the cargo clerks, and whatever local harbor officials came aboard in the various ports. These persons were almost always Negroes, often Africans who had been to England or France to school. They were usually very quiet, educated, and decent black fellows. When all my petty officers were fed, they would come in and eat at the second sitting. I enjoyed waiting on them, and talking to them, if they spoke English.

Deliberately, I think, the Third Engineer would often be late to meals when we were in port, since he knew I had to feed the clerks and port officials. One day, everyone had eaten on my mess list but the Third Engineer. I waited nearly an hour for him to come to luncheon. Then I asked the steward what to do. The steward said: "Call in the customs men and the clerks."

They were entirely Negroes that day, Africans in European clothes, four or five of them, very clean and courteous in their white duck suits. They were in the midst of their meal at the single long table, when the Third Engineer came in.

He ordered: "Get these niggers out of here. I haven't eaten yet."

I said: "You can eat with them if you like. Or I'll serve you afterwards."

"I don't eat with niggers," he said. "And you know damn well an officer don't have to wait for no coons to be fed." He turned on the startled Africans. "Get out of here!" he shouted.

"You get out of here yourself," I said, reaching for the big metal soup tureen on the steam table.

The Third Engineer was a big fellow, and I couldn't fight him barehanded, so I raised the tureen, ready to bring it down on his head.

"I'll report you to the Captain, you black—!"

"Go ahead, you —— and double—!" I said, raising the soup tureen. He went. The Africans finished their meal in peace.

That afternoon I visited the Chief Steward, a grave little Filipino, and told him I would not wait on the Third Engineer any more. No, sir, under no circumstances! But the steward, who had plenty of troubles on his mind, such as an impending meat shortage and sailors who threw whole containers of food into the sea when they didn't like it, and missionaries who complained that the cooking wasn't what they had been used to at home in Iowa, and a German Captain who wanted nothing but sauerkraut—the steward said, forlornly: "Mess boy, in this my life things is not always easible. Sometimes hard like hell! I wish you please help me out and feed the Third."

So, because I liked the steward, I continued to serve the Third Engineer for the rest of the trip, and he continued

to come as late as he could for meals when we were in port
and he knew that there were Negroes to follow him in the
mess hall. But he kept quiet and never referred to the day
of the soup tureen.

It was in Lagos, one afternoon, that there was a pitched
battle between the crew of our ship and the crew of a
British freighter tied up opposite us. It began with one of
our sailors, Chicago Slim, who was drunk, being pushed off
the dock into the river by a limey, as the British seamen
are called.

"Let's go get those limeys," somebody yelled, as Slim was
fished out of the inlet, smelling of whiskey and of mud.
So we went after the limeys.

The main thing I remember is that crew-solidarity out-
weighed race that day, because there were on the British
ship quite a few Negroes—West Indian Negroes, and on
our ship, George and I and the two Puerto Ricans were
definitely colored. But when the white boys on our boat
yelled: "Get them limeys! Get them niggers!" and we
met the British crew on the dock head on, George and the
Puerto Ricans and I yelled, too: "Get them niggers! Get
them limeys!" And after them we went.

In the heat of the fight, we forgot we didn't like the
word *nigger* applied to ourselves.

"Get them Yankees! Get them bloody bastards!" yelled
the Britishers. And everybody had a grand time, until
somebody opened up a salt-water hose on the fray with
such force that the stream knocked us all sprawling, scattering Yankees of every color, West Indians and Britishers
right and left, drenched to the skin, some with the breath
knocked out of them.

A couple of weeks later, I got soaking-wet again, when
I fell in the Congo, trying to climb down a mooring rope

at Boma. Since I couldn't swim, I got out, without being drowned, by paddling dog-fashion.

Late in August, from the blue harbor of Loanda, we turned our prow north and started up the coast again. Somewhere we picked up a stowaway, a Panamanian Indian who had lost his ship and couldn't prove his nationality. At another port we took on a sick seaman, an American Portuguese from Cape Cod, whom the Consul was sending home. Various missionaries came aboard, too, Massachusetts bound. And when we got to the town where we had left the Brooklyn kid, they brought him aboard from the hospital, looking very sick, with his skin all yellow and dry.

BURUTU MOON
~~~~~~~~~~~~~~~~~~~~~~~~~~~~~~~~

Sometimes life is a ripe fruit too delicious for the taste of man: the full moon hung low over Burutu and it was night on the Nigerian delta.

We walked through the quiet streets of the native town, Tom Pey, one of the Kru men from our boat, and I. There were no pavements, no arclights. Only the wide grassy streets, the thatched huts and the near low-hung moon. Dark figures with naked shoulders, a single cloth about their bodies, and bare feet, passed us often, their footsteps making no sounds on the grassy road, their voices soft like the light of the moon. Through the open doors of some of the house fires gleamed. Women moved about preparing food. In the clearing, great mango trees cast purple shadows across the path. There was no wind. Only the moon.

"How still it is," I said to Pey.

"Yes," Pey replied, "but by and by they make Ju-Ju."

"Tonight? Where?" I cried excited. "I want to go."

Pey shook his head, but pointed toward the edge of the town, where the walls of the forest began. "Christian man no bother with Ju-Ju," Pey said politely. "Omali dance no good for Christian man."

"But I want to see it," I insisted.

"No," Pey cried. "White man never go see Ju-Ju. Him hurt you! Him too awful! White man never go!"

"But I'm not a white man," I objected. "I'll—"

"You no black man, neither," said Pey impatiently. So I gave up going to the Ju-Ju.

We were invited into the house of Nagary, the trader. It was a little larger than the other houses of the village. There were two or three small rooms. We sat down on the floor in the first room, the moonlight streaming through the doorway. A large green parrot slept on a wooden ring hung from the ceiling.

Nagary was an old Mohammedan in voluminous long robes. He must have been a large, strong man in his youth. There was a lingering nobleness in his dark old face and proud carriage.

Nagary called his wife. She came, a pretty brown woman, much younger than Nagary. Her body was wrapped in a dull red cloth of rich fiber. She spoke no English, but she smiled. Nagary sent her for two candles and the only chair, which she offered to me. Nagary sent her for three heavy boxes, which she placed before him. He opened two of the boxes and showed us beaten brass from up the Niger, statu-

ettes that skilled hands had made, fiber-cloth woven by
women in far-off villages, the skin of jungle animals, and
the soft, white feathers of birds found in the dangerous
forests of "the bush."

Nagary opened the third box with a rusty key. It contained a fortune in ivory. Great heavy bracelets for women
when they marry; solid ivory tusks, smooth and milk-white;
little figures and tiny panels intricately carved; and one
great white tusk, circled with monkeys and coiled snakes.
Nagary did not ask me to buy any of these things. He
seemed satisfied with my surprise and wonder. He told me
of his trips up the river to Wari and down to Lagos. He
gave me a great spray of feathers. When I left, he said,
with outstretched hands: "God be with you."

When we came out of Nagary's house, the moon had
risen in the sky. It was not so large now, but it was much
brighter. I had never seen a moon so bright.

We turned into a narrow street, where there was a bit
of animation. Men were walking up and down.

"This is where the girls stay," said Pey.

Women of the night stood before low doors, with oiled
hair and henna-dyed nails. In the golden light, they were
like dark flowers offering their beauty to the moon. With
slender bodies wrapped in bright cloths, they waited for
lovers and said no word to those who passed. They simply
stood still, waiting.

In front of one hut three white sailors from a British
ship were bargaining with an old woman. Behind her,
frightened and ashamed, stood a small girl, said to be a
virgin. The price was four pounds. The sailors argued
for a cheaper rate. They hadn't that much money.

We crossed the dry bed of a creek. In the distance, we

heard the drums of Omali, the Ju-Ju. Their measured beating came across the swamp lands at the edge of the forest. Tonight the natives danced to their gods.

We turned back toward the docks and followed the river road. Hundreds of tiny house boats, each with its lantern on a slender pole, lay rocking at their moorings. The long, flat paddle-wheel steamers of the Niger were anchored in mid-stream. The river flowed quietly under the moon.

We came to the docks where the great ships from the white man's land rested—an American boat, a Belgian tramp, an English steamer. Tall, black, sinister ships, high above the water.

"Their men," say the natives, "their white strong men come to take our palm oil and ivory, our ebony and mahogany, to buy our women and bribe our chiefs. . . ."

I climbed the rope ladder to the deck of the *Malone*. Far off, at the edge of the clearing, over against the forest, I heard the drums of Omali, the Ju-Ju. Above, the moon was like a gold ripe fruit in heaven, too sweet for the taste of man.

For a long time I could not sleep.

WRECK OF THE MONKEY CAGE

In one of the Congo ports, I had acquired a monkey. I paid three shillings, an old shirt, and a pair of shoes for him. But every time I touched him, he would bite me. He was a large, red monkey, very wild, just out of the bush. It took me a long time to tame him, but finally, after weeks and weeks, he would no longer bite. Then he grew to love me, and wanted always to hang on my neck or sleep in my arms. But at that stage, out of love for me, he began to bite again, for, whereas formerly he would bite if I picked him up, now he bit if I put him down.

It made him furious to have to get back in his cage, when it was time for me to go to work. He would chatter and swear like mad. Then he would cry, as I disappeared from sight. I called him Jocko and I intended to take him home to my little brother, Kit. But I wish now I could have visualized his antics in America—for thereby hangs a tale.

Even on the boat, the monkeys created plenty of trouble. There were about twenty. Every sailor had either a parrot or a monkey, and one fireman would have purchased a baboon had not the Captain denied it passage.

We built a big cage on deck for the monkeys, and we fed them on the scraps from the sailors' table. They got plenty to eat, for when the sailors did not like a dish, they'd dump it all in the monkeys' cage instead of in the sea, and then send Ramon with a message to the Chinese cook, that threatened him with gruesome murder unless he sent them something else they could eat. They declared the ship's food not fit even for the monkeys.

But monkeys will eat anything, from hash to custard pie, and thrive on it. Our monkeys grew fat and frisky. And all went well until one morning shortly after we'd left the coast of Africa a mild storm came up and the ship began to roll and toss and the waves washed over the deck. A huge wave hit the monkey cage and it broke loose from its moorings, overturning and letting all the monkeys out in a running, leaping, climbing mob, chattering in the spray until they spread all over the boat like a flying phalanx, from stern to prow.

Some of them went up the masts, thinking the masts, no doubt, were jungle trees. Some of the little ones negotiated the wireless cords, swinging by their tails high in the air on the thin wires. Others invaded the saloon and sent the missionaries screaming from their mid-morning prayers. Still other simians made so bold as to invade the Captain's room while he was out inspecting the supercargo's books. They made havoc of his desk, scattering valuable papers to the winds, stealing pencils, and taking a portion of the ship's records aloft with them to the mastheads. They worked swiftly and were as volatile as the wind.

When the Captain saw them he grew too red in the face to speak. Had there not been passengers aboard, he said, he would shoot each monkey down like a dog from the mast or cable where it clung, frolicking in the wind. He threatened to dock everybody's pay who owned a monkey. He gave the men one hour to get them all back into the cage—or into the sea.

But it took two days to get them back. Meanwhile, one or two of them were drowned, and one got in the steering gear and was ground to death. Another was found in a missionary's bathtub. And another in a warm but empty pot in the galley. In the end, most of them were not actually captured. Instead, they frolicked and played in the windy gale from mast to mast until they had had their fill of freedom. Then hunger lured them back to the cage on deck again, where a fine meal of bananas and bread, meat scraps, and saucers of sticky condensed milk had been spread to tempt them home. Eventually, we had them all in. My own Jocko was among the last to give up. But finally he leaped chattering into my arms and devoured a prune.

VOYAGE HOME

The squall that turned over the monkeys' cage was only a prelude to much heavier ones we were to experience as we passed mid-ocean, heading toward America. One night a terrific wind came up, that sent enormous waves crashing over the deck, and made our boat lean until it seemed that it would lie flat on its side in the water. Suitcases beneath bunks went scooting across the floor, back and forth. Everything movable had to be tied down, and the monkeys put in the lamp room. Every few moments, a new mountain of water hit the deck and thunder seemed to strike the S.S. *Malone*. Tons of falling water washed up and over and down upon us with a deafening noise, wave after wave, like one long and consecutive crash of doom, while the wind howled like a thousand furies.

In the morning, when I got up to go forward to the galley, ship-tall sheaves of green water were still breaking over the open deck with such rapidity that I was afraid to cross. I cracked the iron door, and looked out, wondering how I could make it to the galley without being swept into the sea. Just then Ernesto, the Puerto Rican sailor, came out of the sailors' quarters in oilskins, ready to go on watch at four bells. He took my arm and showed me how to run crouching across the open deck between waves, as the ship dived toward the lee side and the swirling rapids swept off the deck into the boiling sea just before another wave broke from the windward.

Ernesto said: "Grab for the railing if the water hits you."

But we made it safely, clambering up the midships steps as a hundred-ton wave thundered across the deck, drenching us both in spray.

That day two of our lifeboats were smashed by the pounding water. The wind blew so strong that it was as dangerous as the waves. No work was done on deck, for the wind could pick a man up and lift him off his feet. The Third Mate said it was a tropical hurricane, and one of the worst, for he had been through many in sailing vessels out of Boston. Twenty-nine times, he had made the African voyage, he told us, and always with a crew of Negro seamen. He said Negroes were splendid sailors, and that it was too bad modern steamers did not, as a rule, employ them. He was a fine old New Englander of abolitionist stock, this Third Mate, who had many thrilling stories to tell of windjammer days and the kind of ships now rapidly disappearing from the Western Ocean.

During the entire storm, next to the cabin where George and I and Puerto Rico slept, in the hospital room the Irish kid and the sick Portuguese rolled and tossed and moaned. The Portuguese often went out of his head, and had to be tied in his bunk. The Irish kid said he didn't have any pain, but he was just weak. And the idea of getting back home to Brooklyn and his people with this strange yellow sickness and dry skin he had made him look as if he wanted to cry.

We put the dying Portuguese off on a stretcher in the Virgin Islands to be rushed to a hospital, because we had no doctor aboard. The Captain also put the Panamanian Indian ashore there. Those of us who had any money made up a collection to give the Indian, who had stowed away with nothing and had no idea now how he would ever get back home to Panama.

The storm had delayed us several days, forcing us off our course. About a week before we got to the Virgin Islands, the food began to run low. This shortage, of course, affected the ordinary members of the crew first. Hardtack appeared aft instead of bread. The sailors' stew had one cube of meat to a quart of watery gravy. There was no more fruit, fresh or canned. Then no more condensed milk for coffee. Finally, no more coffee.

The petty officers' mess felt the shortage shortly after the sailors and the firemen. All the men began to crumble. They cussed the Chinese cook, the Filipino steward, and the Old Man himself for letting things come to such a pass. They accused the steamship company of stinting on rations. The sailors and firemen threw so many of their big tin food containers full of watery stew into the sea (now that the monkeys were out of sight) that the containers ran out, and Puerto Rico, their mess boy, had nothing in which to carry food to them.

The steward began to scrape the bottom of barrels and boxes. For breakfast we had musty oatmeal, full of little worms, hundreds of them, too many to pick out, so we ate them. The sailors went to mob the steward one morning, and chased him from the galley with knives. For once, the Captain sided with the men, and gave the steward an awful bawling out in front of the crew. For by that time the food shortage had reached the saloon where the Captain and the passengers ate, so the Captain was mad himself. The day we pulled into port in the Virgin Islands, all that the passengers had had for dinner the night before was canned sardines.

I felt sorry for Manuel, the Filipino boy from Mindanao, who served the passengers. He had worked hard the whole trip waiting on them, keeping their rooms spotlessly clean, preparing their baths, and even going to prayer meetings to sing hymns with the missionaries, because he was hoping they would tip him well when the boat got to New York. Manuel wanted to marry a Mexican girl in Fourteenth Street, and put a big payment down on new furniture for their flat. Now, the passengers were in an ungrateful mood, angrily pushing their plates away, and calling down the wrath of God on the owners of any steamship line that would send out a boat with such a crew and such a larder, blaming everybody from the mess boy to the Captain for it all. Sardines for dinner! Bah! They were certainly in no mood for tipping generously.

George, who worked in the pantry and who would eat half the passengers' scanty food before it reached the table, said the Captain's face was so red at mealtime he thought the Old Man was burning up. And the night the sardines appeared, George swore the missionaries forgot to bless the table.

That night in the petty officers' mess we had a stew made out of all the scraps of garbage left over from the days that had gone before, and for dessert a tasteless hardtack pudding the second cook had concocted. It was a good thing we sighted the Virgin Islands shortly or there might have been a riot aboard.

We reached New York on an autumn day as beautiful and bright as if all storms had forever passed. We docked at noon. As soon as the gangplank was down, the passengers departed in high dudgeon, giving the Captain and all the officials of the line a large and fluent piece of their mind.

As we tied up at dock, there had been much loud talking in the Captain's quarters. The Chief Engineer, he of the overflowing oil, already had his bags packed. When the paymaster arrived, we were—each and every one of the crew of forty-two—given our walking papers. That was the only job from which I have ever been fired.

This time, there was no chance to quit first.

STANDEE
wwwwwwwwwwwww

We had lived together six months, that crew of the old S.S. *Malone,* pal'd around together in dozens of West African ports, worked together, played together, fought together, slept with the same women, drunk from the same bottles; now, in one short afternoon, given our money and our discharge, the boat emptied quickly of sailors, firemen, mess boys, cooks, officers—everybody gone! Melting into the crowds of lower New York, I never saw a single one of those forty-two men again.

With my monkey, I went to Harlem. My former landlady had moved. Near her old place, I saw a ROOM FOR RENT sign in a window, so I stopped at the apartment door.

A woman opened the door and screamed: "What devilish thing is that you got on your shoulder?"

She shut the door swiftly to only a crack, as Jocko clutched my ear, chattered and trembled in fright.

"A monkey," I said. "He's tame."

"Tame or not, I don't take no monkeys here," she shouted. "Get out of this hallway with that varmint— scarin' the livin' daylights out o' me."

Bang! and the door closed. With the next landlady, I

fared no better. Finally, in desperation, I got a bartender in a speakeasy to let me tie Jocko in his back room for half an hour. Then I went to find a place to sleep. But in Harlem there was no resting place for a monkey, so I had to come back and get Jocko, put him under my coat, and take the subway downtown to a pet shop where animals were boarded, a shop that I had located through the classified telephone book.

At the shop they seemed delighted to have Jocko as a guest. They proclaimed him to be a rare species of red monkey seldom seen in America. Then they put him into a clean cage all to himself and assured me he would be well taken care of, and that the bill would be moderate. They couldn't say offhand just what, but not much. So I left Jocko clinging to the bars, weeping and waving wildly after me as I went out. I hated to leave him there in a strange place in downtown New York, but the women in Harlem didn't seem to like him.

I intended to stay in New York only a day or two, just long enough to get a new suit. Then I planned to go home for a visit to McKeesport, near Pittsburgh, where my mother was then living with my step-father. I wrote my kid brother that I was bringing him a present, but I didn't tell him what it was.

I went from the pet shop to the Pennsylvania station and priced a ticket to McKeesport. Then I walked over to Broadway to window-shop for suits. As I passed the Metropolitan Opera House, I noticed two huge placards posted there, announcing the opening of the American tour of Eleonora Duse, the great Italian actress. My heart stood still and I knew I couldn't go to McKeesport until I had seen Duse!

All my life, it seemed, I had read the legend of Duse—

the hands of Duse, the eyes of Duse, how simply to sit in her presence, the core of your being would be stirred! On the boat up the Hudson, I had read d'Annunzio's romance, *The Flame of Life,* through which she moved as a touring actress on the dusty roads of Italy, a virgin Juliet in the amphitheater of Verona, a wraith of beauty gliding along the leaf-strewn canals of Venice in the autumn, a great artist and a great woman. I had to see Duse.

But the opening was over a week off. Nevertheless, I decided to stay in New York until it occurred, so I paid two weeks' rent. I bought a new suit and a coat. I put aside the fare to McKeesport and I had fifty-two dollars left.

I wanted to take my mother fifty dollars, then I decided forty would do, since I had to eat for ten days. I ate in fifteen-cent lunch rooms, went to the movies, and waited for Duse to come. All the cheaper seats were sold in advance, so I had to depend on standing room. I could not afford anything else.

Finally, the day of Duse's opening arrived. I left Harlem in the early afternoon. There was already a line curving around the Metropolitan into Thirty-ninth Street. It was cold and people had folding stools, some of them sitting in line with blankets on their knees. I had filled my pockets with peanuts and stood in line all afternoon eating them.

Toward evening, it got colder, so I bought a newspaper and put half of it inside my coat across my chest, and the other part around my feet. Slowly the lights came on in the blue November dusk. Horns and headlights cut through the frosty air. People poured into the streets, home-bound from work. Newsboys cried the final editions. Then came that strange Broadway lull that just precedes the theater hour, when the streets are not so busy, nor the traffic so noisy.

But the line for Eleonora Duse had grown and grown. Soon the lights of the huge opera house were lighted and a crowd began to collect at the entrances to the theater. An occasional car glided up to the carriage entrance, some official perhaps, or a patron, or a very early comer.

Now, more often the cars came, and the crowds grew. Finally our line began to move. Slowly. Slowly. Too slowly, and an awful thought struck me! Suppose there was no more standing room left by the time I got to the box office!

The line moved. Halted. And moved. I grew nervous. But the two middle-aged women in front of me, Italians, were not impatient. They calmly edged their stools along as the line moved. After a while they picked them up and folded them over their arms, when we neared the corner. Finally the line turned the corner and we were moving along against the wall on the Broadway side, where two big cops kept outsiders from breaking into the line that we had held so long. My feet were very cold, and I was hungry, but finally I reached the lobby, and the box office, and at last had a ticket in my hand. Then—inside, early enough to get a place at the tall partition, leaning right up against the rail at the rear of the auditorium.

It must have been a good hour before the orchestra filed in, and it was finally time for the curtain to rise. Still it did not rise on time. People kept pouring into the theater—in the orchestra and boxes, a brilliant crowd in top hats and shimmering evening gowns.

Finally the lights darkened and the play began. It was Ibsen's *Lady from the Sea*, in Italian. (I kept wishing it was a real Italian play instead of a Scandinavian drama performed in Italian before an American crowd.) The people were restless. It was very warm in the theater, and I was tired from waiting in line so long. The standees behind pressed against my back and coughed on my shoulders. I began to be sleepier and sleepier, but finally Duse entered—the famous, the legendary, the great Duse— and there was a wave of applause as a slight, weary, gray little woman stopped at the center of the stage.

Then she began to speak. But her voice was lost, and somehow the magic didn't come through. Even when she lifted her famous hands, in the vastness of the Metropolitan Opera House that night the magic didn't come through. She seemed just a tiny little old woman, on an enormous stage, speaking in a foreign language, before an audience that didn't understand. After a while, behind me some of the people began to drift out and it was not so crowded among the standees. Before it was over, there was plenty of room.

JOCKO

The next day I went to the pet shop to get Jocko. Jocko was delighted to see me, chattering and screaming as soon as I stepped in the door. But the proprietors handed me a bill for thirty dollars! I was stunned. Elegantly, they explained that Jocko was a very special kind of monkey and that he had to have very special care. They said he required a diet of Indian rice and milk and fruit. When I told them that he had eaten anything and everything on the boat, they said that couldn't be true, because any-and-everything would not agree with such a monkey. So they charged me thirty dollars. I had almost nothing left in my pockets.

I put Jocko in a little black handbag, with a couple of round holes punched at each end for air. He did not like being in the bag at all, and whined and kicked and kept up an awful racket all the way to the station. I was afraid the conductor on the train would hear him and put him out. The baggage man had already said monkeys could not be checked except in wire cages, and I had no wire cage. But once on the train, it seemed that everything was all right. I was due to reach home about two o'clock in the morning. I went to sleep in the day coach, and I guess Jocko did, too, because he remained quiet.

Then a calamity happened. The conductor came through and said all day coach passengers must change trains at Washington.

"Change for what?" I asked him.

"This train's all Pullman beyond Washington," he said. "Next train for McKeesport is in the morning."

For the second time that day, I was stunned. The ticket agents in New York had not told me that, and I had no money to secure Pullman space, nor to spend the night in a hotel in Washington. In fact, I had less than a dollar, getting home from my African trip with less than a dollar—after Duse and Jocko!

I could hear my mother now: "Coming home with only a monkey, heh?"

But I did want to get home quickly with Jocko. I was afraid that a night in Washington, perhaps in a cold station waiting room, might give him pneumonia. I had to think of some way of going on through to McKeesport on that train in a Pullman.

I spoke to one of the porters on the train. I tried to sell him some African souvenirs I had in my bag, rhinoceros-hide slippers or a hammered-brass tray. But he would have none of them. He didn't believe they were real, and he didn't believe I had been to Africa. He thought I was just some college kid trying to fool him.

The train laid over for half an hour in Washington, dropping the day coaches and making up the Pullmans. I rushed out into the station and asked a policeman where the nearest pawnshop was. That was an error—to ask a policeman about a pawnshop. But in my excitement, I didn't think of the danger of arrest. He looked me up and down, but in my new suit, I guess I didn't look like a suspicious character. Finally, he said slowly: "The nearest pawnshop, young man, is way over yonder in Virginia. There ain't none in the District of Columbia."

So that hope was out! I needed three dollars to get Pullman space to McKeesport, and I had eighty cents. And Jocko and I were both hungry. I tried the red caps in the station. I spoke of Africa and pulled my brass trays and African beads and the vermilion slippers out of my bag, but no takers—not for three dollars. Then, with only ten minutes left, and Jocko whimpering and kicking in his bag, a bright thought struck me. With my new suit, there were two pairs of trousers. It was a nice blue serge suit, and I had never put the extra pair of trousers on. I took the trousers out of my suitcase and offered them to a red-cap for two dollars and a half. The red cap bought them. Without putting the money in my pocket, I rushed to get Pullman space in the parlor car. I just made the train as it pulled out.

I put Jocko down behind the seat, hoping that he would hush his noise, or that the rattle of the train would drown his whimpering. It was bitter cold that autumn night and I was sorry for the poor little beast out of Africa. I took my coat and dropped it over the bag. The conductor came and sniffed the air suspiciously, but punched my ticket and went on. I had been around Jocko so long that I didn't realize he smelt like a zoo at close range—and particularly so tonight, after a long afternoon in that small black bag. I don't know what the conductor thought each time he passed by my seat, sniffed, and looked down. I guess he thought it was me, so I pretended to be asleep. (But I felt bad.)

I was glad to get home. Although I had never been in McKeesport before, I called it home, because my mother had moved there. They all met me at the station, my mother, Dad and my little brother, Kit. But I didn't reveal Jocko until I got to the house, although they surely must have smelt him. I didn't even mention his name. Once home, however, I opened the bag and Jocko leaped out, big as the jungle.

My mother gave a cry of horror. My step-father looked amazed. My little brother fled. Jocko jumped into my arms, and my mother locked me and Jocko into a bedroom together for the night. They were afraid the monkey might get out and attack them.

He was a big red monkey, and if you didn't know him, I guess he did look fierce. But my little brother, who was then about eleven, became very pleased to have him. And Jocko soon became attached to him, too. In fact, Jocko became so attached to my brother, that he would leap into his arms, cuddle there, and be quite content all day. But the moment my brother wanted to put Jocko down, he would scream, kick, and bite. Result, any time Jocko reached Kit's arms, Kit had to hold him until I got home and rescued him from the grasp of the too-contented monkey.

One Saturday when my mother and I went into Pittsburgh, about ten in the morning, Kit picked up the monkey to take him for a walk. He still had Jocko in his arms at six that afternoon, having tried unsuccessfully all day to put him down on the floor.

My mother hated Jocko and, because Jocko knew she was afraid of him, he would tease her by biting at her skirt and leaping up behind her, pulling at her apron strings until he untied them. Sometimes he would make for her sewing basket and fill his mouth with buttons or thimbles. He used also to pack his pouch with phonograph needles and go spitting them out all around the place just for the fun of it.

We had rented the top floor of an old wooden house from an orthodox Jewish family who lived downstairs. The wife wore a wig and the old man a skull cap. It was a house down by the river in McKeesport, and there were trees around it, in which Jocko used to love to climb on warm autumn days, with the bright leaves falling and the sun shining. One day the wife of our landlord came near the tree where Jocko was playing and stood laughing at him. Suddenly Jocko swung by his paw down from a limb and grabbed the elderly Jewish lady by the hair. She fled, leaving her wig in Jocko's paw.

My step-father was amused at Jocko and it was his special pleading with my mother that permitted us to keep him. But Kit and I almost lost the battle when Dad's own mother arrived for a visit from Topeka. She was a neat, elderly lady, the wife of a former presiding elder of the church, and somewhat staid. Before her arrival, we shortened Jocko's rope where he was tied to a table leg in a corner of the kitchen. But during the excitement of her arrival, somehow he got loose, and no sooner did my step-grandmother reach the bottom of the stairs leading to our floor than Jocko leaped chattering on the railing at the top. The old lady set her bags down in shocked amazement and refused to come another step. She said it was her, or Jocko! We could choose. So we had to lock Jocko in a closet for the night, and the next day she insisted we build a cage and put him in it or else she would return to Kansas.

Now, my mother had an ally in the house in her opposition to Jocko. But by this time his fame had spread far and wide. All the school children in my brother's class came to see him. And many adults, as well, whom we had never met, came to call on Jocko. Nobody asked anymore how any member of the family was, but always: "How is Jocko?"

One pay day, my step-father conceived the idea of taking Jocko around to the pool hall on a Saturday night, so all the men of the neighborhood could see him. Washed and combed with a little knitted sweater on, Jocko leaped to dad's shoulder and they started out. The rest is history.

My step-father and Jocko arrived at the pool hall about eight o'clock. It was crowded with Saturday night players, young loungers, spectators, and drunks. It was loud and smoky therein, but Jocko's arrival created a sensation. The men crowded around to see him—the big red monkey, with whiskers and a sweater on.

The better to show the animal off, Dad put him down on the green pool table, holding him by a long leash. But the noise and the people and the smoke and the shouting were too much for Jocko, surrounded on the table by the crowd. He uttered a yell of fright and began to run frantically back and forth on the pool table as far as his leash would permit. The crowd roared with laughter, and the ring of dark faces closed in on poor Jocko, closer and closer, frightening him so badly that suddenly he could no longer control himself, and without warning his bowels began to move all over the table.

The crowd bent double with laughter, but the proprietor almost had apoplexy. Jocko made an awful mess on the green baize, and the boss wanted to have Dad arrested, so he had to pay to have the table redone.

The men kidded my step-father about that for months. But not my mother! Because it cost twenty-five dollars for a new cover for the table, and my step-father had to pay for it, my mother was very mad.

A few days after that I left, to return to New York.

Within a week, my mother sold Jocko to a Pittsburgh pet shop. The first letter I got from home told me that now he would certainly pull at her apron strings no more, the Congo devil! But I was sorry. He was the best pet I ever had. He used to put his arms around my neck. And he cried when I left the house.

BAD LUCK IS GOOD

Back in New York I got a job on a boat bound for Constantinople and Odessa. The former mess boys had all been white, but now they were changing the steward's crew to colored. The boat was anchored in the stream out in New York harbor, waiting to load. One of the white mess boys was still aboard and a new Spanish-speaking colored boy had arrived just before I came. We slept in the same room on tiered bunks. None of us knew each other, but I thought the other two fellows looked all right. That night about ten we locked the door and went to bed.

The next morning when we woke up, as the white boy pulled on his pants, he felt in his pockets, and yelled: "My money's gone!"

The Puerto Rican grabbed his pants, looked, and also cried: "My money's gone, too!"

I jumped down from the top bunk and opened my wallet—and my money was gone, also!

The door was still locked. No one had entered, so we looked from one to another. Who took the money? Some one of the three of us had robbed the other two, that was clear. But nobody quite dared take a chance on making an accusation on less than a twenty-four-hour acquaintance. There was dead silence as we stared at one another suspiciously—the Puerto Rican, the white boy, and I.

"I had four dollars," I said.

"Me, ten," said the Puerto Rican.

"Seven bucks gone," said the white boy. "Damn it!"

"Well, whoever took it, I hope he rot in hell!" said the Puerto Rican.

"Me, too!" I added.

"I hope he drops dead right here!" said the white boy.

But nobody dropped dead. We just glared from one to another as we dressed. All I know is, it wasn't I who took the money, because I was flat broke all the rest of the week, without a penny in the world.

The next day we began to load supplies for the galley. Coming up from the wharf with a bag of potatoes, the

Chief Steward fell from the top of the ladder and broke his arm. He was sent to the hospital and a new steward came aboard, who said he had never worked with a colored crew and therefore was sending for a set of white boys to replace us. When the white boys came, the Puerto Rican and I were promptly discharged. A day later, the boat sailed. And a month later it was at the bottom of the Black Sea! It was blown up by a stray mine, which had been floating there since the Great War, a stray mine that the mine sweepers had missed. The papers said more than half the crew drowned. When I read about it, I thought how lucky it was for me that a bag of potatoes had caused a broken arm. And a broken arm, a change in stewards. And that the new steward didn't like colored folks.

WINTER SEAS TO ROTTERDAM

The next job I got was on a vile-looking tub, running from Hoboken to the West Indies, with a bunch of cut-throats in the crew. I think the boat must have been a rum-runner. They had only one cook, and one mess boy— me. And part of my job was to get up at four-thirty and start the fires going in the galley for the cook. The cook was a vicious old Negro from Barbados, with a scar across his face, six inches long. He informed me early that he was the boss and that I not only had to act as general mess boy, but also peel potatoes, knead the bread, scrub the galley, wash the pots, empty the ashes, shine the brass—and wake him up in the morning as well, with a cup of coffee in hand. I quit.

Then I got a job going to Holland on a big, clean-look-ing freighter, on a regular run between Rotterdam and New York. The first December snow was falling as we passed the Statue of Liberty. Off Sandy Hook, the sea rolled in mountains. The wind blew keen. We had a twenty-day crossing, in a terrific storm all the way.

We got to Rotterdam, Christmas Eve, 1923, and stayed until New Year's. The town was covered with snow and the canals were frozen. But the cozy waterfront taverns were warm and the stone jugs of gin good to the belly. There were hot rum punches at the café concerts, and wonderful food served by the ton in the restaurants. Rotterdam's Chinatown and the famous Schiedamschedyk of the sailors were full of excitement. The canals, and the kids in wooden shoes, and the low, quaint houses of the town were picturesque and beautiful. The Dutch people seemed friendly and kind. The old watchman on the dock took all the Negro boys on our boat to his home to taste his wife's holiday cakes. There I met his daughter, who was married to a French lad. And I began to talk to the Frenchman about Paris, using my high school French. The more I talked to him about Paris, the more I wanted to go there—and not just go, but *stay* long enough really to know the city. I felt sure I would fall in love with Paris, once I saw it.

The day we sailed for New York, another fellow and I drank a whole jug of Hulskamps gin ourselves, in a tavern near the wharf while we were waiting for the ship's whistle to blow. When we hit the English Channel that night, choppy and wind-blown as it was, I began to be seasick for the first and only time in my life. But I thought I was going to die. I rocked! And the sea rocked! And the boat rocked! And the world went round and round! When we got out of the Channel, we ran into one of those North Atlantic gales that lasted half-way to New York. And for over a week, every time the boat would sway, my stomach would sway, too. That cured me of ever again drinking too much gin.

Back in New York, I decided to stay on the ship for another trip, maybe several. The steward was a good guy, the Captain pleasant, and the crew lively. One of our sailors from a well-to-do family in Washington told me his sister was married to Francis Carco, the French writer, and he invited the whole crew to run down to Paris and visit them.

Our second trip across was as bad as the first, so far as weather went. And worse in other respects. Several very unfortunate things happened aboard. Three days out of New York harbor, on a bitter-cold, windy day, our Chief Engineer died. Double pneumonia, and we had no doctor aboard. I saw my first funeral at sea. They sewed his body in a canvas shroud, laid him on a cooling board, covered the board with an American flag, and pushed it up to the edge of the boat. The engines stopped. The crew gathered around and the Captain read a few words out of the Bible. Then the assistant engineers lifted up one end of the board, and the Chief's body slid off into the tossing sea. But they held on to the flag and put it away for the next funeral.

The rough weather continued. We had to tie our suitcases beneath our bunks to keep them from wearing out sliding across the floor. In fact, on the previous trip, what the wear and tear of a rocking boat can do was pretty well impressed on me by what happened to a fellow-messman's suit, which he had bought in Harlem just before we sailed. It was a brand-new, pinch-back suit, tailored in the style of the times. The saloon mess boy, my cabinmate, was very pleased with it. He took it and hung it neatly on a hanger as we passed Sandy Hook. Then very carefully, he draped a sheet around it to keep off the dust. Then he hung the hanger on a peg against the wall. Every time the boat rocked, naturally the suit would swing. For twenty days that suit swung there against the rough wall, back and forth in a wide arc, following the rocking of the boat. When we got to Rotterdam and the mess boy took his suit down to go ashore, the whole back of the suit was worn out, just from swinging against the wall. Right through the sheet and all across the shoulders, completely worn out!

The second trip for this mess boy, Eddie, was even more disastrous. This time he didn't lose a suit, but he had a very painful accident. The cook set a steaming pot of boiling cabbage down on the galley deck one noon, just before meal time. The boat lurched and the pot slid over the tile floor, stopping only when it reached the water bank at the door. Just then Eddie came rushing through the door and stepped straight into the uncovered pot of boiling cabbage.

His foot and ankle were so badly scalded that he could not work for the rest of the trip, and I was changed from the P.O. mess to the officers' saloon, taking over his job—which meant I had to get up an hour earlier every morning to take the Captain's coffee to him on the bridge at five, struggling in oilskins through the howling storm, since on a freight boat there are very few protected passageways or staircases. Almost everything is wide open to the wind and wave, and all cabin doors give directly on the elements. You must have oilskins and boots to work on the Western Ocean in the winter time, and you can't be seasick, and you can't be scared. If you were scared, you'd never get across the deck when the big waves come over, roaring like thunder and dangerous as hundred-ton mountains falling.

Sometimes waves would hit our boat with such violence that she would shake and rattle as though she were going to splinter into a million pieces—but she didn't break. She always went on. Sometimes she'd be down in a trough of water twice as tall as the masts. Then the water would lift her up again, so high in the air you could see miles of rolling ocean around her, restless and angry. But she always went on. The strength of a ship and the strength of water, and the strength of a handful of men going on through the storm, against distance and wind and waves until they get where they are going is thrilling—still thrilling—even if ships are run by steam now and sails no longer blow white before the masts.

But, to cap the climax of misfortunes, in mid-ocean, this trip, our wireless operator went crazy. Sparks, as sailors call him, went to pieces and imagined he had killed the Chief Engineer. He refused to leave his cabin. He brooded and talked out of his head. He wouldn't eat. He couldn't work. So we had no use of the wireless in mid-Atlantic in one of the worst storms in years. But we went on, ploughing through the waves. Finally, we reached the Channel.

When we got to Rotterdam, however, I thought maybe there might be a jinx on our ship, so I got off. I had twenty-five dollars coming. I drew it, packed my bags, and caught the night train for Paris. Good-bye, old freight boat!

I will never forget the thrill of *La Frontière*. In the middle of the night the French customs inspectors came through, throwing open all the many doors of our third-class coach, and letting in the snow and the cold night wind that swirled about the little station. I was in France.

La Frontière!

La France!

The train to Paris. A dream come true.

MONTMARTRE

My ticket and the French visa had taken nearly all my money. I got to the Gare du Nord in Paris early one February morning with only seven dollars in my pockets. I didn't know anybody in Paris. I didn't know anybody in the whole of Europe, except the old Dutch watchman's family in Rotterdam. But I had made up my mind to pass the rest of the winter in Paris.

I checked my bags at the parcel stand, and had some coffee and rolls in the station. I found that my high school French didn't work very well, and that I understood nothing anyone said to me. They talked too fast. But I could read French.

I went outside the station and saw a bus marked *Opéra*. I knew the opera was at the center of Paris, so I got in the bus and rode down there, determined to do a little sight-seeing before I looked for work, or maybe starved to death. When I got to the Opéra, a fine wet snow was falling. People were pouring out of the Métro on their way to work. To the right and left of me stretched the Grands Boulevards. I looked across the street and saw the Café de la Paix. Ahead the Vendôme. I walked down the

rue de la Paix, turned, and on until I came out at the
Concorde. I recognized the Champs Elysées, and the great
Arc de Triomphe in the distance through the snow.

Boy, was I thrilled! I was torn between walking up the
Champs Elysées or down along the Seine, past the Tui-
leries. Finally, I took the river, hoping to see the book-
stalls and Notre Dame. But I ended up in the Louvre
instead, looking at Venus.

It was warmer in the Louvre than in the street, and the
Greek statues were calm and friendly. I said to the statues:
"If you can stay in Paris as long as you've been here and
still look O.K., I guess I can stay a while with seven dollars and make a go of it." But when I came out of the
Louvre, I was tired and hungry. I had no idea where I
would sleep that night, or where to go about finding a
cheap hotel. So I began to look around for someone I
could talk to. To tell the truth, I began to look for a colored person on the streets of Paris.

As luck would have it, I came across an American Negro
in a doorman's uniform. He told me most of the American
colored people he knew lived in Montmartre, and that
they were musicians working in the theaters and night
clubs. He directed me to Montmartre. I walked. I passed
Notre Dame de Lorette, then on up the hill. I got to
Montmartre about four o'clock. Many of the people there
were just getting up and having their breakfast at that
hour, since they worked all night. I don't think they were
in a very good humor, because I went into a little café
where I saw some colored musicians sitting, having their
coffee. I spoke to them, and said: "I've just come to Paris,
and I'm looking for a cheap place to stay and a job."

They scowled at me. Finally one of them said: "Well,
what instrument do you play?"

They thought I was musical competition.

I said: "None. I'm just looking for an ordinary job."

Puzzled, another one asked: "Do you tap dance, or what?"

"No," I said, "I've just got off a ship and I want any kind of a job there is."

"You must be crazy, boy," one of the men said. "There ain't no 'any kind of a job' here. There're plenty of French people for ordinary work. 'Less you can play jazz or tap dance, you'd just as well go back home."

"He's telling you right," the rest of the fellows at the table agreed, "there's no work here."

But one of them indicated a hotel. "Go over there across the street and see if you can't get a little room cheap."

I went. But it was high for me, almost a dollar a day in American money. However, I had to take the room for that night. Then I ate my first dinner in Paris—*bœuf au gros sel,* and a cream cheese with sugar. Even with the damp and the slush—for the snow had turned to a nasty rain—I began to like Paris a little, and to take it personally.

The next day I went everywhere where people spoke English, looking for a job—the American Library, the Embassy, the American Express, the newspaper offices. Nothing doing. Besides I would have to have a *carte d'identité.* But it would be better to go back home, I was advised, because there were plenty of people out of work in Paris.

"With five dollars, I can't go back home," I said.

People shrugged their shoulders and went on doing whatever they were doing. I tramped the streets. Late afternoon of the second day came. I went back to Montmartre, to that same little café in front of my hotel, where

I had no room that night—unless I paid again. And if I did take the same room again, with supper, I'd have scarcely four dollars left!

My bags were still checked at the station, so I had no clean clothes to put on. It was drizzling rain, and I was cold and hungry. I had had only coffee and a roll all day. I felt bad.

I slumped down at a table in the small café and ordered another *café crème* and a *croissant*—the second that day. I ate the croissant (a slender, curved French roll) and wondered what on earth I ought to do. I decided tomorrow to try the French for a job somewhere, maybe the Ritz or some other of the large hotels, or maybe where I had seen them building a big building on one of the boulevards. Perhaps they could use a hodcarrier.

The café had begun to be crowded, as the afternoon darkened into a damp and murky dusk. A tall, young colored fellow came in and sat down at the marble-topped table where I was. He ordered a *fine*, and asked me if I wanted to play dominoes.

I said no, I was looking for a cheap room.

He recommended his hotel, where he lived by the month, but when we figured it out, it was about the same as the place across the street, too high for me. I said I meant a *really* cheap room. I said I didn't care about heat or hot water or carpets on the floor right now, just a place to sleep. He said he didn't know of any hotels like that, as cheap as I needed.

Just then a girl, with reddish-blond hair, sitting on a bench that ran along the wall, spoke up and said: "You say you look at one hotel?"

I said: "Yes."

She said: "I know one, not much dear."

"Where?" I asked her. "And how much?"

"Almost not nothing," she said, "not dear! No! I will show you. Come."

She put on her thin coat and got up. I followed her. She was a short girl, with a round, pale Slavic face and big dark eyes. She had a little rouge on her cheeks. She had on a wine-red hat with a rain-wilted feather. She was pretty, but her slippers were worn at the heels. We walked up the hill in silence, across the Place Blanche and up toward the rue Lepic. Finally I said to her, in French, that I had very little money and the room would have to be very cheap or I would have nothing left to eat on, because I had no *travaille*. No *travaille* and no prospects, and I was not a musician.

She answered that this was the cheapest hotel in Montmartre, where she was taking me. *"Pas de tout cher."* But, as she spoke, I could tell that her French was almost as bad as mine, so we switched back to English, which she spoke passably well.

She said she had not been in Paris long, that she had come from Constantinople with a ballet troupe, and that she was Russian. Beyond that, she volunteered no information. The drizzling February rain wet our faces, the water was soggy in my shoes, and the girl looked none too warm in her thin but rather chic coat. After several turns up and down a narrow, winding street, we came to the hotel, a tall, neat-looking building, with a tiled entrance hall. From a tiny sitting room came a large French woman. And the girl spoke to her about the room, the very least dear, for *m'sieu.*

"Oui," said the woman, "a quite small room, by the week, fifty francs."

"I'll take it," I said, "and pay two weeks." I knew it would leave me almost nothing, but I would have a place to sleep.

I thanked the girl for bringing me to the hotel and I invited her to a cup of coffee with me next time we met at the café. We parted at the Place Blanche, and I went to the station to get my bags, now that I had some place to put them. After paying for the room and the storage of my bags, I had just about enough money left for coffee and rolls for a week—if I ate nothing *but* coffee and one roll a meal.

I was terribly hungry and it took me some time to get to the station by Métro. I got back to the hotel about nine that night, through a chilly drizzle. My key was not hanging on the hallboard, but the landlady pointed up, so I went up. It was a long climb with the bags, and I stopped on each landing to rest. I guess I was weak with hunger, having only eaten those two croissants all day. When I got to my room, I could see a light beneath the door, so I thought maybe I was confused about the number. I hesitated, then knocked. The door opened and there stood the Russian girl.

I said: "Hello!"

I didn't know what else to say.

She said: "I first return me," and smiled.

Her coat was hanging on a nail behind the door and a small bag sat beneath the window. She was barefooted, her wet shoes were beneath the heatless radiator, and her stockings drying on the foot of the bed.

I said: "Are you going to stay here, too?"

She said: "Of course! *Mais oui!* Why you think, I find one room?"

She had her hat off. Her red-blond hair was soft and wavy. She laughed and laughed. I laughed, too, since I didn't know what to say.

"I have no mon-nee nedder," she said.

We sat down on the bed. In broken English, she told me her story. Her name was Sonya. Her dancing troupe had gone to pieces in Nice. She had bought a ticket to Paris. And here we were—in a room that was all bed, just space barely to open the door, that was all, and a few nails in the barren wall, on which to hang clothes. No heat in the radiator. No table, no washstand, no chair, but a deep window seat that could serve as a chair and a place to put things on. It was cold, so cold you could see your breath. But the rent was cheap, so you couldn't ask for much.

We didn't ask for anything.

I put my suitcase under the bed. Sonya hung her clothes on the nails. She said: "If you have some francs I go *chez l'épicerie* and get white cheese and one small bread and one small wine and we have supper. Eat right here. That way are less dear."

I gave her ten francs and she went out shopping for the supper. We spread the food on the bed. It tasted very good and cost little, cheese and crisp, fresh bread and a bottle of wine. But I could see my francs gone in a few days more. Then what would we do? But Sonya said she was looking for a job, and perhaps she would find one soon, then we both could eat.

Not being accustomed to the quick friendship of the dispossessed, I wondered if she meant it. Later, I knew she did. She found a job first. And we both ate.

The day after I took the room, I wrote to my mother in McKeesport, requesting a loan. It was the first time I had ever written home asking for money. I told her that I was stranded in Paris, and would she or Dad please cable me twenty dollars. But I wondered how I would live the ten or twelve days I'd have to wait for the letter to reach America and the answer to come back. I was sure, however, that the money would come if my step-father had it. He was always generous and a good sport, my step-father.

Before I would have written my own father for a penny, I would have died in Paris, because I knew his answer would be: "I told you you should have listened to me, and gone to Switzerland to study, as I asked you!" So I would not write my father, though hunger reduced me to a skeleton, and I died of malnutrition on the steps of the Louvre.

Hunger came, too. Bread and cheese once a day couldn't keep hunger away. Selling your clothes, when you didn't have many, couldn't keep hunger away. Going to bed early and sleeping late couldn't keep hunger away. Looking for a job and always being turned down couldn't keep hunger away. Not sleeping alone couldn't keep hunger away.

Sonya did her stretching exercises on the bed every morning. There wasn't room to do them on the floor, and she wanted to keep in shape in case she got a job dancing. But Montmartre was full of Russian dancers—and no jobs.

She was twenty-four, older than I was. Her father had been on the wrong side in the Russian Revolution and had escaped to Turkey. He died in Roumania. Then Sonya danced in Bucharest, Budapest, Athens and Constantinople, Trieste, and Nice, where the troupe of dancers went to pieces because the manager fell ill, and contracts and working permits ran out. So Sonya, who, like me, had never seen Paris before, had packed up and come north.

Now, her costumes were all in pawn, and her best clothes, too. Still, she didn't look bad when she went out.

She walked with her head up. And from the hands of the usurer she had managed to hold back one evening gown of pearl-colored sequins, hanging limp against our wall.

WORK

Sonya found work as a danseuse at Zelli's famous night club in the rue Fontaine. Not as a dancer in the show, but as a dancer with the patrons—a girl who sits at tables, dances with the guests and persuades them to order one more drink—and then another—usually champagne. She got no pay, but drew a commission on every bottle of champagne, beyond the first, she could persuade a guest to buy. Result, she drank a great many glasses of champagne every night, because the faster she could aid a bottle of champagne to disappear, the sooner a new one would appear, and like lightning, be opened by the attentive waiters, with an additional commission added in Sonya's column at the *caisse*.

Most of the danseuses in the clubs did not really enjoy drinking champagne night after night, and they would dump it into the ice bucket if they got a chance, or the waiters would help them by carrying off each bottle half-emptied, if the guest was not observant. Then, with the bottle gone, the little danseuse would sigh: "It is so ver-ree warm this night. Couldn't we have just another one lee-tle drink champagne, please?" And if the guest was at all a good sport, he would naturally give the waiter the nod to open another 200-franc quart of *Cordon Rouge* that had already appeared like magic in the ice bucket on his table, waiting for the word for the cork to pop.

Some nights Zelli's did good business and some nights not, so Sonya's income varied greatly. It was never large, because it was a big club and Zelli had a great many girls working there, and it was not summer, with the American tourist trade to help out. So after a time, Sonya went to work in another smaller club, where there were only two danseuses. That was after we had known one another some three weeks, and I hadn't found a job yet, and most of my clothes were sold.

But one morning at daybreak, Sonya came home and woke me up with a joyous shout. "Loo-oo-ook-ee here!" she cried. She opened her pocketbook and it was full of money that fell out all over the bed.

"Where did you get it?" I asked sleepily.

"Took it," she said, "from a Danish who waste it anyhow."

It seems that a visiting Dane (in Paris for the first time) had got very drunk on the eight bottles of champagne Sonya helped him order. So when closing time came, Sonya kindly helped him pay his bill, too. And, in doing so, simply helped herself to a large handful of the Dane's francs.

"I deedn't take him all," she said, "just some lee-tle I need."

She was very happy to have money, and so was I. So we both dressed and went to the barber shop and got our hair cut. I got a shine, and Sonya, a manicure. Then we had luncheon at a café on the Place Pigalle. After that we went to a movie on the Boulevards, my first theater in Paris. And at dusk, we came back up to the little café on the rue Bruyère, where the Montmartre performers hung out in the late afternoon, a place the Negroes called "The Flea Pit."

The café was crowded. We were sitting just inside the big window overlooking the street with our *fines*, when all of a sudden, Sonya went down under the table.

Startled, I thought she had fainted. But no; she had not fainted. She sat on the floor under the table, motioning everyone to be quiet and pay her no mind. She whispered to me that the big Dane was just passing the window outside! Fortunately, he didn't look in. He continued ambling along down the hill in the dusk, out of sight.

By now, I'd been in Paris a month and still had no job. At some of the places where I sought work, the French employees had almost run me away, particularly on one big construction job, where I thought the irate workmen, for a moment, intended to shower me with bricks.

"*Salaud!*" they screamed. "*Sale étranger!*"

It seems that there was a bitter anti-foreign feeling then among the French workers, because so many Italians and Poles had come to Paris and were working for even lower wages than the underpaid Frenchmen. I wasn't an Italian or a Pole, but they knew I was a foreigner of some kind, and they didn't like me, so they shouted insults.

And still there was no letter from my mother in McKeesport, much less a cable for twenty dollars. Finally, when a letter did arrive from home, it contained the longest list of calamities I have ever seen on one sheet of paper.

In the first place, my mother wrote, my step-father was seriously ill in the city hospital with pneumonia; she herself had no job and no money; my little brother had been expelled from school for fighting; and besides all that, the river was rising in McKeesport. The water was already knee-deep at the door, and if it got any higher she would have to get a rowboat and move out of the house. The Jewish people downstairs had fled to stay with relatives. But my mother had no place to go, and she couldn't even send me a two-cent stamp, much less twenty dollars. Besides, what was I doing way over there in France? Why didn't I stay home like decent folks, get a job, and go to work and help her—instead of galavanting all over the world as a sailor, and writing from Paris for money?

Well, I felt bad. I wondered how I would ever get back home, and how my mother would get along with so much trouble on her hands.

Fortunately, a few days after that letter came, I got a job myself. I had tried all the big night clubs in Montmartre, now I decided to try the little ones; so I started out early one evening. I noticed a little club in the rue Fontaine that had no doorman. I went in and asked for the owner. The owner turned out to be a colored woman, a *Martiniquaise*. I addressed her politely in my best French and asked if she needed a *chausseur*. She looked at me a moment, and finally said: *"Oui! Cinq francs et le dîner."* Naturally, I accepted.

Then and there, she showed me the way to the kitchen, where the cook fed me. And at ten o'clock that night, I took up my post outside the door on the rue Fontaine. The heavy dinner the cook gave me and the big bottle of wine that went with it made me so sleepy that I went to sleep standing up in the street outside the door. I couldn't help it. I slept almost all night.

I had no uniform, but the next day, at the Flea Market, I bought a blue cap with gold braid on it, which gave me an air of authority. My salary, five francs a night, was less than a quarter in American money, but it was a great help in Paris until I could do better.

Shortly after I began working for the Martinique lady, Sonya secured a contract to dance at Le Havre, so one rainy March afternoon I went to the Gare St. Lazare with her to say good-bye. She cried and I felt bad seeing her cry. She had been a swell friend and I liked her. She waved at me through the window as the long train pulled out. I waved back. And I never saw her any more.

That night I felt lonesome and sad standing outside the door of the little *boîte* in the cold, damp, winter night, my collar turned up and my cap with the gold braid pulled down as far over my ears as it would come. Every so often, I would step inside the door to get warm. Business was dull.

It was a very small night club of not more than ten tables and a tiny bar. There was a little Tzigane orchestra, and one entertainer. And a great many fights in the place.

Since they sold no cigarettes, the way I made my tips was largely by going to the corner to the *tabac* for packages of smokes for the guests. But whenever a fight would break out, I made an especial point of heading for the tabac so that I would not be called upon to stop it. I didn't know when I took the job that I was expected to be a bouncer as well as a doorman, and I didn't like the task of fight-stopping, because the first fight I saw there was between ladies, who shattered champagne glasses on the edge of the table, then slashed at each other with the jagged stems.

Madame's friend was a tall Roumanian girl, with large green circles painted on her eyes, who often came to the club in a white riding habit, white boots and hat, carrying a black whip. And madame herself would fight if the girl were insulted by any of the guests. For such a job, five francs was not enough, and the fights were too much, so I was glad when I found other work. Rayford Logan told me about an opening at a popular club on the rue Pigalle.

Rayford Logan is now a professor of history at Howard University in Washington. Then, he had been in France since the war, one of the Negro officers who stayed over there instead of coming home. That winter he was around Montmartre on crutches, having broken his leg in a bus accident. He received the *Crisis* all the time in Paris, and had read my poems, so when he knew I was a poet, he tried to help me find a job. One day he sent for me to tell me they needed a second cook at the Grand Duc, a well-known night club.

I couldn't cook, but I decided to say I could. Fortunately the title, second cook, really meant dishwasher, so I got the job. They fired another boy to give it to me. Strangely enough, the other boy happened to be from Cleveland, too, a tall brownskin fellow named Bob. He was discharged, the bosses said, because he came late to work, was unreliable, broke too many dishes, and cussed out the proprietors.

Gene Bullard, the colored manager, told me to be at work at eleven o'clock. Salary, fifteen francs a night and breakfast.

I was coming up in the world.

LE GRAND DUC

The cook at the Grand Duc's name was Bruce. He was an enormous brownskin fellow, with one eye, stout, and nearing fifty. He wore a white apron, a white cap, and a very fierce frown. He could look at you so fiercely out of his one eye that you would quake in your shoes. His other eye was closed tight. But the one he had looked like three.

Bruce was boss in his own domain, the kitchen. During his hours there, from 11 P.M. to 7 A.M., he would let no one else come in the kitchen, not even the boss or the manager. Only his helper, myself, was permitted. The others called for what they wished at the service window, and woe to the impatient waiter who set foot inside the door. Bruce had once hung a pan of pancake batter over such a waiter's head, and several others had often seen the threat of a raised knife. Bruce was highly respected by the employees of the Grand Duc, and addressed with great gentility.

Because he could fry the best chicken à la Maryland in Paris, with corn fritters and gravy, because he could bake beans the way Boston bakes them, and make a golden brown Virginia corn bread that would melt in your mouth, Bruce had a public all his own, was a distinct asset to the place, and his little vagaries were permitted.

They had to be permitted or he would quit.

It was good, working with Bruce, because he would let no one else give you any orders of any kind, neither the French owners nor the Negro manager. And if any waiter said to me: "Hurry up, boy, and hand me some butter,"

Bruce would bellow: "If you're in such a rush, why don't you tell *me* to hurry up? I'm in charge of this kitchen."

Not another peep out of the waiter, for Bruce's one big eye would petrify him.

Bruce was no respecter of persons, from the star entertainer, Florence, to the star patrons, such as Belle Livingston and Fannie Ward. If something about his food displeased a customer and it was sent back to the kitchen, Bruce would sometimes leave the kitchen himself, stick his head through the pantry curtains opening on the main room of the club, and glare down with his Cyclops eye on whatever unsuspecting patron had dared return a dish of *his*. If the patron's reasons were satisfactory, however, Bruce would go back to the kitchen and send out as tempting a new plate as mortal ever prepared. But if the patron was rude or drunk, he would get nothing from the hand of Bruce. Then Bruce would turn the order over to me, the dishwasher, without even the benefit of his advice on how to cook what was wanted. In my early days there, I turned out many strange concoctions—so strange that they embarrassed even the waiters.

Bruce did not like Fannie Ward and would never prepare an order for her table if he knew where the order originated—so I usually did the cooking for Miss Ward. I hope she never suffered indigestion.

A great many celebrities and millionaires came to the Grand Duc in those days, drawn by the fame of Florence Embry—known simply as Florence—the beautiful brown-skin girl from Harlem who sang there. Anita Loos and John Emerson, young William Leeds, the Dolly Sisters, Lady Nancy Cunard, various of the McCormicks. the writer, Robert McAlmon, and Belle Livingston with her son and daughter, Fannie Ward, looking not so very young,

Prince Tuvalou of Dahomey, Sparrow Robertson of the *Paris Herald*'s sport page, Joe Alix, who became Josephine Baker's dancing partner, the sur-realist poet, Louis Aragon, all came—and Florence would notice none of them unless they were very celebrated or very rich.

Part of Florence's reputation was based on snobbishness, no doubt, a professional snobbishness which she deliberately cultivated, because outside the club she was as kind and sociable a person as you would ever wish to find. And those who worked with her, from musicians to waiters, loved her. But to the patrons, she adopted an air of unattainable aloofness. She would sing a requested song with only the most casual glance at the table she was singing for—unless a duke, or a steel magnate, or a world celebrity sat there.

Rich, but lowly, patrons could tip Florence ever so heavily, and she would not even condescend to accept a glass of champagne with them. But the amazing thing was that they would come back and tip her even better for her songs the next time. In the snob world of *de luxe boîte de nuit* society it was considered a mark of distinction for Florence to sit for a moment at your table.

Most of the time when Florence was not singing she would remain at her own table by the orchestra saying: "Tell them, 'No, thank you!'" to the waiters who came with offers of champagne from guests who admired her looks or her singing. These frequent "No, thank you's" greatly infuriated the management, who were too short-sighted to see that that was, no doubt, a part of Florence's spell over her following—because she was by no means a great singer of popular songs. She was no Raquel Meller or Yvette Guilbert. But she was very pretty and brown, and could wear the gowns of the great Paris couturières as few other women could. At that time she went home every morning and got plenty of sleep, and would come to work every night looking as fresh and lovely as a black-eyed susan from some unheard-of Alabama *jardin de luxe,* where sophisticated darkies grow.

In the early part of the evening Florence would often laugh and talk with the waiters and the musicians, or with Bruce and me—but an hour later be as remote as you please to a party of well-to-do tourists from Wisconsin, spending a thousand francs at the front table. It was the first time I had ever seen a colored person deliberately and openly snubbing white people, so it always amused me no end to watch Florence move away from a table of money-spending Americans, who wanted nothing in the world so much as to have her sit down with them.

Her full name was Florence Embry Jones and her husband's name was Palmer Jones. Palmer was a fine piano player, and they frequently sang together. But Palmer at that time was working at the Ambassadeurs, and didn't arrive at the Grand Duc until about three in the morning so, until he came, Florence sang with the orchestra—perhaps a couple of songs an hour between dances, the popular American tunes of the day. Then when Palmer arrived, she would do a group of special numbers with him at the piano, if they felt like it.

Palmer himself knew a great many old blues and folksongs, like "Frankie and Johnnie" and "Henrico." He would occasionally sing one or two of those songs for the guests, inserting off-color lyrics if the crowd was that kind of crowd.

Then when all the other clubs were closed, the best of the musicians and entertainers from various other smart places would often drop into the Grand Duc, and there'd be a jam session until seven or eight in the morning—only in 1924 they had no such name for it. They'd just get together and the music would be on. The cream of the Negro musicians then in France, like Cricket Smith on the trumpet, Louis Jones on the violin, Palmer Jones at the piano, Frank Withers on the clarinet, and Buddy Gilmore at the drums, would weave out music that would almost make your heart stand still at dawn in a Paris night club in the rue Pigalle, when most of the guests were gone and you were washing the last pots and pans in a two-by-four kitchen, with the fire in the range dying and the one high window letting the soft dawn in.

Blues in the rue Pigalle. Black and laughing, heart-breaking blues in the Paris dawn, pounding like a pulse-beat, moving like the Mississippi!

> *Lawd, I looked and saw a spider*
> *Goin' up de wall.*
> *I say, I looked and saw a spider*
> *Goin' up de wall.*
> *I said where you goin', Mister Spider?*
> *I'm goin' to get my ashes hauled!*

Through the mist of smoke and champagne, you laughed at the loneliness of a tiny little spider, going up a great big wall to get his ashes hauled. And the blues went on:

> *I did more for my good gal*
> *Than de good Lawd ever done.*
> *Did more for my good gal*
> *Than de good Lawd ever done.*
> *I bought her some hair—*
> *Cause de Lawd ain't give her none.*

Play it, Mister Palmer Jones! Lawd! Lawd! Lawd! Play it, Buddy Gilmore! What you doin' to them drums? Man, you gonna bust your diamond studs in a minute!

> *Is you ever seen a*
> *One-eyed woman cry?*
> *I say, is you ever seen a*
> *One-eyed woman cry?*
> *Jack, she can cry so good*
> *Just out of that one old eye!*

PARIS IN THE SPRING

In April I moved to 15, rue Nollet near the Place Clichy in a room with slanting roofs up under the eaves, over-looking the chimney pots of Paris. It was a tall, old house, with very old furniture in the room, and a big bed with a feather tick. I don't believe the hotel had a name, simply HOTEL. (In France every rooming house is a hotel, but not all have names.)

The elderly French couple who ran the place were good people, and the rent was cheap. It was a quiet, working folks' hotel, with a little restaurant across the street, and a grocery store on the corner, and a cream and cheese shop next to the grocery.

That room was right out of a book, and I began to say to myself that I guess dreams do come true, and sometimes life makes its own books, because here I am living in a Paris garret, writing poems and having champagne for breakfast (because champagne is what we had with our breakfast at the Grand Duc from the half-empty bottles left by unsuspecting guests, in their ice buckets—thanks to their fleet removal by the waiters).

For a while I occupied my attic room alone. Then one night on my way to work I ran across Bob, the boy whose job I had taken at the cabaret. It was a cold, rainy night, depressingly wet and unpleasant, as so many early spring nights in Paris are. Bob was sitting at a café table, with his head in his arms, staring through the windowpane. He said he hadn't been able to find another job and he had no place to sleep and no money. So I gave him the key to my room and told him he could stay there. He moved in with me.

Then I found out why Bob couldn't keep a job. Although I seldom saw him, because he slept at night and I slept in the day, sometimes I would wake up in the late afternoon to find him there, sitting in a chair with his head in his hands staring into space.

I'd say: "Hey, Bob, what's the matter?"

And he would look up, glassy-eyed, and it would take him a long time to say anything. Gradually, it dawned on me that Bob used dope. And there was nothing you could do about it. He couldn't stop, he said.

So I was glad when Bob found work as a valet for an Englishman, and went away. Unfortunately, he didn't stay long.

One day, Rayford Logan, who was crippled and had helped me get the job at the Grand Duc, asked me to do him a favor and carry a note to a young lady living in the Latin Quarter. I took the note, got on a bus, and went over to the Boulevard St. Michel. The young lady lived just in front of the Luxembourg Gardens. She was an English-African girl named Mary. Her roommate was a Jamaican girl named Rosalie. They offered me tea and little cakes. I liked Mary, and was pleased to meet such a charming and cultured, good-looking colored girl. She said I might come back to see her again.

I went back. We became good friends and often went dancing together and to the theaters, and shortly we began to be in love. It was spring in Paris.

Mary's family divided their time between Lagos and London, for her father had business interests in West Africa, and so was frequently back and forth between England and the Nigerian coast. Mary had been educated in London and spoke very *English* English. And she thought I spoke very *American* American. Our accents were mutually amusing, and we used to laugh over the simplest words.

Mary was a soft, doe-skin brown. Perhaps her mother, now deceased, had been a white English woman. I never knew. But her father was an African of culture and money. Mary had read my poems in the *Crisis*, and she knew quite a lot about America, although she had never been there. But I think she had met Claude McKay, the Negro poet, in London. We both adored his "Spring in New Hampshire." But Rosalie, Mary's friend from the West Indies, said she did not like Claude McKay because he was too black. Rosalie was a light-skinned Jamaican, who had a violent prejudice toward dark Negroes—as, unfortunately, so many West Indian mulattoes have.

I said that color had nothing to do with the quality of one's writing. But Rosalie said it had to do with the quality of one's affections, and that was that. I didn't like Rosalie much, so I was glad when she went away to Seville for Easter.

Mary had been sent to Paris for a season by her father, because she had got herself engaged to an official in the colonial service of His Majesty's government, and now she didn't want to marry the official. All of which was very embarrassing to her father, who thought it a good match and was insisting that she carry it through. Mary still said no. Meantime, she was studying weaving at Raymond Duncan's school in Paris. Although she did not go about in a tunic and sandals like Raymond, she was, nevertheless, a great admirer of him and of Isadora, whom she had seen dance during her school days in London. So Mary, out of Africa, spent a great deal of her time talking about Isadora, out of Greece (by grace of San Francisco). And Mary gave me a piece of cloth woven with her own hands at Raymond Duncan's school.

She was amusing, Mary. We went dancing at the Moulin Rouge and walking in the forest at Versailles. I seldom had any money to spend, but she always had money, and would spend it with me. That embarrassed me at first, but then that was the only way we could go around much together, at all. And since we liked each other, after a while it didn't matter whose money we spent. We both liked shows, but seldom could go together except in the afternoons, since I had to be at work in the kitchen of the Grand Duc by eleven, and most French plays lasted much, much past that hour. But we often went to matinées at the varieties to hear Raquel Meller sing, and Damia, and Chevalier.

Spring came late in Paris that year, but when it did come, it was as golden-green a spring as I have ever seen, fresh and beautiful, and utterly Parisian. In June, Mary wanted to elope with me and run away to Florence and get married, then send her father a cable and tell him what she had done and tell him to tell the colonial official to go on back to his colony.

I was in love with Mary and the idea appealed to me immensely—until I felt my empty pocketbook. Then I said: "What would we live on in Italy?"

Mary said: "My father's allowance, until you set up in business."

"What business?" I wondered. "And suppose he cuts off your allowance?"

"He wouldn't dare cut off my allowance," said Mary.

But I thought he might dare, knowing fathers. And anyway, I couldn't see married life on a girl's money, when I myself didn't have the price of even a ring or a new suit to get married in.

But Rosalie must have written Mary's father, because Mary's sister suddenly showed up from London and began to chaperon us around—every date we had. She asked me about my family, and since it amused me to pretend that I had no ancestors, like an Alger boy, I wouldn't tell her anything. After a week, Mary's sister wanted to take Mary back to England, but Mary wouldn't go. She said she still had some important weaving to do at Raymond Duncan's school. So we took her sister to the boat train and gave her some candy to eat on the way to Dieppe.

One day, about noon, when I was sleeping good and deep in my feather tick under the eaves, tired from the night's work, there was a loud knock on the door, and a boy stood there with a note. Half asleep, I tore it open. It was from Mary. She said to come to her at once. She needed me. It was urgent.

Quickly, I dressed and went across Paris to the Latin Quarter to the big old house opposite the Luxembourg. Mary was in tears, packing. Her father had not only refused to continue her monthly allowance, but he had sent a friend of his to Paris, a distinguished Negro doctor,

well known in London, with an order to bring Mary back
at once to England. The doctor was returning on an early
evening boat train and Mary had to go with him.

She and I decided to have dinner together, far from the
Latin Quarter, so the doctor could not find us. We went
to a little restaurant in the Place du Tertre almost up to
Sacre-Cœur on top of the hill of Montmartre. We had
wine and *épaule de veau* and a *salade de saison* and *cœur
à la crème*. And then we went walking down the winding
old streets of the hill, and across the Boulevard Clichy.
And somehow we came to my house, and we went climbing up the steep stairs in the cool, half-dark hall, up, up,
up, until we came to where the roof slanted and my room
was under the eaves.

On the way to the house we had seen a pile of tiny
strawberries, the wild French *fraises de bois*, in a grocer's
window, so we bought a paper coneful, and two little jars
of yellow cream. And we sat in my room on the wide stone
window seat, in an open gabled window that looked over
the chimney pots of Paris, and ate the strawberries and
cream, dipping each berry into the cream and feeding
each other, and sadly watching the sun set over Paris. And
we felt very *tristes* and very young and helpless, because we
could not do what we wanted to do—be happy together
with no money and no fathers to worry us.

When the roof tops were gleaming like reddish brass,
and the sun was a great golden ball over the Bois, and
the cool evening breeze began to blow from the meadows
outside Paris, we knew that the doctor would be very, very
angry (mad in American) if Mary kept him waiting much
longer, so we went down to the street and found an old,
open horse carriage, with a wrinkled coachman in a black
coat, and arranged with him to drive us across the Seine,

past the Odéon, and the Gardens, to the house where Mary lived.

Driving in the dusk through Paris, very close together, we didn't say anything to each other, as the first stars came out and the early lights were lighted along the Seine and new green leaves rustled softly in the trees on the Boulevard St. Germain and the sound of auto horns and rumbling busses came faintly to the ear, though they were all around us and the scent of gasoline and *café crème* mingled on the Boulevard at the corner, where we turned past the Gardens, where children were still playing in the blue dusk—but the old people had closed their books and papers, because it was too dark to read.

The doctor, a dignified and very angry colored man, was pacing the sidewalk, up and down before Mary's apartment. But Mary and I hadn't noticed that we were in front of the house until the old coachman said: *"Arrêtez!"* to his horse. Then we saw the doctor glaring at us. Suddenly, he darted across the sidewalk and, before Mary could even tell me good-bye, he had reached up and pulled her from the carriage.

"I'll lose our places on the train," he cried. "Will you kindly hurry!"

The doctor hustled Mary toward the doorway of the house, as she called back weakly: "Good-bye! Darling! Good-bye! Good-bye!"

"Good-bye," I said, standing up in the carriage as the old coachman cried: *"Allons!"* to his horse. But Mary had disappeared into the doorway with the irate doctor.

Clop! Clop! . . . Clop! Clop! went the horse's hooves on the pavement. Clop! Clop! . . . Clop! Clop! as I drove away.

The lights grew bright along the Boulevard St. Michel

and the café terraces filled with people. Notre Dame loomed on its island as we crossed the Seine. Night settled like a blue blanket over Paris. The old coachman cut through Les Halles toward Montmartre.

Clop! Clop! . . . Clop! Clop! . . . Clop! Clop! . . . Clop! Clop!

POEM

Sitting in my little attic room that spring, I thought a lot about Mary after she went away. Then after a while, I didn't think about her so much. But when I did, I felt sad. So one day I wrote this poem (that later Grant Still set to music) which I called, "The Breath of a Rose": [1]

> *Love is like dew*
> *On lilacs at dawn:*
> *Comes the swift sun*
> *And the dew is gone.*

> *Love is like star-light*
> *In the sky at morn:*
> *Star-light that dies*
> *When day is born.*

> *Love is like perfume*
> *In the heart of a rose:*
> *The flower withers,*
> *The perfume goes—*

[1] Reprinted by permission of G. Schirmer, Inc., from whom the musical setting may be obtained.

Love is no more
Than the breath of a rose,
No more
Than the breath of a rose.

DON'T HIT A WOMAN

One night there was a terrific fight in the Grand Duc.

It began like this: a little French danseuse named Annette was going to have a child. Still, to make a living, she had to come to work every night, dance with the patrons and drink as much champagne as she could, in order to get her commission. But she was not well and she shouldn't have been there. Of course, if she had had any other way of making a living, she wouldn't have been there, but she didn't have any other way.

Feeling badly, no doubt, Annette began to be very spiteful to those clients who didn't think that they could afford another bottle of champagne, so one night the owner of the place asked her not to come back any more. He was French and she was French, and they spoke the same language fluently, so Annette said some very unpleasant things to the owner. He called an attendant to eject her. Annette would not go. The attendant laid hands on her and pushed her, struggling in her satin evening gown, toward the door.

As she passed the last table, Annette seized a patron's champagne bucket—ice, bottle, and all—and flung it straight at the proprietor at his cash desk behind the bar;

whereupon the attendant slapped Annette to the floor with one blow of his hand.

Then it was that Florence, the famous entertainer, that same Florence who snubbed millionaires nightly, arose from her table near the orchestra to defend the poor little French danseuse in her troubles. Florence wore an evening gown of gold and a spray of orchids in her hair. She swept across the floor like a handsome tigress, blocking the path of the waiters, who, at the bidding of the management, rushed to eject the little danseuse.

Florence said: "Don't touch that woman! She's a woman and I'm a woman, and can't nobody hit a woman in any place where I work! Don't put your hands on that woman."

By that time the little danseuse had risen from the floor and seized another ice bucket, which she sent whirling into space. Customers dodged behind tables. The orchestra struck up "Tuck me to sleep in my Old Kentucky Home," to drown out the noise.

A waiter did lay hands on the danseuse, but Florence laid hands on the waiter. Then the Negro manager laid hands on Florence, and a battle royal began between the women (and those who sided with the women) and the management (and those who sided with the men).

"*Je suis une femme,*" screamed the little French girl, hurling whatever she could lay hands on. "*Je suis une femme.*"

"A woman and a mother," cried Florence, "and nobody can hit a woman and a mother. I've got a mother and nobody can't hit my mother."

The orchids fell from Florence's hair and her nails dug into the face of any man who came near her, boss, manager, waiters, or customers. But suddenly an unknown client sprang from his table to the protection of Florence and the embattled danseuse, a big man, a foreigner, never seen in the Grand Duc before or since, but who effectively defended all womankind with his fists that evening.

At that moment a strange thing happened—something you wouldn't believe in fiction—but it's true. A girl named Cornelia had been waiting since midnight for a fellow named Joe to arrive. He was late; in fact, he was very late, for it was now about four o'clock. (And Cornelia suspected him of going about with other women.) But just at the height of the fight, who should walk in the door but Joe, cigar in mouth.

Cornelia, already in sympathetic tears about the fate of womankind, beset on all sides by evil men, suddenly saw her lover across the room, standing by the door. Through the mêlée of fleeing guests and struggling fighters crowding the floor, Cornelia went, and with one mighty blow knocked his cigar down his throat.

Joe was taken by surprise, stunned and amazed. But he recovered himself sufficiently to slap Cornelia completely across two tables.

One of the members of the orchestra said: "Doggone if I can stand to see a colored woman abused by a colored man." So he lit in on Joe and the two fought from the bar to the kitchen door.

By then the customers had either fled or joined the battle on one side or another but most of them had gone, in their flight leaving wraps and unpaid checks behind. The owner quickly locked the door to keep the fight from spreading to the street, so there was now no way of getting out. Bruce had already left with the first customers, saying he would have nothing to do with such affairs—since "who hit who" was no concern of his. So he put on his street coat and went to the corner bistro for a drink. I was left alone in the kitchen, looking out through the red curtains of the serving pantry at the fray.

Detached from the rest of the fighting, Joe and the musician approached the curtain opening to the pantry, blow by blow. The musician knocked Joe through the curtains, and leaped toward him. I retreated into the kitchen. They rose, locked in struggle. They fell backward. They panted and turned, and Joe threw the musician against the hot range. His rear sizzled. I then got on top of the icebox. Pots and pans fell to the floor with a mighty clatter, eggs were broken, beans overturned. I reached down from the icebox and grabbed the two huge kitchen knives from their racks and dropped them behind the box, not wishing to view a murder before my eyes. Joe and the musician fought terrifically all over the kitchen.

Outside in the cabaret, curses, shouts, groans, grunts, cries, and the clatter of glass filled the night. No music now, only good, hard, steady fighting. The women did not even scream as they fought. Suddenly Cornelia came into the kitchen and began to pull the musician off her boyfriend, imploring him to stop before he killed Joe dead.

The two men stopped, panting and spent, so I went outside into the cabaret to see how things were there. They had finally declared a truce, due, no doubt, to exhaustion. Bedraggled, but triumphant in that she left of her own accord and nobody put her out, the little French danseuse spat a last insult at the proprietor and backed through the door on the arm of the unknown foreigner, who said, in bad French: *"Faut pas frapper une femme."*

Florence, saying plenty in English and loud, still occupied the center of the floor in the midst of the wreckage, hair awry, orchids gone, tears of triumph in her eyes and a run of golden sequins dripping from her dress.

"Nobody'll mistreat a woman in front of me," she said, "'cause I'm a woman, and nobody's gonna mistreat a woman in front of me. Everybody's got a mother."

"Yes," said Cornelia, "I'm a woman, too."

"And that poor little French girl's going to have an *enfant*," said Florence. "You men ought to be proud of any woman what has an *enfant*, 'cause it takes guts to have an *enfant*. None of you men ever had a baby! *Écoutez! Je dis*, it takes all kinds of guts to be a mother! You hear me?"

"I got a mother, and I love her," said Cornelia. "*Mais oui*, I do!"

"I love my mother, too, honey," said Joe, emerging from the kitchen, "but she never hit me no such blow as you hit me tonight." He rubbed a rueful hand across his face. "You mighty nigh cold-cocked me, Cornelia!"

Cornelia melted: "Aw, baby, bend down and lemme kiss it," she said. "I didn't really aim to hurt you."

"*Chérie*, you take the cake!" sighed Joe. "*Sans blague.*"

It took the waiters and me until almost noon to clean up the place after Florence left. Bruce never came back until the following evening. He just went home. He said if he'd stayed there, he would have killed somebody sure, probably the proprietor—since he never did like a boss, nohow. Furthermore, Bruce said, half the women in this world need to be beat—not once but plenty of times.

"Women have tried my soul," said Bruce, "so I ought to know. Somebody has to slap one down once in a while."

BRICKTOP

Relations between the management of the Grand Duc and Florence were never any too cordial, and after the fight, they were worse. Some evenings she would not sing a single song for the customers. Often, long before dawn, she would wrap her evening cloak about her and depart.

Shortly, she quit to join forces with Louis Mitchell and open the famous Chez Florence that became, and remained, *the* place in Montmartre for a number of years, blessed by theatrical celebrities, millionaires, and the Prince of Wales.

Florence's departure left the Grand Duc with no drawing card—with summer and the tourist season approaching. The manager tried Jarahal, a female impersonator with a double voice. He tried tap dancers. He tried a Charleston expert. No crowds. Finally, they sent to New York posthaste for a new girl to feature—any new girl. New York sent Bricktop Ada Smith of Connie's Inn.

The evening that Bricktop arrived, Gene Bullard, the manager, went to Le Havre to meet her. Returning, he reached Paris about midnight, bringing Bricktop directly to the Grand Duc to look the place over. It was empty. But the band had a habit of playing every time the door opened, thinking customers might be arriving, so the musicians burst into a popular tune, the hired dancers got up and twirled about the floor, the waiters rushed forward— but it was nobody but Gene Bullard and a plain little mulatto girl with freckles. So the music stopped, and the danseuses sat down, and everybody gazed at Bricktop.

She was short and freckled and slightly lighter than mustard. She was plainly dressed. She had reddish hair and was not very pretty. But she went around and met everybody in the place and shook hands with each one, and smiled.

And you liked her right away.

Then she began to ask if that one little room was all there was to the Grand Duc. (French night clubs, as a rule, are small and intimate, not acres of tables with a stage, and spotlights, like New York.) So Bricktop was surprised at the tiny little room she was expected to work in, with its small tables very close together, its eight-foot bar, and a dance floor for only a dozen couples. Bricktop said it was about the size of a lunch room in Harlem.

"Just a three-piece orchestra?" she asked.

"That's all," said the manager.

She looked sad. Bricktop had been used to big bands, like Leroy Smith's, to back her up, and amber spotlights, and feathered costumes, and all the build-up a New York club gives even to its chorus girls. Here she found a small room, a small band, no light effects, no chorus, and not even a dressing room to make a change. She was expected simply to stand up and sing in an evening gown under the house lights.

"I don't know!" said Brick. "It looks funny to me."

They opened a bottle of champagne to cheer her up, and she sat down at a table. One o'clock came. Two o'clock. Three. Nobody. House empty.

"Where are all the people?" said Bricktop.

"Well, you see, this is a late place," the manager explained.

Four o'clock. Five. Almost dawn. But nobody at all.

Finally Brick got up and went out in the kitchen, where Bruce and I were.

"I want to see what you all got back here," she said to us.

I offered her our only chair, and Bruce invited her to eat some corn bread and a piece of chicken.

Bricktop said she wasn't hungry, that she felt bad, that what kind of a joint was this she had come all the way across the Atlantic to work in and there was no customers to work to. Where in the world were all the people?

Bruce told her frankly what had happened—that everybody had followed Florence to her new place, all the customers, and that was why they had sent for her, to build up a new crowd for the Grand Duc.

Bricktop said, well, she would try, but she sure would be starting from scratch—no customers and no money—because in the excitement of landing at Le Havre, she had lost her pocketbook, with every penny she had in the world in it. So she was starting out in Paris with nothing, in a club that had nothing, and she felt bad, way over here by herself in a foreign country with no friends and no money. She began to cry, leaning on the table in the kitchen.

I told her not to worry about losing her money. I said I had only seven dollars myself when I got to Paris—and I was still living.

But she sobbed and sobbed.

Bruce said: "Life's a bitch, but you can beat it if you try."

Bricktop sobbed: "I'm gonna try."

And Bruce said: "Here, have a piece of corn bread."

Ten years later, Florence was dying on Welfare Island in New York, and Bricktop was the toast of Montmartre, with dukes and princes at her tables.

LATE PLACE

That spring and early summer, practically nobody came to the Grand Duc except the colored entertainers when they got off from work in the wee hours of the morning—Olley Cooper of the golden voice, and Louis Douglas, the great dancer and pantomimist, Cricket Smith, Sammy Richardson, Buddy Gilmore of the magic drums, and Crutcher and Evans, two singing colored boys that everybody liked and who died tragically, one shot by his French mistress, the other of a quick disease.

These Negro entertainers liked Bricktop and they rallied around her. Late, any morning, the Grand Duc was almost like a Harlem night club, except for the French boss, and Luigi and Romeo.

Luigi was the barman, and Romeo the only waiter left since business had fallen off—that is, the only waiter except myself, for I had now become a waiter. Because they could no longer afford to keep me in the kitchen, Bruce held the culinary fort alone, and I had been moved out in front as a helper to Romeo. Louis Douglas gave me one of his old stage tuxedos to work in, a funny, comedian's tuxedo with wide lapels, but it served as a waiter's uniform, and Romeo taught me how to wait table.

Luigi and Romeo were Italians, youths in their twenties who had come to Paris to make a livelihood. They were pleasant, jolly fellows, who taught me all I know about waiting table and serving drinks. It was fun working in the Grand Duc that spring, with practically nothing to do all night except sit around and listen to the musicians and Bricktop talking about when they first started in the show business, and telling marvelous stories of Florence Mills and Bojangles and Bert Williams and others they had worked with in their travels.

Then about four in the morning, more and more dusky tale-tellers and singers and dancers would come in, and drinks would be ordered (at professional rates) and from then on until seven or eight, the gaiety of professional merrymakers no longer being professionally merry—but just themselves—would obtain.

The Charleston had but recently come to Europe. It hadn't yet caught Paris by storm, as it would a year later with the arrival of the lanky Josephine Baker, but Negro dancers had brought it over with them, and were now busy demonstrating it to the old timers who hadn't been home in years. For a while, the Grand Duc was a colored Charleston school.

Gradually people began to hear about the gay doings at our club in the early morning, and a clientele began to form around that group of Negroes who came there to clown the dawn away amusing themselves. This new clientele liked Bricktop, too, and so customers finally began to come earlier, just to hear her sing—as early as one or two o'clock.

Bricktop sang in a cute little voice, with nice, wistful notes. She danced a few cute little steps, tossed her head and smiled, and went around to all the tables and was pleasant to everybody—from guests who could afford only one quart of champagne to those who bought a dozen bottles. French, or American, tourist or diplomat, white or colored, were all the same to Brick—and really all the same. She liked everybody and made everybody like her. Her professional manner was simply her own manner, in the club or out. And her attraction was just the opposite of Florence's. Bricktop was simply a good old girl of the kind folks called "regular." But Florence was a brownskin princess, remote as a million dollars.

Chez Florence, however, made a great deal of money that spring and the Grand Duc didn't—for our new customers were not really big-monied ones, nor *très chic*. At our place there was a definite air of uncertainty about the future. So I began to save my francs—just in case a rainy day came.

CHEF ONE-EYE

That spring Bruce of the one eye had become very temperamental, often threatening to quit—for lack of respect, he said. If it hadn't been for him, he declared, after Florence left there would have been no trade at all—since the customers who continued to come to the Grand Duc now came only to eat his food. Yet, Bruce said, the management put up in big letters the names of various knock-kneed tap dancers and a male soprano as the featured attractions, and never mentioned the name of the chef in any of their publicity. Bruce's feelings were hurt and, before Bricktop came, he would sometimes roll his one big eye ominously and look toward the French proprietor at the caisse or the Negro manager at the door, as though he could cut them in two. Then he would go out to a corner bistro and drink a whole bottle of black rum. Often he would come back rolling drunk and sit down in the coal box—which made it very difficult for me to keep the fire going. He sat in the coal box, he said, because it would not be right for him to occupy the only chair in the kitchen all the evening—since, when he got drunk, he meant to sit down a *long* time. So he politely left the chair to me.

One night, the French proprietor decided to fire Bruce, his salary being high and the income of the place low, and Bruce's temper that week having been surlier than ever. So the boss came back with his pay, and told Bruce in polite French that he wouldn't need him any more.

Bruce said: *"Y quoi?"*

The boss said: *"Oui,* you may go right now, if you like. I'm tired of your impudence and that frown of yours you carry all the time."

Bruce said: *"Alors?"*

The boss said: *"Allez!"* and went back to his cash desk behind the bar, leaving Bruce's money on the kitchen table.

Bruce was a very big fellow, six feet or so, and in his white apron and tall chef's hat he looked even bigger. The white hat made his huge dark face stand out like a round Dixie moon. And tonight, with its single eye, it looked like a moon in a cyclone cloud, as he regarded the money on the table.

Silently, Bruce selected the longest of the butcher knives from the kitchen rack. He calmly parted the red curtains that separated the kitchen and pantry from the club proper. He walked slowly across the dance floor, where a few couples were dancing as the band played. Then he stopped at the cash desk at the end of the bar and calmly raised the butcher knife as he demanded of the boss, "Now, *qu'est-ce que vous voulez, m'sieu?"*

The Frenchman looked up and saw the knife descending. He dived beneath the bar.

The colored manager rushed up to Bruce and said:

"Say! You're fired! Get out of here."

"What?" said Bruce, brandishing the knife. "Who's fired? Do you want some of this, too?"

The manager backed right on out into the street.

Bruce then went without haste around behind the bar, which move sent the proprietor and the bartender leaping for safety over the counter, across the dance floor and out the door. His long knife gleamed. The customers fled. The danseuses screamed. The house emptied. By this time Bruce had the place to himself, except for the orchestra, that stopped playing to laugh.

Bruce then calmly returned to the kitchen, put the butcher knife back in the rack, and sat down. "Jim, did you see me?" he asked.

"I saw you, Bruce," I said. "You really did your stuff."

"Talking about *I'm fired*!" he snorted indignantly. "You saw *who* left here, didn't you?"

"The boss!" I said.

"And all his assistants, little and big! Lit out and gone!" He rolled his one good eye and it rested on me. "But we still here, ain't we?"

"We're right here," I said.

"And here we'll be," he affirmed. "Life's a bitch, but I'll beat it—and stay here, too."

His final statement was absolutely correct.

The piano player went out and told the boss Bruce had quieted down. The manager came back in from the street, and Bruce was not fired. And that is how I got my job as a waiter, because, the following week, when they wanted to discharge me, saying they couldn't afford two men in the kitchen with business so bad, Bruce said: "If he goes, I go! And I'll go mad! Give him a job as a waiter." So I got a job as a waiter.

DISTINGUISHED VISITOR

After Mary left, I took to sleeping all day long to keep from eating any meals, because I wanted to save a little money. One day Bob came banging on the door and woke me up. He was dopey to the point of incoherence, but I gathered that he wanted a place to sleep again and that he was down and out, having lost his job as valet. So I had to let him stay.

But now, almost daily he was trembling and pitiful for lack of drugs. Or wild-eyed, when he had them. I was afraid he would go mad. So I moved out, leaving him with the room rent paid up a month ahead. I moved to another attic chamber, high up on the hill toward Sacre Cœur in the rue de Trois Frères—the Street of the Three Brothers.

One day before I moved to the rue de Trois Frères, I had an early morning caller. I had just got home from work and was sound asleep, when there came a knock on the door.

I mumbled sleepily: *"Qui est-il?"*

A mild and gentle voice answered: "Alain Locke."

And sure enough, there was Dr. Alain Locke of Washington, a little, brown man with spats and a cultured accent, and a degree from Oxford. The same Dr. Locke who had written me about my poems, and who wanted to come to see me almost two years before on the fleet of dead ships, anchored up the Hudson. He had got my address from the *Crisis* in New York, to whom I had sent some poems from Paris. Now, in Europe on vacation, he had come to call.

I was covered with confusion at finding so distinguished

and learned a visitor in my room and me groggy with sleep, and Bob likely to enter at any moment groggy with dope. But I found Doctor Locke a charming and delightful conversationalist.

He said he had come to invite me to luncheon, and to talk with me about a special Negro number of the *Survey Graphic* that he was preparing. So I dressed, and we had luncheon at a restaurant near the Place Clichy on a sidewalk terrace.

Dr. Locke said he was going to Germany, and wanted to see my new poems before he left in order to consider some of them for the *Survey*. So I promised to copy them off for him and bring them to his hotel near the Madeleine.

I did, and he liked the poems. Later he wrote me a nice note about them and invited me to hear *Manon* at the Opéra Comique.

A few days after he left for Germany, I received a *pneumatique* asking me to luncheon at the Café Royale near the Louvre. The note was signed: Albert C. Barnes. Then I recalled that Dr. Locke had spoken to me about Mr. Barnes, the Argyrol magnate, who had the finest collection of modern art in America at his foundation in Merion, Pennsylvania. So I went down to the café at one o'clock and found Mr. Barnes and his assistant, Thomas Monroe, already eating. They had had to start promptly, they told me, because they were doing the Louvre for a study of modern art, and they were behind schedule. Mr. Barnes on art sounded like my father talking about business—only Mr. Barnes was interested in painting. He and Mr. Monroe were very up on it. But I ordered some *fraises de bois* and thought about Mary, away off in London, as I ate them, because I didn't know anything about modern art then, so my mind wandered. But I was grateful to Dr.

Locke for having arranged that I meet Mr. Barnes.

Another thing Alain Locke did for me before he went off to his spa was to arrange that I see the famous collection of African sculpture belonging to Paul Guillaume. He gave me a note to M. Guillaume and I went there one day and looked a long time at all the treasures he had from Benin and the Sudan and the Congo.

Again I was grateful to Dr. Locke, who seemed to me a gentleman of culture, happy to help others enjoy the things he had learned to enjoy.

ITALY

In July, with business very bad, the management of the Grand Duc decided to close up entirely until September; re-decorate, get a new band, and figure out how they were going to build up their former *de luxe* trade again. The night before the Grand Duc closed, Romeo asked me what I was going to do until the place re-opened in the fall.

I said: "Just stay in Paris, I guess."

He said: "Why don't you come to Italy with me and Luigi? We're going home on a vacation. You can stay at my house."

I said: "How much is the fare?"

Third-class, it turned out to be very little. I had saved several hundred francs, so I decided to go with them. I wanted very much to see Italy, especially Venice, where I had read that all the streets were streets of water. Luigi lived in Turin, so we stayed there a day or so with his parents. Then we went on to Dezenzano, where Romeo lived.

Dezenzano is a very old village on the shore of the Lago di Gardo, not far from where d'Annunzio died. It is a postcard village, with a lake so blue that in any other land it would only be a picture lake—not real. The village itself begins with the fishing port and runs up a slight rise to end in flowery fields, crossed by an ancient aqueduct bringing water from the mountains. The fishing boats had red sails, and orange-colored sails, and brown sails billowing softly in the wind, as the landward breeze brought the boats to dock with their catch of silver fish.

The girls were black-haired and pretty. Romeo had a nice girl in the village near the port, by whom he had had a child. But Romeo's patrician mother lived in a big, old, stone house on a cobblestone square at the top of the town, across from a church and near the town's sole moving picture theater, which had pictures only on Sundays after the angelus.

The night we arrived was Sunday and the whole village had gone to the movies. There was no one home at Romeo's house and he had no key, so we left our baggage piled in the doorway and went to the movies, too. It was one of those theaters where the screen is at the front of the house beside the front door, so you come in facing the audience. Just as we came in, the house lights went on between reels, as they were changing the film. The place was crowded, but as we entered and the people saw us, the whole crowd arose and began to make for the doorway. Soon they became a shouting, pushing mass. I didn't know what they were saying, for they were speaking Italian, of course, and I didn't understand Italian. But Romeo and I were swept into the street and surrounded by curious but amiable men, women, and children. Finally, Romeo's mother got to him through the crowd and threw her arms about his neck. I gathered that almost all of the people of the village were Romeo's friends, but I didn't know why so many of them clung to me and shook my hands, while a crowd of young boys and men pulled and pushed until they had me in the midst of them in a wine shop, with a dozen big glasses of wine in front of me.

Later that night Romeo explained to me that never in Dezenzano, so far as he knew, had there been a Negro before, so naturally everybody wanted to look at me at close hand, and touch me, and treat me to a glass of *vino nero*. Romeo said they were all his friends, but hardly would the whole theater have rushed into the street between reels had it not been for me, a Negro, being with him. They would have contented themselves with simply shouting greetings at him from their seats, except for his bosom friends, who would have hurried down the aisle to throw their arms around him and pat him affectionately on the back.

For a week I was the town curiosity, and the town guest. It seems that the darkest person they had ever seen in Dezenzano had been an East Indian, who had come through there many years before. But the curiosity was kindly, and their hospitality simple and well meant.

The men would take me with them to the village inns near the port and ply me with wine, or to the village dances on the sandy lake shore under the moonlight, or on picnics to the ancient olive groves, where Virgil used to walk. And the boys would often lend me their bicycles to ride in the bright sun, down the fine paved highroad that led to other villages around the shores of the lake.

Romeo's mother prepared the best of *pastas* and *minestrones* and dishes of mixed wild birds for her son and me. So I had a marvelous time in that postcard village by the too-blue-to-be-real lake. And I forgot that soon I would have to go back to Paris and look for another job—or trust to luck that the Grand Duc would reopen before my remaining francs were gone.

Then, one day, I had a note from Dr. Alain Locke, saying he was coming to Italy for two weeks before sailing for the opening of his teaching year at Howard University. And since he had heard me speak of wishing to see Venice, he would be glad to guide me through the museums there and show me the Titians and the Tintorettos. So I decided to go to Venice and see the streets of water. On the way, I spent a night in Verona, where I saw the amphitheater and looked at the cards the tourists had dropped in Juliet's tomb.

Venice, the Rialto, and the Doge's Palace, and the Bridge of Sighs and the pigeons in St. Mark's were all that I had dreamed they would be. The night I arrived, there was a band concert in the Piazza San Marco and fireworks and somebody in the band playing a marvellous trumpet, sweet as a human voice.

Dr. Locke knew Venice like a book. He knew who had painted all the pictures, and who had built all the old buildings, and where Wagner had died. He also knew the good restaurants for eating, and was gracious enough to invite me to dine with him.

But before the week was up, I got a little tired of palaces and churches and famous paintings and English tourists. And I began to wonder if there were no back alleys in Venice and no poor people and no slums and nothing that looked like the districts down by the markets on Woodland Avenue in Cleveland, where the American Italians lived. So I went off by myself a couple of times and wandered around in sections not stressed in the guide books.

And I found that there were plenty of poor people in Venice and plenty of back alleys off canals too dirty to be picturesque.

Dr. Locke told me that the fine Negro poet, Claude McKay, was then living in Toulon on the Riviera. Since I liked his poems so much, I wanted to meet him and talk to him about poetry and about Russia, where he had lived shortly after the revolution. So I wrote Claude McKay a card and told him I would return to Paris by way of the Riviera, and would stop off to see him then.

On the way back across Italy, in a very crowded third-class carriage, I went to sleep in the train. I had pinned my money and my passport in my inside coat pocket—the way my grandmother used to tell me to do in order to protect my valuables when, as a child, she put me on the train in Lawrence to go visit my mother in Topeka or Kansas City. For that purpose then, I kept a safety pin always handy when travelling. So I slept deeply and soundly, sitting up in the train. When I awoke, the safety pin, my passport, and all my money were gone! Someone had picked my pocket.

BEACHCOMBER

After the robbery, I had just a few lire left in a trousers pocket. I got out of the train at Genoa. I could not go into France without a passport and with no money at all. So I went to the American Consul. He was kind and nonchalant, but he said he could do nothing for me except, since I was a seaman, sign me on a boat to work my way home, should a boat wish to take me. He said he had no funds to help Americans stranded in Italy.

"Good day!" he dismissed me.

So I went to the Albergo Populare, the municipal flop house, and for two lire a night had a bed there. It was a big, modern building, several stories high, with clean wire-cage rooms, having a number of beds in each of them. It had very strange rules. If you had no money at all, you could stay there for ten nights, sleeping in bed. Then if you still had no money and no place to go, you could sleep for ten more nights on the cement floor in the basement. But after that you had to pay the regulation fee of two lire a night or move out altogether. I never had to move out, because I found a few days' work every so often relieving some seaman, who wanted a whole day off to carouse around away from his ship.

The only trouble with the Albergo Populare was that you could not come in the place at all in the daytime. It opened at four in the afternoon for the nightly registration, and you could sleep until seven in the morning. Then all out, until evening again. So I got plenty of fresh air daily, rain or shine, living on the water front. I became a beach-comber on the Genoa beach—a seaman without a ship and no positive source of income.

Some days I went hungry, and most days I worried. I thought of trying to hitch hike to Turin or back to Dezen-zano, but I was not sure but that Luigi and Romeo had by now returned to Paris. And even if they hadn't, as hospit-able as they had been already, it seemed to me ungracious to expect them or their families to play host to me further. Besides, how could they help me to get a new passport, which cost ten dollars and took a long time and a lot of affidavits to secure?

I thought perhaps if I could find work, I might stay in Italy for a while. But in Genoa there was no work for surplus Italians, let alone me, and I knew nobody. The only name I knew in Italy was that of Gordon Craig, for I had read that he lived and worked at Florence. I wanted very badly to see Florence, of course, so I thought perhaps I might go there on foot and ask Gordon Craig for a job, maybe as a second cook—in case he liked chicken à la Maryland that Bruce had taught me how to make. But the week that idea came to me, it rained cloudbursts in Genoa, so I did not start out on foot as I had planned.

But it is pretty hard to starve to death. I got as hungry in Genoa as I've ever been in my life (except in Madrid, years later, during the Civil War). Sometimes I was so hungry I would stand in front of a bakery window or a store show case and wonder how I could steal something to eat and not get caught and locked up. But I never had the nerve, nor the ultimate necessity of stealing, for something always seemed to turn up just when I was the hungriest, so that I didn't starve to death. In the first place, I was lucky about getting odd jobs in the harbor, and in the second place, I soon discovered and went around with a bunch of resourceful fellows, who had been on the beach in more countries than one, and who knew how to hustle up a few lire almost every day.

There were about a half-dozen of us who spoke English on the Genoa waterfront that autumn: two American white fellows and I, a Scotchman, a Limey or so, and one gigantic West Indian Negro, very tall, big-boned, and dark. The West Indian posed as a prize fighter and made quite a few lire letting much smaller and weaker Italian boxers knock him out, while the crowd roared at the prowess of Italy. No doubt, he is quite rich by now, this Negro, and is probably posing as an Ethiopian, and still getting knocked out.

The rest of us couldn't very well pose as anything but the plain beachcombers that we were. But there was one Texas American, who was mighty clever at the technique of beachcombing. At the approach of a party of tourists, English or American, he would slump down on his water front park bench and look like the most woebegone mortal in the world. His eyes would droop and his mouth sag. But he would listen acutely to the twang of the tourists' voices, as they paused to look down on the panorama of Genoa harbor spread out beneath them. As they walked on, Kenny, the Texan, would get up and run breathlessly after them and say: "Aren't you from Vermont?" Or Kansas? Or Wales? Or Australia? Or whatever, to him, their voices seemed to indicate. And often he would hit it exactly right. He had an uncanny faculty for regional intonations, besides being a great actor.

If they said: "Yes," Kenny would say: "I am, too. I'm from New England. And look at me, friends! A man from Vermont here, penniless in this Godforsaken wop country. And no ship to go home on."

Sometimes the tourists would give him enough for all of us to live on for a week.

The Scotch lad in our gang had a trick almost as good, but not quite. Perhaps it aroused suspicion sometimes. If it was raining, he would take off his coat and give it to me or someone else to hold. Then he would approach a party of tourists hurrying for shelter and, in the name of a white man in a dark land with winter coming on, he would ask for enough to buy himself a second-hand garment of some kind to protect him from the chill mistral.

If it was a sunny day instead, he would quickly remove

his shoes at the approach of tourists and hide them under a newspaper blowing on the ground or behind a tree. Then he would say that someone had stolen them off his feet while he slept on a park bench, and that now all the Italians were laughing at him, and surely an Englishman or an American—people of decent blood—would help him buy another pair. The party approached would usually help him, sometimes to the extent of half a crown, or a dollar bill.

Downright servile begging was beneath both Kenny and the Scotchman. They always put on an act. And none of the boys, so far as I know, tried stealing. The Italian police, in making an arrest, were said to be most inconsiderate of one's feelings.

Some of the beachcombers courted buxom market women or water front barmaids. And one of the American lads lived with a prostitute, on whom he had spent all his wages the night his ship pulled out prematurely and left him in her bed. So now the girl was reciprocating by giving him a place to eat and sleep.

The six of us, a mixed crowd, roamed around the water front all day together. And whatever we lucked up on, we shared. But toward sundown, everybody scattered. Some of the boys always tried to get on a boat in the harbor for dinner with the crew. The big Negro would seek out some Italian café or farmers' inn, where often just to look at him and feel his mat of hair, some peasant, who had never seen a Negro before, would buy him a dinner.

I usually had spaghetti in gravy, or spaghetti in butter, or spaghetti in sea-food sauce, or spaghetti in cheese, or spaghetti in tomato sauce, or spaghetti in any of the different ways the Italians serve it, or just spaghetti, at a little restaurant facing toward the sea, where the single plate, steaming hot and full of *pasta,* was very cheap—with a roll and a bottle of red wine, to boot. Then I would go to my flop house and go to sleep.

But one night I had an overwhelming desire for a piece of meat. I was dying for just one good, solid, hard, non-spaghetti-like piece of meat. I hadn't had a piece of meat since I left Venice weeks before. (How far off the art museums were.) So I looked down the list of meats on the café menu and I couldn't read one. I didn't know what the Italian words meant, but I knew they were meats, so I put my finger on one that said "3 lire" after it and I nodded to the waitress to bring that.

Please, quick! Meat! At last meat! My mouth watered. When it came, I could smell it afar off. It was liver. And ripe. In small restaurants in Italy they have no ice boxes. Besides, it seems the Italians are used to eating their meats somewhat gamey and advanced in age. Anyway, this was an old piece of liver. A *very old* piece. But I was hungry and I didn't know how to ask for anything else, or get my money back, or make a scene, and I couldn't afford to go supperless nor lose my three lire, so I ate it, every leaping morsel, and washed it down with red wine. And went to bed at the flop house.

That night there was an earthquake in Genoa. The town trembled and shook and everybody ran out into the streets. The Albergo Populare was in an uproar. The cries of men rushing to get into their clothes woke me up and I felt the building shaking. But I woke up sick! And the more the building shook, the sicker I got. Not from the earthquake and not from fear. It was the liver! I could taste it in my mouth and it was a thousand years old. I could feel it boiling in my stomach. I could smell it green as maggots on my breath.

One of those Germans of the sort who hike all over Europe in schoolboy trunks with a pack on his back, came by my cot and saw me lying there. He shook me and said: "Vake up! The earth ist falling downt."

I said: "I wish it would fall down! I'm sick." So the German went on, rushing out with the others, and left me there.

I really didn't care how much the earth shook, because I thought I was going to die anyhow. But it didn't shake long. Shortly, everybody came back and went to bed. But I was sick for two days, and could just barely make it to a park bench every morning when we were ejected from the Albergo Populare.

One day, I sat down in the park and wrote an article about my trip to Africa and sent it to the *Crisis* and asked them please to pay me twenty dollars for it, because I was stranded and starving in Italy—but would try to live until the money got there. It was the first time I had asked the *Crisis* to pay me anything, or expected it. Now I desperately hoped they would like the article.

A lot of bad luck always comes at once. A few days after my illness, the six of us on the water front were chased by the Blackshirts, who knocked one of the American boys down because they had seen us laughing at a clown on a circus poster near the harbor. And the Fascisti thought we were laughing at a message from Mussolini, pasted up next to the circus poster.

A day or so after that, I got a job painting an old hulk of a boat in the harbor, anchored way out in deep water. They wanted the sides beneath the poop painted—a job that called for riding a painter's stage with some skill. I didn't even know how to raise or lower a painter's stage and I didn't know how to swim. But some kind sailor let me down and tied the ropes for me. So I swung out there all day over the water in one spot, painting away at the same six feet of bulkhead, not daring to let myself up or down farther, for fear of releasing the board, the paint, and me into the sea.

Shortly, I began to get acutely weary of Genoa, and I wanted to get away. But even way over there, the American color line stretched out its inconvenient prejudices. Several American boats came into the harbor during my weeks in port and, one by one, the white boys were signed on. But they would not take a Negro in the crew. I had to wait for a ship that had an all-colored crew or a colored stewards' department, before I could have a chance. Finally such a boat came along, and the Captain agreed to sign me on as a workaway with no pay for the return trip to New York. I was put under the bo'sun to chip decks and wash paint with the ordinary sailors.

I was glad to be gone from Genoa.

WORKAWAY

We went to Livorno, then to Naples. In Naples I saw the ribald treasures of Pompeii in the dusty old museum there, but I did not have time to visit Pompeii itself. We sailed by Capri on the way out and I remembered Bunin's *Gentleman from San Francisco*. We visited the Lipari Islands, gleaming-white and dusty in the brilliant sun, barren and chalk-like and terrible. (Mussolini has his prison colony there now, they say.)

In Catania we saw a marvelous fight in one of the plazas. It must have been a family feud, because there were men, women, and children on each side. Stones flew and knives flashed, and we got out of the way in a wine shop.

Around the island of Sicily we went to Palermo, where I saw the mosaics of La Martorana. Then we headed for Spain across the dancing Mediterranean.

In Valencia the Captain let the crew draw money, and we all went ashore. I had not a penny, being a workaway, but there was a colored boy named Beard aboard, who invited me to come along with him to see the town. From the port, we took a street car and I kept staring out of the windows in the dusk, because I didn't want to miss anything. The *Cuentos Valencianos* of Blasco Ibañez kept coming back to me, and I was perhaps looking for his little girl who sold flowers.

Beard wanted to go to a show in an open-air garden, where castanets were clicking and the guitar strings sounded gaily. We went in and drank sweet yellow wine, while girls in spangled gowns and red petticoats stamped their heels, and whirled and cried, and let their hips sway to the rhythm of the guitars.

An old Spaniard in a black suit came up to our table and asked us if we gentlemen wanted to go drink wine where there were only girls and no big crowd of people, so we went with the Spaniard. Through the narrow, winding streets of Valencia we walked under tall archways over the streets, past high grilled gates opening on flowered patios, where the moon cast silver shadows.

A bell tolled midnight. I said: "Maybe we'd better start back to the ship."

The Spaniard said: *"Ya no hay tranvias."*

The street cars had stopped running! The port was

miles away. Beard said: "If we stay here with the girls, we'll wake up early in the morning and go."

So I said: "O.K."

But we didn't wake up early in the morning. Everybody in the house where we stayed was still asleep at nine o'clock. Finally the madame came and knocked on our doors and said: *"Oigan! Marineros, levantense! Ya es tarde."*

Ya es tarde was right! It was very late for sailors to be getting back to their ship. The girls brought us black coffee to drink and followed us with great concern to the door, jabbering directions. It was a long walk to a street car line. Then we were not sure which way to ride, so we decided to walk to the center of the city. We had thick chocolate and buns at a café across from the flower market and I kept thinking about the Ibañez story of the little girl who sold flowers, as I ate my porridge-like chocolate with a heavy spoon.

Beard said there was no use to hurry now. He would surely get docked a day's pay anyhow. And as for me, they couldn't dock me anything, because I was a workaway. So about noon we returned to the ship in order to eat. But we sadly mis-timed our arrival.

Our boat was anchored offshore, several hundred yards from the wharf, and was being loaded from tenders. We had to pay a rowboat to carry us out to the ship. Just as the boatman was about to pull off, a voice on the pier cried: "Hey! Wait a minute! Another passenger." We looked up, and who should we see crossing the dock but the Captain himself?

The Old Man stepped rather unsteadily down into the boat, took out his peseta for the boatman, then looked up and saw us sitting in front of him! He began to cuss. The

Old Man had no doubt been out all night, too—but that was his privilege. He was the Captain. We were merely a mess boy and a workaway, and colored at that. He continued to cuss.

As the boatman shoved off, the Captain called Beard all kinds of illegitimate names and threatened to dock him to the limit of the law for coming aboard at that hour of the day. As for me—he called to the boatman to turn back. "Ashore! Turn around! Go back!" But the boatman didn't understand English, or pretended not to, so the Captain turned on me again. He threatened to put me ashore, bag and baggage, leave me stranded in Spain, since I seemed to prefer (sarcastically) the pleasures of Valencia to my work aboard ship. He called me a variety of illegitimate names, too, and offered to lock me up in the hold in irons.

(But with all his profanity, the Old Man did not use a single racial epithet. So I sort of always liked him for that afterwards.)

But then I didn't say a word, having learned from many months in Mexico that silence is as good as the next best thing in the face of wrath. (And the next best thing is to evaporate! Get away, leave.) But there was no way of leaving that rowboat in the middle of Valencia harbor, except to jump into the water, and I couldn't swim. So Beard and I just sat staring at the Captain's feet, planted in the bottom of the rowboat. We sat and took it. But that was the most uncomfortable boat ride I ever had.

Aboard ship, the Captain gave orders to the Mate not to permit us ashore again until we reached New York. There, he said, we could go ashore and stay! Again referring to our parentage.

A few days later we steamed on down the Spanish coast

to Alicante's beautiful beach of sand, bordered by a long row of palm trees, and a white town facing the water. The second cook still had some money left, so he invited Beard and me to go ashore. When the Old Man wasn't around, we went. We had a swell time in Alicante, but we came back to the ship well before dawn that time.

When we passed Gibraltar, all I could see was lights, because it was dark and moonless. Being so close to Africa, I made up a poem about the face of England looking into the face of the Dark Continent, but I lost it, so it was never published, my poem about Gibraltar.

On the way across the Atlantic, I washed the Chief Mate's shirt and he gave me a quarter, the first American money I had seen in a long time. When we docked early on November 24th down at the tip of Manhattan Island, I took a nickel of that quarter and rode the subway to Harlem.

Ten months before, I had got to Paris with seven dollars. I had been in France, Italy, and Spain. And after the Grand Tour of the Mediterranean, I came home with a quarter, so my first European trip cost me exactly six dollars and seventy-five cents!

In Harlem I bought a pack of cigarettes and still had a nickel left.

WASHINGTON SOCIETY

Besides the quarter, I landed with a few poems. I took them that afternoon to show to Countee Cullen, whose work I admired. Cullen told me the National Association for the Advancement of Colored People was having a benefit cabaret party that night at Happy Rhone's Club on Lenox Avenue. So I went—and got in free, being a writer for the *Crisis*. It was a very gay and very crowded party, sprinkled with celebrities. Alberta Hunter was singing a song about, "Everybody loves my baby, but my baby don't love nobody but me."

At the door I met Walter White and he introduced me to Mary White Ovington, James Weldon Johnson, and Carl Van Vechten. I sat at a table with Walter's charming and very beautiful wife, and I was properly dazed. She looked like a Moorish princess.

I wanted to ask her for a dance, but I still had my sea-legs on. Besides, I was bashful.

All the *Crisis* people were at the party and I asked if they had liked my article and they said: "Yes." They told me their office had cabled me twenty dollars to Genoa. But the cable came back. The next day they showed me the cable receipt, and the date indicated that it reached the Albergo Populare the day after I sailed. I was glad it had missed me, because now I had twenty dollars to start life anew in my New World, like an immigrant from Europe. So I went to see Jeanne Eagels in *Rain*, and then *What Price Glory*, before I went home.

My mother and kid brother were in Washington. This time, she wrote, she and my step-father had separated for good, and she had decided to come to Washington to live with our cousins there, who belonged to the more intellectual and high-class branch of our family, being direct descendants of Congressman John M. Langston. She asked me to join her. It all sounded risky to me, but I decided to try it. My cousins extended a cordial invitation to come and share their life with them. They were proud of my poems, they said, and would be pleased to have a writer in the house.

By now, I wanted to go back to college, anyhow. And I thought that Howard, in Washington, would be a good place to start, if I could manage to get together the tuition. So I bought a ticket to Washington. The twenty dollars from the *Crisis* would not cover both a ticket and an over-coat, which I needed, so I arrived in Washington with only a sailor's peajacket protecting me from the winter winds. All my shirts were ragged and my trousers frayed. I am sure I did not look like a distinguished poet, when I walked up to my cousin's porch in Washington's Negro society section, LeDroit Park, next door to the famous colored surgeon and heart specialist, Dr. Carson.

Listen, everybody! Never go to live with relatives if you're broke! That is an error. My cousins introduced me as just back from Europe, but they didn't say I came by chipping decks on a freight ship—which seemed to me an essential explanation.

The nice, cultured colored people I met in Washington seemed to think that by just being a poet I could get a dignified job, such as a page boy in the Library of Congress. I thought such a job would be nice, too, so they sent me to see Mary Church Terrell and some other famous Negro leaders who had political influence. But to be a page boy in the Library of Congress seems to require a tremendous list of qualifications and influential connec-tions, and a great capacity for calling on politicians and race leaders, as well as a vast patience for waiting and wait-ing. So, being broke, I finally got a job in a wet wash laundry instead.

I had to help unload the wagons, and open the big bags of dirty clothes people send to wet wash laundries. Then

I had to sort out and pin the clothes together with numbered pins so that, once washed, they could be reassembled again. I never dreamed human beings sent *such* dirty clothes to a laundry. But I knew that, as a rule, only very poor people use wet wash laundries. And very poor people cannot afford to be changing clothes every day. Nor every week, either, I guess, from the look of those I handled.

Cultured Washington, I mean cultured colored Washington, who read my poems in the *Crisis*, did not find it fitting and proper that a poet should work in a wet wash laundry. Still, they did nothing much about it. And since none of them had any better jobs to offer me, I stayed there. The laundry at least paid twelve dollars a week.

I spoke with Dean Kelly Miller at Howard University about the possibility of trying for a scholarship at the college. And he spoke grandiloquently about my grand-uncle, who had been the first Dean of the Howard Law School, and what a fine man he was. But it seems that there were no scholarships forthcoming. I spoke with Dr. Alain Locke, who said my poems were about to appear in the New Negro Issue of the *Survey Graphic*, and who declared I was the most racial of the New Negro poets. But he didn't have any scholarship up his sleeve, either.

So I began to try to save a dollar a week toward entering college. But if you ever started out with nothing, maybe you know how hard it is to work up even to an overcoat.

I wanted to return to college mostly in order to get a better background for writing and for understanding the world. I wanted to study sociology and history and psychology, and find out why countries and people were the kind of countries and people they are. Somebody lent me *This Believing World*, which I put on the sorting table at the laundry and read between bundles of wet wash. Comparative religions interested me, but I didn't believe the end of *This Believing World* was necessarily true.

One day my mother came to the laundry, crying. She said she couldn't stay at our cousin's house a minute longer, not one minute! It seems that in some way they had hurt both her pride and her feelings. So I took my lunch hour off to help her find a new place to stay. We located two small rooms on the second floor in an old brick house not far from where I worked. The rooms were furnished, but they had no heat in them, so we bought a second-hand oil stove, which we had to take turns using, carrying it back and forth between my room and my mother's room, since we couldn't afford two oil stoves that winter.

My little brother, Kit, was in school then and could kick out a pair of shoes as fast as any boy his age in America. My mother worked in service, but wages were very low in Washington. So, together, we made barely enough to get along. Hard as I tried, I could not save a dollar a week to go to college. I could not even save enough to buy a heavy coat.

Folks! Start out with nothing sometime and see how long it takes to work up to something.

I felt very bad in Washington that winter, so I wrote a great many poems. (I wrote only a few poems in Paris, because I had had such a good time there.) But in Washington I didn't have a good time. I didn't like my job, and I didn't know what was going to happen to me, and I was cold and half-hungry, so I wrote a great many poems. I began to write poems in the manner of the Negro blues and the spirituals.

Seventh Street in Washington was the nearest thing I had known to the South up to that time, never having been in Dixie proper. But Washington is like the South. It has all the prejudices and Jim Crow customs of any Southern town, except that there are no Jim Crow sections on the street cars.

Negro life in Washington is definitely a ghetto life and only in the Negro sections of the city may colored people attend theaters, eat a meal, or drink a Coca-Cola. Strangely undemocratic doings take place in the shadow of "the world's greatest democracy."

In Europe and in Mexico I have lived with white people, worked and eaten and slept with white people, and no one seemed any the worse for it. In New York I have sat beside white people in theaters and movie houses and neither they nor I appeared to suffer. But in Washington I could not see a legitimate stage show, because the theaters would not sell Negroes a ticket. I could not get a cup of coffee on a cold day anywhere within sight of the Capitol, because no "white" restaurant would serve a Negro. I could not see the new motion pictures, because they did not play in the Negro houses.

I asked some of the leading Washington Negroes about this, and they loftily said that they had their own society and their own culture—so I looked around to see what that was like.

To me it did not seem good, for the "better class" Washington colored people, as they called themselves, drew rigid class and color lines within the race against Negroes who worked with their hands, or who were dark in complexion and had no degrees from colleges. These upper class colored people consisted largely of government workers, professors and teachers, doctors, lawyers, and resident politicians. They were on the whole as unbearable and snobbish a group of people as I have ever come in contact with anywhere. They lived in comfortable homes, had fine cars, played bridge, drank Scotch, gave exclusive "formal" parties, and dressed well, but seemed to me altogether lacking in real culture, kindness, or good common sense.

Lots of them held degrees from colleges like Harvard and Dartmouth and Columbia and Radcliffe and Smith, but God knows what they had learned there. They had all the manners and airs of reactionary, ill-bred *nouveaux riches*—except that they were not really rich. Just middle class. And many of them had less fortunate brothers or cousins working as red-caps and porters—so near was their society standing to that of the poorest Negro. (Their snobbishness was so precarious, that I suppose for that very reason it had to be doubly reinforced.)

To seem people of culture, they performed in an amazing fashion. Perhaps, because I was very young and easily hurt, I remember so well some of the things that happened to me. When Dr. Locke's fine collection of articles, stories, pictures, and poems by and about Negroes was published, *The New Negro,* Washington's leading colored literary club, decided to honor the "New Negro" writers by inviting them to their annual dinner, a very "formal" event in the city. To represent the younger poets, they invited Countee Cullen and me. Mr. Cullen wrote from New York that he accepted the invitation.

I dropped them a note saying that I could not come, because, among other reasons, I had no dinner clothes to wear to a formal dinner. They assured me that in such a case I could attend their dinner without dinner clothes—just so I would read some of my poems. They also stated that their invitation included my mother, who, they knew, would be proud to see me so honored.

I did not want to go to the dinner, but finally I agreed. On the evening of the dinner, however, I came home from work to find my mother in tears. She had left her job early to get ready to go with me. But about five o'clock, one of the ladies of the committee had telephoned her to say that, after all, she didn't feel it wise for her to come— since it was to be a formal dinner, and perhaps my mother did not possess an evening gown.

We didn't go.

Again, some months later, at the home of a prominent hostess, at a supper for Roland Hayes after his first big Washington concert, I was placed near the end of the table. The lady next to me kept her back turned all the time, talking up the table in the direction of Mr. Hayes. A few days later, however, (amusingly enough) I got a note from this lady, saying she was extremely sorry she hadn't known she was sitting next to *Langston* Hughes, the poet, because we could have talked together!

One of the things that amused me in Washington, though, was that with all their conventional-mindedness, a number of the families in the best colored society made proud boast of being directly decended from the leading Southern white families, "on the colored side"—which, of course, meant the *illegitimate* side. One prominent Negro family tree went straight back to George Washington and his various slave mistresses.

From all this pretentiousness Seventh Street was a sweet relief. Seventh Street is the long, old, dirty street, where the ordinary Negroes hang out, folks with practically no family tree at all, folks who draw no color line between mulattoes and deep dark-browns, folks who work hard for a living with their hands. On Seventh Street in 1924 they played the blues, ate watermelon, barbecue, and fish sandwiches, shot pool, told tall tales, looked at the dome of the Capitol and laughed out loud. I listened to their blues:

> Did you ever dream lucky—
> Wake up cold in hand?

And I went to their churches and heard the tamborines play and the little tinkling bells of the triangles adorn the gay shouting tunes that sent sisters dancing down the aisles for joy.

I tried to write poems like the songs they sang on Seventh Street—gay songs, because you had to be gay or die; sad songs, because you couldn't help being sad sometimes. But gay or sad, you kept on living and you kept on going. Their songs—those of Seventh Street—had the pulse beat of the people who keep on going.

Like the waves of the sea coming one after another, always one after another, like the earth moving around the sun, night, day—night, day—night, day—forever, so is the undertow of black music with its rhythm that never betrays you, its strength like the beat of the human heart, its humor, and its rooted power.

> I'm goin' down to de railroad, baby,
> Lay ma head on de track.
> I'm goin' down to de railroad, babe,
> Lay ma head on de track—
> But if I see de train a-comin',
> I'm gonna jerk it back.

I liked the barrel houses of Seventh Street, the shouting churches, and the songs. They were warm and kind and didn't care whether you had an overcoat or not.

In one of the little churches one night I saw something that reminded me of my own unfortunate "conversion." A revival had been going full swing since early evening. It was now nearing one o'clock. A sinner, overcome by his guilt, had passed out in front of the mourners' bench and was lying prone on the floor. All the other sinners by now had been brought to Jesus, but this fellow looked distinctly as if he had fallen asleep.

It was a Sanctified Church, so the Saints came and gathered around the prostrate soul in prayer. They prayed and prayed and they sang and sang. But some of the less devout, as the hour grew late, had to get up and go home, leaving the unsaved soul for another day. Others prayed on. Still the man did not rise. He was resting easy. Neither prayer nor song moved him until, finally, one old lady bent down, shook him, and said sternly: "Brother! You get up—'cause de Saints is gettin' tired!"

VACHEL LINDSAY

Working in the steam of the wet wash laundry that winter, I caught a bad cold, stayed home from work a week—and found my job gone when I went back. So I went to work for a colored newspaper. But I only made eighty cents in two weeks, so I quit the newspaper game. Then an old school friend of my mother's, Amanda Grey Hilyer, who once owned a drug store, spoke to Dr. Carter G. Woodson about me, and Dr. Woodson gave me a job in the offices of the Association for the Study of Negro Life and History as his personal assistant.

My new job paid several dollars more a week than the wet wash laundry. It was what they call in Washington "a position." But it was much harder work than the laundry.

I had to go to work early and start the furnace in the morning, dust, open the office, and see that the stenographers came in on time. Then I had to sort the mail, notify Dr. Woodson of callers, wrap and post all book orders, keep the office routine going, read proof, check address lists, help on the typing, fold and seal letters, run errands, lock up, clean the office in the evening—and then come back and bank the furnace every night at nine!

At that time Dr. Woodson was working on his compilation, *Thirty Thousand Free Negro Heads of Families*. My job was to put the thirty thousand in alphabetical order from *Ab, Abner* on down to *Zu, Zucker,* or whatever the last name might be—from the first letter of each name alphabetically through to the last letter of each name, in absolute order. They were typed on thirty thousand slips of paper. The job took weeks. Then checking the proofs took weeks more. It was like arranging a telephone book, and only myself to do it—along with my other work.

Although I realized what a fine contribution Dr. Woodson was making to the Negro people and to America, publishing his histories, his studies, and his *Journal of Negro History*, I personally did not like the work I had to do. Besides, it hurt my eyes. So when I got through the proofs, I decided I didn't care to have "a position" any longer, I preferred a job, so I went to work at the Wardman Park Hotel as a bus boy, where meals were thrown in and it was less hard on the sight, although the pay was not quite the same and there was no dignity attached to bus boy work in the eyes of upper class Washingtonians, who kept insisting that a colored poet should be a credit to his race.

But I am glad I went to work at the Wardman Park Hotel, because there I met Vachel Lindsay. Diplomats and cabinet members in the dining room did not excite me much, but I was thrilled the day Vachel Lindsay came. I knew him, because I'd seen his picture in the papers that morning. He was to give a reading of his poems in the little theater of the hotel that night. I wanted very much to hear him read his poems, but I knew they did not admit colored people to the auditorium.

That afternoon I wrote out three of my poems, "Jazzonia," "Negro Dancers," and "The Weary Blues," on some pieces of paper and put them in the pocket of my white bus boy's coat. In the evening when Mr. Lindsay came down to dinner, quickly I laid them beside his plate and went away, afraid to say anything to so famous a poet,. except to tell him I liked his poems and that these were poems of mine. I looked back once and saw Mr. Lindsay reading the poems, as I picked up a tray of dirty dishes from a side table and started for the dumb-waiter.

The next morning on the way to work, as usual I bought a paper—and there I read that Vachel Lindsay had discovered a Negro bus boy poet! At the hotel the reporters were already waiting for me. They interviewed me. And they took my picture, holding up a tray of dirty dishes in the middle of the dining room. The picture, copyrighted by Underwood and Underwood, appeared in lots of newspapers throughout the country. It was my first publicity break.

Mr. Lindsay had gone, but he left a package for me at the desk, a set of Amy Lowell's *John Keats,* with this note written on the fly leaves:

December 6, 1925
Wardman Park Hotel,
Washington, D. C.

My dear Langston Hughes:

The "New Poetry" movement has been going on in America since 1912. Two members of that army have died—Joyce Kilmer in the war, and Amy Lowell very recently. Already one hundred distinguished books of verse or criticism have been written, and hundreds of poems set going.

Eleven of the distinguished books are by Amy Lowell—and are listed in the front of this one. Please read the books and ignore the newspapers. I should say "Tendencies in Modern American Poetry" by Miss Lowell is a good book to start on. You may know all of this better than I do.

Miss Lowell has re-written the story of Keats from the standpoint of the "New Poetry." I hope you care to go into the whole movement for study from Edwin Arlington Robinson to Alfred Kreymborg's "Troubadour."

Do not let any lionizers stampede you. Hide and write and study and think. I know what factions do. Beware of them. I know what flatterers do. Beware of them. I know what lionizers do. Beware of them.

Good wishes to you indeed,
(Signed) Nicholas Vachel Lindsay

Permanent address:
Room 1129
Davenport Hotel
Spokane, Washington

This note was written in ink in great, flowing, generous handwriting, spread over six pages—all the pages there were before the book proper began. A few days later Mr. Lindsay and his wife came back to the hotel, passing through Washington on the way to another engagement, and I had a short, encouraging talk with him. He was a great, kind man. And he is one of the people I remember with pleasure and gratitude out of my bewildered days in Washington.

POETRY IS PRACTICAL

The widespread publicity resulting from the Vachel Lindsay incident was certainly good for my poetic career, but it was not good for my job, because from then on, very often the head waiter would call me to come and stand before some table whose curious guests wished to see what a Negro bus boy poet looked like. I felt self-conscious and embarrassed, so when pay day came, I quit.

I went home, went to bed, and stayed in bed ten days. I was not sick, just tired of working. My mother said she was tired of working, too, and I could either get up from there and go back to work, or I would not eat! But I was really tired, so I stayed right on in bed and rested and read—and got hungry. My mother refused to feed me on the food she prepared for my little brother when she got home from work. And I didn't blame her, if she didn't want to feed me.

One day a young Howard student named Edward Lovette came by the house to show me something that he had written. I had never met him before, but I told him that I was hungry, so he invited me to come with him to a restaurant and have lunch. Every day for several days the same student came by and bought me a meal, although he didn't have much money. I will never forget him, because I needed those meals.

While in Washington I won my first poetry prize. *Opportunity* magazine, the official publication of the National Urban League, held its first literary contest. In succeeding years, two others were held with funds given by Casper Holstein, a wealthy West Indian numbers banker who did good things with his money, such as educating boys and girls at colleges in the South, building decent apartment houses in Harlem, and backing literary contests to encourage colored writers. Mr. Holstein, no doubt, would have been snubbed in polite Washington society, Negro or white, but there he was doing decent and helpful things that it hadn't occurred to lots of others to do. Certainly he was a great help to poor poets.

I sent several poems to the first contest. And then, as an afterthought, I sent "The Weary Blues," the poem I had written three winters before up the Hudson and whose ending I had never been able to get quite right. But I thought perhaps it was as right now as it would ever be. It was a poem about a working man who sang the blues all night and then went to bed and slept like a rock. That was all. And it included the first blues verse I'd ever heard way back in Lawrence, Kansas, when I was a kid.

> *I got de weary blues*
> *And I can't be satisfied.*
> *Got de weary blues*
> *And can't be satisfied.*
> *I ain't happy no mo'*
> *And I wish that I had died.*

That was my lucky poem—because it won the first prize.

The prizes were to be awarded at a banquet in New York. The poetry prize was forty dollars. I spent it going after it. But it was a good banquet, where I met Clement Wood and again saw James Weldon Johnson, who, with Witter Bynner and John Farrar, were the poetry judges. Also I met Zora Hurston and Eric Walrond, who were among the prize winners in other fields.

James Weldon Johnson read my poem aloud to the assemblage in awarding me the prize. And after the banquet was over, Carl Van Vechten came up to congratulate me. It was the first time I had seen him since being introduced to him at the N.A.A.C.P. benefit party in Harlem, but he remembered me, and asked if I had enough poems by now to make a book. I told him I thought I had, so he asked me to send them to him to read.

When I got back to Washington, I promptly sent Mr. Van Vechten my poems. He wrote saying that he liked them, and asked permission to submit my manuscript to his publishers, Alfred A. Knopf. And shortly there came a letter from Blanche Knopf, saying my poems were to be accepted for publication. I called the book *The Weary Blues*.

When I was tired of resting after the Wardman Park, I got a job at a fish and oyster house in downtown Washington. (I always liked jobs in places where you eat.) I wore a tall white cap like Bruce's, and I stood behind a counter twelve hours a day, making oyster stews and oyster cocktails to order. My first week there I ate so many oysters myself that I broke out all over in an oyster rash. Now that I had won a prize, I began to meet all the other young colored poets in Washington. Georgia Douglas Johnson, a charming woman poet, who had two sons in college, turned her house into a salon for us on Saturday nights. Marietta Bonner, Dutton Ferguson, Esther Popel, Richard Bruce Nugent, Mae Miller, Lewis Alexander, John P. Davis, Willis Richardson, Hallie Queen, and Clarissa Scott used to come there to eat Mrs. Johnson's cake and drink her wine and talk poetry and books and plays. Sometimes Alain Locke would drop in, too. And that year I met Angelina Grimke.

My two years in Washington were unhappy years, except for poetry and the friends I made through poetry. I wrote many poems. I always put them away new for several weeks in a bottom drawer. Then I would take them out and re-read them. If they seemed bad, I would throw them away. They would all seem good when I wrote them and, usually, bad when I would look at them again. So most of them were thrown away.

The blues poems I would often make up in my head and sing on the way to work. (Except that I could never carry a tune. But when I sing to myself, I think I am singing.) One evening, I was crossing Rock Creek Bridge, singing a blues I was trying to get right before I put it down on paper. A man passing on the opposite side of the bridge stopped, looked at me, then turned around and cut across the roadway.

He said: "Son, what's the matter? Are you ill?"

"No," I said. "Just singing."

"I thought you were groaning," he commented. "Sorry!" And went his way.

So after that I never sang my verses aloud in the street any more.

It seems that Carl Van Vechten had spoken to Margaret Case about my work, so *Vanity Fair* bought some of my poems, the first I sold. And paid well for them. Next I believe the *New Republic* and the *Bookman* bought my work, sending checks that were small, but encouraging. I was particularly glad that Ridgeley Torrence at the *New Republic* had liked my poems.

Then I won another literary prize, one of the Amy Spingarn prizes offered by the *Crisis*. In New York I met Mrs. Spingarn, and was invited to her home for tea. She lived then in West 73rd Street in a tall house with an elevator. I had never seen a private house with an elevator before, so I was much intrigued by it. Mrs. Spingarn had a studio at the top of the house, where she made some sketches of me that later developed into a portrait in oils. As she sketched, the maid brought tea and cinnamon toast, and Mrs. Spingarn recited Wordsworth and Shelley in a deep voice.

During that same trip to New York, Winold Reiss made a portrait of me in colored crayons, and at Eric Walrond's place in Harlem, I met a young Mexican artist named Miguel Covarrubias, who was fascinated by Harlem and made wonderful caricatures in rhythm of dancers and blues singers. About that time I met Aaron Douglas, too, and Augusta Savage, the sculptress, and Gwendolyn Bennett, who was both an artist and a poet. I began to form my first literary and artistic friendships.

In those days, Charles S. Johnson, writer, speaker, and social scientist, was the editor of *Opportunity*. Mr. Johnson, I believe, did more to encourage and develop Negro writers during the 1920's than anyone else in America. He wrote them sympathetic letters, pointing out the merits of their work. He brought them together to meet and know each other. He made the *Opportunity* contests sources of discovery and help.

Jessie Fauset at the *Crisis*, Charles Johnson at *Opportunity*, and Alain Locke in Washington, were the three people who midwifed the so-called New Negro literature into being. Kind and critical—but not too critical for the young—they nursed us along until our books were born. Countee Cullen, Zora Neale Hurston, Arna Bontemps, Rudolph Fisher, Wallace Thurman, Jean Toomer, Nella Larsen, all of us came along about the same time. Most of us are quite grown up now. Some are silent. Some are dead.

One day on a street car in Washington, I first met Waring Cuney. He had a *Chicago Defender,* oldest American Negro newspaper, in his hand, and my picture was in the *Defender* with the announcement of the forthcoming publication of *The Weary Blues.* Cuney looked from the picture to me, then asked if I were one and the same. I said yes. Then he said he wrote poetry, too. I said I'd like to see it, so later he brought some of his poems to show me.

Cuney was a student at Lincoln University, near Philadelphia. He told me it was a fine college, because you had plenty of time there to read and write. He said the tuition was cheaper than at Howard. So I sent for a catalogue of the college courses at Lincoln, since it seemed I would never be able to enter Howard, anyway.

One afternoon I had had tea with a woman in New York to whom I mentioned that I was trying to find a way to go back to college. I said I wanted to find out what makes the world the kind of world it is. She had one son in college herself, and so was very sympathetic. The next time I saw her, I told her about Lincoln. She listened and at Christmas, the Christmas of 1925, there came a letter from her, offering me a scholarship at Lincoln. It was the happiest holiday gift I've ever received. My poems had caused me to meet her. My poems—through the kindness of this woman who liked poetry—sent me to college. So at the mid-year I entered Lincoln, and remained there until I received my degree.

III

Black Renaissance

WHEN THE NEGRO WAS IN VOGUE

The 1920's were the years of Manhattan's black Renaissance. It began with *Shuffle Along, Running Wild,* and the Charleston. Perhaps some people would say even with *The Emperor Jones,* Charles Gilpin, and the tom-toms at the Provincetown. But certainly it was the musical revue, *Shuffle Along,* that gave a scintillating send-off to that Negro vogue in Manhattan, which reached its peak just before the crash of 1929, the crash that sent Negroes, white folks, and all rolling down the hill toward the Works Progress Administration.

Shuffle Along was a honey of a show. Swift, bright, funny, rollicking, and gay, with a dozen danceable, singable tunes. Besides, look who were in it: The now famous choir director, Hall Johnson, and the composer, William Grant Still, were a part of the orchestra. Eubie Blake and Noble Sissle wrote the music and played and acted in the show. Miller and Lyles were the comics. Florence Mills skyrocketed to fame in the second act. Trixie Smith sang "He May Be Your Man But He Comes to See Me Sometimes." And Caterina Jarboro, now a European prima donna, and the internationally celebrated Josephine Baker were merely in the chorus. Everybody was in the audience —including me. People came back to see it innumerable times. It was always packed.

To see *Shuffle Along* was the main reason I wanted to go to Columbia. When I saw it, I was thrilled and delighted. From then on I was in the gallery of the Cort Theatre every time I got a chance. That year, too, I saw Katharine Cornell in *A Bill of Divorcement*, Margaret Wycherly in *The Verge*, Maugham's *The Circle* with Mrs. Leslie Carter, and the Theatre Guild production of Kaiser's *From Morn Till Midnight*. But I remember *Shuffle Along* best of all. It gave just the proper push—a pre-Charleston kick—to that Negro vogue of the 20's, that spread to books, African sculpture, music, and dancing.

Put down the 1920's for the rise of Roland Hayes, who packed Carnegie Hall, the rise of Paul Robeson in New York and London, of Florence Mills over two continents, of Rose McClendon in Broadway parts that never measured up to her, the booming voice of Bessie Smith and the low moan of Clara on thousands of records, and the rise of that grand comedienne of song, Ethel Waters, singing: "Charlie's elected now! He's in right for sure!" Put down the 1920's for Louis Armstrong and Gladys Bentley and Josephine Baker.

White people began to come to Harlem in droves. For several years they packed the expensive Cotton Club on Lenox Avenue. But I was never there, because the Cotton Club was a Jim Crow club for gangsters and monied whites. They were not cordial to Negro patronage, unless you were a celebrity like Bojangles. So Harlem Negroes did not like the Cotton Club and never appreciated its Jim

Crow policy in the very heart of their dark community. Nor did ordinary Negroes like the growing influx of whites toward Harlem after sundown, flooding the little cabarets and bars where formerly only colored people laughed and sang, and where now the strangers were given the best ringside tables to sit and stare at the Negro customers—like amusing animals in a zoo.

The Negroes said: "We can't go downtown and sit and stare at you in your clubs. You won't even let us in your clubs." But they didn't say it out loud—for Negroes are practically never rude to white people. So thousands of whites came to Harlem night after night, thinking the Negroes loved to have them there, and firmly believing that all Harlemites left their houses at sundown to sing and dance in cabarets, because most of the whites saw nothing but the cabarets, not the houses.

Some of the owners of Harlem clubs, delighted at the flood of white patronage, made the grievous error of barring their own race, after the manner of the famous Cotton Club. But most of these quickly lost business and folded up, because they failed to realize that a large part of the Harlem attraction for downtown New Yorkers lay in simply watching the colored customers amuse themselves. And the smaller clubs, of course, had no big floor shows or a name band like the Cotton Club, where Duke Ellington usually held forth, so, without black patronage, they were not amusing at all.

Some of the small clubs, however, had people like Gladys Bentley, who was something worth discovering in those days, before she got famous, acquired an accompanist, specially written material, and conscious vulgarity. But for two or three amazing years, Miss Bentley sat, and played a big piano all night long, literally all night, without stopping—singing songs like "The St. James Infirmary," from ten in the evening until dawn, with scarcely a break between the notes, sliding from one song to another, with a powerful and continuous underbeat of jungle rhythm. Miss Bentley was an amazing exhibition of musical energy —a large, dark, masculine lady, whose feet pounded the floor while her fingers pounded the keyboard—a perfect piece of African sculpture, animated by her own rhythm.

But when the place where she played became too well known, she began to sing with an accompanist, became a star, moved to a larger place, then downtown, and is now in Hollywood. The old magic of the woman and the piano and the night and the rhythm being one is gone. But everything goes, one way or another. The '20's are gone and lots of fine things in Harlem night life have disappeared like snow in the sun—since it became utterly commercial, planned for the downtown tourist trade, and therefore dull.

The lindy-hoppers at the Savoy even began to practise acrobatic routines, and to do absurd things for the entertainment of the whites, that probably never would have entered their heads to attempt merely for their own effortless amusement. Some of the lindy-hoppers had cards printed with their names on them and became dance professors teaching the tourists. Then Harlem nights became show nights for the Nordics.

Some critics say that that is what happened to certain Negro writers, too—that they ceased to write to amuse themselves and began to write to amuse and entertain white people, and in so doing distorted and over-colored their material, and left out a great many things they thought would offend their American brothers of a lighter complexion. Maybe—since Negroes have writer-racketeers, as has any other race. But I have known almost all of them, and most of the good ones have tried to be honest, write honestly, and express their world as they saw it.

All of us know that the gay and sparkling life of the so-called Negro Renaissance of the '20's was not so gay and sparkling beneath the surface as it looked. Carl Van Vechten, in the character of Byron in *Nigger Heaven,* captured some of the bitterness and frustration of literary Harlem that Wallace Thurman later so effectively poured into his *Infants of the Spring*—the only novel by a Negro about that fantastic period when Harlem was in vogue.

It was a period when, at almost every Harlem upper-crust dance or party, one would be introduced to various distinguished white celebrities there as guests. It was a period when almost any Harlem Negro of any social importance at all would be likely to say casually: "As I was remarking the other day to Heywood—," meaning Heywood Broun. Or: "As I said to George—," referring to George Gershwin. It was a period when local and visiting royalty were not at all uncommon in Harlem. And when the parties of A'Lelia Walker, the Negro heiress, were filled with guests whose names would turn any Nordic social climber green with envy. It was a period when Harold Jackman, a handsome young Harlem school teacher of modest means, calmly announced one day that he was sailing for the Riviera for a fortnight, to attend Princess Murat's yachting party. It was a period when Charleston preachers opened up shouting churches as sideshows for white tourists. It was a period when at least one charming colored chorus girl, amber enough to pass for a Latin American, was living in a pent house, with all her bills paid by a gentleman whose name was banker's magic on Wall Street. It was a period when every season there was at least one hit play on Broadway acted by a Negro cast. And when books by Negro authors were being published with much greater frequency and much more publicity than ever before or since in history. It was a period when white writers wrote about Negroes more successfully (commercially speaking) than Negroes did about themselves. It was the period (God help us!) when Ethel Barrymore appeared in blackface in *Scarlet Sister Mary*! It was the period when the Negro was in vogue.

I was there. I had a swell time while it lasted. But I thought it wouldn't last long. (I remember the vogue for things Russian, the season the Chauve-Souris first came to town.) For how could a large and enthusiastic number of people be crazy about Negroes forever? But some Harlemites thought the millennium had come. They thought the race problem had at last been solved through Art plus Gladys Bentley. They were sure the New Negro would lead a new life from then on in green pastures of tolerance created by Countee Cullen, Ethel Waters, Claude McKay, Duke Ellington, Bojangles, and Alain Locke.

I don't know what made any Negroes think that—except that they were mostly intellectuals doing the thinking. The ordinary Negroes hadn't heard of the Negro Renaissance. And if they had, it hadn't raised their wages any. As for all those white folks in the speakeasies and night clubs of Harlem—well, maybe a colored man could find *some* place to have a drink that the tourists hadn't yet discovered.

Then it was that house-rent parties began to flourish—and not always to raise the rent either. But, as often as not, to have a get-together of one's own, where you could do the black-bottom with no stranger behind you trying to do it, too. Non-theatrical, non-intellectual Harlem was an unwilling victim of its own vogue. It didn't like to be stared at by white folks. But perhaps the downtowners never knew this—for the cabaret owners, the entertainers, and the speakeasy proprietors treated them fine—as long as they paid.

The Saturday night rent parties that I attended were often more amusing than any night club, in small apartments where God knows who lived—because the guests seldom did—but where the piano would often be augmented by a guitar, or an odd cornet, or somebody with a pair of drums walking in off the street. And where awful bootleg whiskey and good fried fish or steaming chitterling were sold at very low prices. And the dancing and singing and impromptu entertaining went on until dawn came in at the windows.

These parties, often termed whist parties or dances, were usually announced by brightly colored cards stuck in the grille of apartment house elevators. Some of the cards were highly entertaining in themselves:

We got yellow girls, we've got black and tan
Will you have a good time? - YEAH MAN !

A Social Whist Party
—GIVEN BY—
MARY WINSTON
147 West 145th Street   Apt. 5

SATURDAY EVE., MARCH 19th, 1932

GOOD MUSIC   REFRESHMENTS

H U R R A Y

COME AND SEE WHAT IS IN STORE FOR YOU AT THE

TEA CUP PARTY

GIVEN BY MRS. VANDERBILT SMITH

at 409 EDGECOMBE AVENUE
NEW YORK CITY

Apartment 10-A

on Thursday evening, January 23rd, 1930

at 8:30 P. M.

ORIENTAL - GYPSY - SOUTHERN MAMMY - STARLIGHT
and other readers will be present

Music and Talent   —   —   Refreshments Served

Ribbons-Maws and Trotters A Specialty

Fall in line, and watch your step, For there'll be
Lots of Browns with plenty of Pep At

A Social Whist Party

Given by

Lucille & Minnie

149 West 117th Street, N. Y. Gr. floor, W,

Saturday Evening, Nov. 2nd 1929

Refreshments Just It   Music Won't Quit

If Sweet Mamma is running wild, and you are looking
for a Do-right child, just come around and
linger awhile at a

SOCIAL WHIST PARTY

GIVEN BY

PINKNEY & EPPS

260 West 129th Street   Apartment 10

SATURDAY EVENING, JUNE 9, 1928

GOOD MUSIC   REFRESHMENTS

Railroad Men's Ball

AT CANDY'S PLACE

FRIDAY, SATURDAY & SUNDAY,

April 29-30, May 1, 1927

Black Wax, says change your mind and say they
do and he will give you a hearing, while MEAT
HOUSE SLIM, laying in the bin
killing all good men.
L. A. VAUGH, *President*

OH BOY   OH JOY

The Eleven Brown Skins

of the

Evening Shadow Social Club

are giving their

Second Annual St. Valentine Dance

Saturday evening, Feb. 18th, 1928

At 129 West 136th Street, New York City

Good Music   Refreshments Served

Subscription   **25 Cents**

Some wear pajamas, some wear pants, what does it matter
just so you can dance, at

A Social Whist Party

GIVEN BY

MR. & MRS. BROWN

AT 258 W. 115TH STREET, APT. 9

SATURDAY EVE., SEPT. 14, 1929

The music is sweet and everything good to eat!

Almost every Saturday night when I was in Harlem I went to a house-rent party. I wrote lots of poems about house-rent parties, and ate thereat many a fried fish and pig's foot—with liquid refreshments on the side. I met ladies' maids and truck drivers, laundry workers and shoe shine boys, seamstresses and porters. I can still hear their laughter in my ears, hear the soft slow music, and feel the floor shaking as the dancers danced.

HARLEM LITERATI

The summer of 1926, I lived in a rooming house on 137th Street, where Wallace Thurman and Harcourt Tynes also lived. Thurman was then managing editor of the *Messenger*, a Negro magazine that had a curious career. It began by being very radical, racial, and socialistic, just after the war. I believe it received a grant from the Garland Fund in its early days. Then it later became a kind of Negro society magazine and a plugger for Negro business, with photographs of prominent colored ladies and their nice homes in it. A. Phillip Randolph, now President of the Brotherhood of Sleeping Car Porters, Chandler Owen, and George S. Schuyler were connected with it. Schuyler's editorials, à la Mencken, were the most interesting things in the magazine, verbal brickbats that said sometimes one thing, sometimes another, but always vigorously. I asked Thurman what kind of magazine the *Messenger* was, and he said it reflected the policy of whoever paid off best at the time.

Anyway, the *Messenger* bought my first short stories. They paid me ten dollars a story. Wallace Thurman wrote me that they were very bad stories, but better than any others they could find, so he published them.

Thurman had recently come from California to New York. He was a strangely brilliant black boy, who had read everything, and whose critical mind could find something wrong with everything he read. I have no critical mind, so I usually either like a book or don't. But I am not capable of liking a book and then finding a million things wrong with it, too—as Thurman was capable of doing.

Thurman had read so many books because he could read eleven lines at a time. He would get from the library a great pile of volumes that would have taken me a year to read. But he would go through them in less than a week, and be able to discuss each one at great length with anybody. That was why, I suppose, he was later given a job as a reader at Macaulay's—the only Negro reader, so far as I know, to be employed by any of the larger publishing firms.

Later Thurman became a ghost writer for *True Story,* and other publications, writing under all sorts of fantastic names, like Ethel Belle Mandrake or Patrick Casey. He did Irish and Jewish and Catholic "true confessions." He collaborated with William Jordan Rapp on plays and novels. Later he ghosted books. In fact, this quite dark young Negro is said to have written *Men, Women, and Checks.*

Wallace Thurman wanted to be a great writer, but none of his own work ever made him happy. *The Blacker the Berry,* his first book, was an important novel on a subject little dwelt upon in Negro fiction—the plight of the very dark Negro woman, who encounters in some communities a double wall of color prejudice within and without the race. His play, *Harlem,* considerably distorted for box office purposes, was, nevertheless, a compelling study—and the only one in the theater—of the impact of Harlem on a Negro family fresh from the South. And his *Infants of the Spring,* a superb and bitter study of the bohemian fringe of Harlem's literary and artistic life, is a compelling book.

But none of these things pleased Wallace Thurman. He wanted to be a *very* great writer, like Gorki or Thomas Mann, and he felt that he was merely a journalistic writer. His critical mind, comparing his pages to the thousands of other pages he had read, by Proust, Melville, Tolstoy, Galsworthy, Dostoyevski, Henry James, Sainte-Beauve, Taine, Anatole France, found his own pages vastly wanting. So he contented himself by writing a great deal for money, laughing bitterly at his fabulously concocted "true stories," creating two bad motion pictures of the "Adults Only" type for Hollywood, drinking more and more gin, and then threatening to jump out of windows at people's parties and kill himself.

During the summer of 1926, Wallace Thurman, Zora Neale Hurston, Aaron Douglas, John P. Davis, Bruce Nugent, Gwendolyn Bennett, and I decided to publish "a Negro quarterly of the arts" to be called *Fire*—the idea being that it would burn up a lot of the old, dead conventional Negro-white ideas of the past, *épater le bourgeois* into a realization of the existence of the younger Negro writers and artists, and provide us with an outlet for publication not available in the limited pages of the small Negro magazines then existing, the *Crisis, Opportunity,* and the *Messenger*—the first two being house organs of inter-racial organizations, and the latter being God knows what.

Sweltering summer evenings we met to plan *Fire*. Each of the seven of us agreed to give fifty dollars to finance the first issue. Thurman was to edit it, John P. Davis to handle the business end, and Bruce Nugent to take charge of distribution. The rest of us were to serve as an editorial board to collect material, contribute our own work, and act in any useful way that we could. For artists and writers, we got along fine and there were no quarrels. But October came before we were ready to go to press. I had to return to Lincoln, John Davis to Law School at Harvard, Zora Hurston to her studies at Barnard, from whence she went about Harlem with an anthropologist's ruler, measuring heads for Franz Boas.

Only three of the seven had contributed their fifty dollars, but the others faithfully promised to send theirs out of tuition checks, wages, or begging. Thurman went on with the work of preparing the magazine. He got a printer. He planned the layout. It had to be on good paper, he said, worthy of the drawings of Aaron Douglas. It had to have beautiful type, worthy of the first Negro art quarterly. It had to be what we seven young Negroes dreamed our magazine would be—so in the end it cost almost a thousand dollars, and nobody could pay the bills.

I don't know how Thurman persuaded the printer to let us have all the copies to distribute, but he did. I think Alain Locke, among others, signed notes guaranteeing payments. But since Thurman was the only one of the seven of us with a regular job, for the next three or four years his checks were constantly being attached and his income seized to pay for *Fire*. And whenever I sold a poem, mine went there, too—to *Fire*.

None of the older Negro intellectuals would have anything to do with *Fire*. Dr. DuBois in the *Crisis* roasted it. The Negro press called it all sorts of bad names, largely because of a green and purple story by Bruce Nugent, in the Oscar Wilde tradition, which we had included. Rean Graves, the critic for the *Baltimore Afro-American,* began his review by saying: "I have just tossed the first issue of *Fire* into the fire." Commenting upon various of our contributors, he said: "Aaron Douglas who, in spite of himself and the meaningless grotesqueness of his creations, has gained a reputation as an artist, is permitted to spoil three perfectly good pages and a cover with his pen and ink hudge pudge. Countee Cullen has written a beautiful poem in his 'From a Dark Tower,' but tries his best to obscure the thought in superfluous sentences. Langston Hughes displays his usual ability to say nothing in many words."

So *Fire* had plenty of cold water thrown on it by the colored critics. The white critics (except for an excellent editorial in the *Bookman* for November, 1926) scarcely noticed it at all. We had no way of getting it distributed to bookstands or news stands. Bruce Nugent took it around New York on foot and some of the Greenwich Village bookshops put it on display, and sold it for us. But then Bruce, who had no job, would collect the money and, on account of salary, eat it up before he got back to Harlem.

Finally, irony of ironies, several hundred copies of *Fire* were stored in the basement of an apartment where an actual fire occurred and the bulk of the whole issue was burned up. Even after that Thurman had to go on paying the printer.

Now *Fire* is a collector's item, and very difficult to get, being mostly ashes.

That taught me a lesson about little magazines. But since white folks had them, we Negroes thought we could have one, too. But we didn't have the money.

Wallace Thurman laughed a long bitter laugh. He was a strange kind of fellow, who liked to drink gin, but *didn't* like to drink gin; who liked being a Negro, but felt it a great handicap; who adored bohemianism, but thought it wrong to be a bohemian. He liked to waste a lot of time, but he always felt guilty wasting time. He loathed crowds, yet he hated to be alone. He almost always felt bad, yet he didn't write poetry.

Once I told him if I could feel as bad as he did *all* the time, I would surely produce wonderful books. But he said you had to know how to *write*, as well as how to feel bad. I said I didn't have to know how to feel bad, because, every so often, the blues just naturally overtook me, like a blind beggar with an old guitar:

> *You don't know,*
> *You don't know my mind—*
> *When you see me laughin',*
> *I'm laughin' to keep from cryin'.*

About the future of Negro literature Thurman was very pessimistic. He thought the Negro vogue had made us all too conscious of ourselves, had flattered and spoiled us, and had provided too many easy opportunities for some of us to drink gin and more gin, on which he thought we would always be drunk. With his bitter sense of humor, he called the Harlem literati, the "niggerati."

Of this "niggerati," Zora Neale Hurston was certainly the most amusing. Only to reach a wider audience, need she ever write books—because she is a perfect book of entertainment in herself. In her youth she was always getting scholarships and things from wealthy white people, some of whom simply paid her just to sit around and represent the Negro race for them, she did it in such a racy fashion. She was full of side-splitting anecdotes, humorous tales, and tragicomic stories, remembered out of her life in the South as a daughter of a travelling minister of God. She could make you laugh one minute and cry the next. To many of her white friends, no doubt, she was a perfect "darkie," in the nice meaning they give the term—that is a naïve, childlike, sweet, humorous, and highly colored Negro.

But Miss Hurston was clever, too—a student who didn't let college give her a broad *a* and who had great scorn for all pretensions, academic or otherwise. That is why she was such a fine folk-lore collector, able to go among the people and never act as if she had been to school at all. Almost nobody else could stop the average Harlemite on Lenox Avenue and measure his head with a strange-looking, anthropological device and not get bawled out for the attempt, except Zora, who used to stop anyone whose head looked interesting, and measure it.

When Miss Hurston graduated from Barnard she took an apartment in West 66th Street near the park, in that row of Negro houses there. She moved in with no furniture at all and no money, but in a few days friends had given her everything, from decorative silver birds, perched atop the linen cabinet, down to a footstool. And on Saturday night, to christen the place, she had a *hand*-chicken dinner, since she had forgotten to say she needed forks.

She seemed to know almost everybody in New York. She had been a secretary to Fannie Hurst, and had met dozens of celebrities whose friendship she retained. Yet she was always having terrific ups-and-downs about money. She tells this story on herself, about needing a nickel to go downtown one day and wondering where on earth she would get it. As she approached the subway, she was stopped by a blind beggar holding out his cup.

"Please help the blind! Help the blind! A nickel for the blind!"

"I need money worse than you today," said Miss Hurston, taking five cents out of his cup. "Lend me this! Next time, I'll give it back." And she went on downtown.

Harlem was like a great magnet for the Negro intellectual, pulling him from everywhere. Or perhaps the magnet was New York—but once in New York, he had to live in Harlem, for rooms were hardly to be found elsewhere unless one could pass for white or Mexican or Eurasian and perhaps live in the Village—which always seemed to me a very arty locale, in spite of the many real artists and writers who lived there. Only a few of the New Negroes lived in the Village, Harlem being their real stamping ground.

The wittiest of these New Negroes of Harlem, whose tongue was flavored with the sharpest and saltiest humor, was Rudolph Fisher, whose stories appeared in the *Atlantic Monthly*. His novel, *Walls of Jericho,* captures but slightly the raciness of his own conversation. He was a young medical doctor and X-ray specialist, who always frightened me a little, because he could think of the most incisively clever things to say—and I could never think of anything to answer. He and Alain Locke together were great for intellectual wise-cracking. The two would fling big and witty words about with such swift and punning innuendo that an ordinary mortal just sat and looked wary for fear of being caught in a net of witticisms beyond his cultural ken. I used to wish I could talk like Rudolph Fisher. Besides being a good writer, he was an excellent singer, and had sung with Paul Robeson during their college days. But I guess Fisher was too brilliant and too talented to stay long on this earth. During the same week, in December, 1934, he and Wallace Thurman both died.

Thurman died of tuberculosis in the charity ward at Bellevue Hospital, having just flown back to New York from Hollywood.

GURDJIEFF IN HARLEM

One of the most talented of the Negro writers, Jean Toomer, went to Paris to become a follower and disciple of Gurdjieff's at Fontainebleau, where Katherine Mansfield died. He returned to Harlem, having achieved awareness, to impart his precepts to the literati. Wallace Thurman and Dorothy Peterson, Aaron Douglas, and Nella Larsen, not to speak of a number of lesser known Harlemites of the literary and social world, became ardent neophytes of the word brought from Fontainebleau by this handsome young olive-skinned bearer of Gurdjieff's message to upper Manhattan.

But the trouble with such a life-pattern in Harlem was that practically everybody had to work all day to make a living, and the cult of Gurdjieff demanded not only study and application, but a large amount of inner observation and silent concentration as well. So while some of Mr. Toomer's best disciples were sitting long hours concentrating, unaware of time, unfortunately they lost their jobs, and could no longer pay the handsome young teacher for his instructions. Others had so little time to concentrate, if they wanted to live and eat, that their advance toward cosmic consciousness was slow and their hope of achieving awareness distant indeed. So Jean Toomer shortly left his Harlem group and went downtown to drop the seeds of Gurdjieff in less dark and poverty-stricken fields.

They liked him downtown because he was better-looking than Krishnamurti, some said. He had an evolved soul, and that soul made him feel that nothing else mattered, not even writing. From downtown New York, Toomer carried Gurdjieff to Chicago's Gold Coast—and the Negroes lost one of the most talented of all their writers—the author of the beautiful book of prose and verse, *Cane*.

The next thing Harlem heard of Jean Toomer was that he had married Margery Latimer, a talented white novelist, and maintained to the newspapers that he was no more colored than white—as certainly his complexion indicated. When the late James Weldon Johnson wrote him for permission to use some of his poems in the *Book of American Negro Poetry*, Mr. Johnson reported that the poet, who, a few years before, was "caroling softly souls of slavery" now refused to permit his poems to appear in an anthology of *Negro* verse—which put all the critics, white and colored, in a great dilemma. How should they class the author of *Cane* in their lists and summaries? With Dubose Heyward and Julia Peterkin? Or with Claude McKay and Countee Cullen? Nobody knew exactly, it being a case of black blood and white blood having met and the individual deciding, after Paris and Gurdjieff, to be merely American.

One can't blame him for that. Certainly nobody in Harlem could afford to pay for Gurdjieff. And very few there have evolved souls.

Now Mr. Toomer is married to a lady of means—his second wife—of New York and Santa Fe, and is never seen on Lenox Avenue any more. Harlem is sorry he stopped writing. He was a fine American writer. But when we get as democratic in America as we pretend we are on days when we wish to shame Hitler, nobody will bother much about anybody else's race anyway. Why should Mr. Toomer live in Harlem if he doesn't care to? Democracy is democracy, isn't it?

PARTIES

In those days of the late 1920's, there were a great many parties, in Harlem and out, to which various members of the New Negro group were invited. These parties, when given by important Harlemites (or Carl Van Vechten) were reported in full in the society pages of the Harlem press, but best in the sparkling Harlemese of Geraldyn Dismond who wrote for the *Interstate Tattler*. On one of Taylor Gordon's fiestas she reports as follows:

What a crowd! All classes and colors met face to face, ultra aristocrats, Bourgeois, Communists, Park Avenuers galore, bookers, publishers, Broadway celebs, and Harlemites giving each other the once over. The social revolution was on. And yes, Lady Nancy Cunard was there all in black (she would) with 12 of her grand bracelets. . . . And was the entertainment on the up and up! Into swell dance music was injected African drums that played havoc with blood pressure. Jimmy Daniels sang his gigolo hits. Gus Simons, the Harlem crooner, made the River Stay Away From His Door and Taylor himself brought out everything from "Hot Dog" to "Bravo" when he made high C.

A'Lelia Walker was the then great Harlem party giver, although Mrs. Bernia Austin fell but little behind. And at the Seventh Avenue apartment of Jessie Fauset, literary soirées with much poetry and but little to drink were the order of the day. The same was true of Lillian Alexander's, where the older intellectuals gathered.

A'Lelia Walker, however, big-hearted, night-dark, hair-straightening heiress, made no pretense at being intellectual or exclusive. At her "at homes" Negro poets and Negro number bankers mingled with downtown poets and seat-on-the-stock-exchange racketeers. Countee Cullen would be there and Witter Bynner, Muriel Draper and Nora Holt, Andy Razaf and Taylor Gordon. And a good time was had by all.

A'Lelia Walker had an apartment that held perhaps a hundred people. She would usually issue several hundred invitations to each party. Unless you went early there was no possible way of getting in. Her parties were as crowded as the New York subway at the rush hour—entrance, lobby, steps, hallway, and apartment a milling crush of guests, with everybody seeming to enjoy the crowding. Once, some royal personage arrived, a Scandinavian prince, I believe, but his equerry saw no way of getting him through the crowded entrance hall and into the party, so word was sent in to A'Lelia Walker that His Highness, the Prince, was waiting without. A'Lelia sent word back that she saw no way of getting His Highness in, either, nor could she herself get out through the crowd to greet him. But she offered to send refreshments downstairs to the Prince's car.

A'Lelia Walker was a gorgeous dark Amazon, in a silver turban. She had a town house in New York (also an apartment where she preferred to live) and a country mansion at Irvington-on-the-Hudson, with pipe organ programs each morning to awaken her guests gently. Her mother made a great fortune from the Madame Walker Hair Straightening Process, which had worked wonders on unruly Negro hair in the early nineteen hundreds—and which continues to work wonders today. The daughter used much of that money for fun. A'Lelia Walker was the joy-goddess of Harlem's 1920's.

She had been very much in love with her first husband, from whom she was divorced. Once at one of her parties she began to cry about him. She retired to her boudoir and wept. Some of her friends went in to comfort her, and found her clutching a memento of their broken romance.

"The only thing I have left that he gave me," she sobbed, "it's all I have left of him!"

It was a gold shoehorn.

When A'Lelia Walker died in 1931, she had a grand funeral. It was by invitation only. But, just as for her parties, a great many more invitations had been issued than the small but exclusive Seventh Avenue funeral parlor could provide for. Hours before the funeral, the street in front of the undertaker's chapel was crowded. The doors were not opened until the cortège arrived—and the cortège was late. When it came, there were almost enough family mourners, attendants, and honorary pall-bearers in the procession to fill the room; as well as the representatives of the various Walker beauty parlors throughout the country. And there were still hundreds of friends outside, waving their white, engraved invitations aloft in the vain hope of entering.

Once the last honorary pallbearers had marched in, there was a great crush at the doors. Muriel Draper, Rita Romilly, Mrs. Roy Sheldon, and I were among the fortunate few who achieved an entrance.

We were startled to find De Lawd standing over A'Lelia's casket. It was a truly amazing illusion. At that time *The Green Pastures* was at the height of its fame, and there stood De Lawd in the person of Rev. E. Clayton Powell, a Harlem minister, who looked exactly like Richard B. Harrison in the famous role in the play. He had the same white hair and kind face, and was later offered the part of De Lawd in the film version of the drama. Now, he stood there motionless in the dim light behind the silver casket of A'Lelia Walker.

Soft music played and it was very solemn. When we were seated and the chapel became dead silent, De Lawd said: "The Four Bon Bons will now sing."

A night club quartette that had often performed at A'Lelia's parties arose and sang for her. They sang Noel Coward's "I'll See You Again," and they swung it slightly, as she might have liked it. It was a grand funeral and very much like a party. Mrs. Mary McCleod Bethune spoke in that great deep voice of hers, as only she can speak. She recalled the poor mother of A'Lelia Walker in old clothes, who had labored to bring the gift of beauty to Negro womanhood, and had taught them the care of their skin and their hair, and had built up a great business and a great fortune to the pride and glory of the Negro race—and then had given it all to her daughter, A'Lelia.

Then a poem of mine was read by Edward Perry, "To

A'Lelia." And after that the girls from the various Walker beauty shops throughout America brought their flowers and laid them on the bier.

That was really the end of the gay times of the New Negro era in Harlem, the period that had begun to reach its end when the crash came in 1929 and the white people had much less money to spend on themselves, and practically none to spend on Negroes, for the depression brought everybody down a peg or two. And the Negroes had but few pegs to fall.

But in those pre-crash days there were parties and parties. At the novelist, Jessie Fauset's, parties there was always quite a different atmosphere from that at most other Harlem good-time gatherings. At Miss Fauset's, a good time was shared by talking literature and reading poetry aloud and perhaps enjoying some conversation in French. White people were seldom present there unless they were very distinguished white people, because Jessie Fauset did not feel like opening her home to mere sightseers, or faddists momentarily in love with Negro life. At her house one would usually meet editors and students, writers and social workers, and serious people who liked books and the British Museum, and had perhaps been to Florence. (Italy, not Alabama.)

I remember, one night at her home there was a gathering in honor of Salvador de Madariaga, the Spanish diplomat and savant, which somehow became a rather self-conscious gathering, with all the Harlem writers called upon to recite their poems and speak their pieces. But afterwards, Charles S. Johnson and I invited Mr. Madariaga to Small's Paradise where we had a "ball" until the dawn came up and forced us from the club.

In those days, 409 Edgecombe, Harlem's tallest and

most exclusive apartment house, was quite a party center. The Walter Whites and the Aaron Douglases, among others, lived and entertained there. Walter White was a jovial and cultured host, with a sprightly mind, and an apartment overlooking the Hudson. He had the most beautiful wife in Harlem, and they were always hospitable to hungry literati like me.

At the Aaron Douglases', although he was a painter, more young writers were found than painters. Usually everybody would chip in and go dutch on the refreshments, calling down to the nearest bootlegger for a bottle of whatever it was that was drunk in those days, when labels made no difference at all in the liquid content—Scotch, bourbon, rye, and gin being the same except for coloring matter.

Arna Bontemps, poet and coming novelist, quiet and scholarly, looking like a young edition of Dr. DuBois, was the mysterious member of the Harlem literati, in that we knew he had recently married, but none of us had ever seen his wife. All the writers wondered who she was and what she looked like. He never brought her with him to any of the parties, so she remained the mystery of the New Negro Renaissance. But I went with him once to his apartment to meet her, and found her a shy and charming girl, holding a golden baby on her lap. A year or two later there was another golden baby. And every time I went away to Haiti or Mexico or Europe and came back, there would be a new golden baby, each prettier than the last—so that was why the literati never saw Mrs. Bontemps.

Toward the end of the New Negro era, E. Simms Campbell came to Harlem from St. Louis, and began to try to sell cartoons to the *New Yorker*. My first memory of him is at a party at Gwendolyn Bennett's on Long Island. In the midst of the party, the young lady Mr. Campbell had brought, Constance Willis, whom he later married, began to put on her hat and coat and gloves. The hostess asked her if she was going home. She said: "No, only taking Elmer outside to straighten him out." What indiscretion he had committed at the party I never knew, perhaps flirting with some other girl, or taking a drink too many. But when we looked out, there was Constance giving Elmer an all-around talking-to on the sidewalk. And she must have straightened him out, because he was a very nice young man at parties ever after.

At the James Weldon Johnson parties and gumbo suppers, one met solid people like Clarence and Mrs. Darrow. At the Dr. Alexander's, you met the upper crust Negro intellectuals like Dr. DuBois. At Wallace Thurman's, you met the bohemians of both Harlem and the Village. And in the gin mills and speakeasies and night clubs between 125th and 145th, Eighth Avenue and Lenox, you met everybody from Buddy de Silva to Theodore Dreiser, Ann Pennington to the first Mrs. Eugene O'Neill. In the days when Harlem was in vogue, Amanda Randolph was at the Alhambra, Jimmy Walker was mayor of New York, and Louise sang at the old New World.

DOWNTOWN

Downtown there were many interesting parties in those days, too, to which I was sometimes bidden. I remember one at Florine Stettheimer's, another at V. F. Calverton's, and another at Bob Chandler's, where the walls were hung

with paintings and Louise Helstrom served the drinks.
Paul Haakon, who was a kid then whom Louise had "discovered" somewhere, danced and everybody Oh'ed and
Ah'ed, and said what a beautiful young artist! What an
artist! But later when nobody was listening, Paul Haakon
said to me: "Some baloney—I'm no artist. I'm in vaudeville!"

I remember also a party at Jake Baker's, somewhere on
the lower East Side near the river, where I do not recall any
whites being present except Mr. Baker himself. Jake
Baker then had one of the largest erotic libraries in New
York, ranging from the ancient to the modern, the classic
to the vulgar, the *Kama Sutra* to T. R. Smith's anthology
of *Poetica Erotica*. But since Harlemites are not very
familiar with erotic books, Mr. Baker was never able to
get the party started. His gathering took on the atmosphere of the main reading room at the public library with
everybody hunched over a book—trying to find out what
white folks say about love when they really come to the
point.

I remember also a big cocktail party for Ernestine Evans
at the Ritz, when she had got a new job with some publishing firm and they were celebrating her addition to the
staff. Josephine Herbst was there and we had a long talk
near the hors-d'œuvres, and I liked Josephine Herbst very
much. Also I recall a dinner party for Claire Spencer at
Colin McPhee's and Jane Belo's in the village, where
Claire Spencer told about a thrilling night flight over Manhattan Island in a monoplane and also another party in the
Fifties for Rebecca West, who knew a lot of highly amusing gossip about the Queen of Rumania. I remember
well, too, my first party after a Broadway opening, the
one Horace Liveright gave for Paul Robeson and Fredi

Washington, following the premiere of Jim Tully's *Black Boy*. And there was one grand New Year's Eve fête at the Alfred A. Knopf's on Fifth Avenue, where I met Ethel Barrymore and Jascha Heifetz, and everybody was in tails but me, and all I had on was a blue serge suit—which didn't seem to matter to anyone—for Fifth Avenue was not nearly so snooty about clothes as Washington's Negro society.

Downtown at Charlie Studin's parties, at Arthur and Mrs. Spingarn's, Eddie Wasserman's, at Muriel Draper's, or Rita Romilly's, one would often meet almost as many Negro guests as in Harlem. But only Carl Van Vechten's parties were *so* Negro that they were reported as a matter of course in the colored society columns, just as though they occurred in Harlem instead of West 55th Street, where he and Fania Marinoff then lived in a Peter Whiffle apartment, full of silver fishes and colored glass balls and ceiling-high shelves of gaily-bound books.

Not only were there interesting Negroes at Carl Van Vechten's parties, ranging from famous writers to famous tap dancers, but there were always many other celebrities of various colors and kinds, old ones and new ones from Hollywood, Broadway, London, Paris or Harlem. I remember one party when Chief Long Lance of the cinema did an Indian war dance, while Adelaide Hall of *Blackbirds* played the drums, and an international assemblage crowded around to cheer.

At another of Mr. Van Vechten's parties, Bessie Smith sang the blues. And when she finished, Margarita D'Alvarez of the Metropolitan Opera arose and sang an aria. Bessie Smith did not know D'Alvarez, but, liking her voice, she went up to her when she had ceased and cried: "Don't let nobody tell you you can't sing!"

Carl Van Vechten and A'Lelia Walker were great

friends, and at each of their parties many of the same people were to be seen, but more writers were present at Carl Van Vechten's. At cocktail time, or in the evening, I first met at his house Somerset Maugham, Hugh Walpole, Fannie Hurst, Witter Bynner, Isa Glenn, Emily Clark, William Seabrook, Arthur Davison Ficke, Louis Untermeyer, and George Sylvester Viereck.

Mr. Viereck cured me of a very bad habit I used to have of thinking I had to say something nice to every writer I met concerning his work. Upon being introduced to Mr. Viereck, I said, "I like your books."

He demanded: "Which one?"

And I couldn't think of a single one.

Of course, at Mr. Van Vechten's parties there were always many others who were not writers: Lawrence Langner and Armina Marshall of the Theatre Guild, Eugene Goossens, Jane Belo, who married Colin McPhee and went to Bali to live, beautiful Rose Rolanda, who married Miguel Covarrubias, Lilyan Tashman, who died, Horace Liveright, Blanche Dunn, Ruben Mamoulian, Marie Doro, Nicholas Muray, Madame Helena Rubinstein, Richmond Barthe, Salvador Dali, Waldo Frank, Dudley Murphy, and often Dorothy Peterson, a charming colored girl who had grown up mostly in Puerto Rico, and who moved with such poise among these colorful celebrities that I thought when I first met her she was a white girl of the grande monde, slightly sun-tanned. But she was a Negro teacher of French and Spanish, who later got a leave of absence from her school work to play Cain's Gal in *The Green Pastures*.

Being interested in the Negro problem in various parts of the world, Dorothy Peterson once asked Dali if he knew anything about Negroes.

"Everything!" Dali answered. "I've met Nancy Cunard!"

Speaking of celebrities, one night as one of Carl Van Vechten's parties was drawing to a close, Rudolph Valentino called, saying that he was on his way. That was the only time I have ever seen the genial Van Vechten hospitality waver. He told Mr. Valentino the party was over. It seems that our host was slightly perturbed at the thought of so celebrated a guest coming into a party that had passed its peak. Besides, he told the rest of us, movie stars usually expect a lot of attention—and it was too late in the evening for such extended solicitude now.

Carl Van Vechten once wrote a book called *Parties*. But it is not nearly so amusing as his own parties. Once he gave a gossip party, where everybody was at liberty to go around the room repeating the worst things they could make up or recall about each other to their friends on opposite sides of the room—who were sure to go right over and tell them all about it.

At another party of his (but this was incidental) the guests were kept in a constant state of frightful expectancy by a lady standing in the hall outside Mr. Van Vechten's door, who announced that she was waiting for her husband to emerge from the opposite apartment, where he was visiting another woman. When I came to the party, I saw her standing grimly there. It was her full intention to kill her husband, she said. And she displayed to Mrs. Van Vechten's maids the pistol in her handbag.

At intervals during the evening, the woman in the hall would receive coffee from the Van Vechten party to help her maintain her vigil. But the suspense was not pleasant. I kept feeling goose pimples on my body and hearing a gun in my mind. Finally someone suggested phoning the apartment across the way to inform the erring husband of the fate awaiting him if he came out. Perhaps this was done. I don't know. But I learned later that the woman waited until dawn and then went home. No husband emerged from the silent door, so her gun was not fired.

Once when Mr. Van Vechten gave a bon voyage party in the Prince of Wales suite aboard the Cunarder on which he was sailing, as the champagne flowed, Nora Holt, the scintillating Negro blonde entertainer de luxe from Nevada, sang a ribald ditty called, "My Daddy Rocks Me With One Steady Roll." As she ceased, a well-known New York matron cried ecstatically, with tears in her eyes: "My dear! Oh, my dear! How beautifully you sing Negro spirituals!"

Carl Van Vechten moved about filling glasses and playing host with the greatest of zest at his parties, while his tiny wife, Fania Marinoff, looking always very pretty and very gay, when the evening grew late would sometimes take Mr. Van Vechten severely to task for his drinking—before bidding the remaining guests good night and retiring to her bed.

Now, Mr. Van Vechten has entirely given up drinking (as well as writing books and smoking cigarettes) in favor of photography. Although his parties are still gaily liquid for those who wish it, he himself is sober as a judge, but not as solemn.

For several pleasant years, he gave an annual birthday party for James Weldon Johnson, young Alfred A. Knopf, Jr., and himself, for their birthdays fall on the same day. At the last of these parties the year before Mr. Johnson died, on the Van Vechten table there were three cakes, one red, one white, and one blue—the colors of our flag. They honored a Gentile, a Negro, and a Jew—friends and fellow-

Americans. But the differences of race did not occur to me until days later, when I thought back about the three colors and the three men.

Carl Van Vechten is like that party. He never talks grandiloquently about democracy or Americanism. Nor makes a fetish of those qualities. But he lives them with sincerity—and humor.

Perhaps that is why *his* parties were reported in the Harlem press.

SHOWS

During the *Fire* summer, I earned my living by writing lyrics and sketches for an intimate musical revue for Caroline Dudley (then Mrs. Reagan), sister of Dorothy Dudley, who wrote a fine study of Theodore Dreiser, and who introduced the Italian poet Carnevali to America.

Mrs. Reagan lived in an apartment in an old house in, I believe, West 11th Street, with a courtyard garden in the rear. And the apartment was all aflurry with excitement over the prospect of an intimate Negro revue, to star Paul Robeson, and to include the sparkling Nora Holt. And to present many of the then unexploited Negro folk-songs. All the material, music, and sketches were to be by Negro writers. I was helping Mrs. Reagan plan the revue, and later Rudolph Fisher came in on some of the skits. The house was alive with the continual comings and goings of Negro artists having auditions, tap dancers in one room, tramp bands in another, the ear-splitting voice of George Dewey Washington bursting the walls of the parlor, and comedians looking dumb in the courtyard.

In the midst of it all, Dorothy Dudley, who had suffered a broken toe, lay on a chaise longue, looking very pretty and bird-like, taking it all in, making charming comments, and waiting for her husband, Henry Harvey, to come home from his office. Then, if we were still working in the early evening, Mrs. Reagan would send out for a chicken or two, some peas and beans and cucumbers, and put them all in a grilling pan and run them in the oven, where everything cooked at once and automatically came out tasting very good, while everybody went on talking about the revue and writing things down and only looking once or twice in the oven to see what the chicken and cucumbers and peas were doing. And they would be doing very nicely, and would be eaten in the midst of writing, talking, and singing.

I continued to come up to New York from college weekends most of the winter to work on the revue. But meanwhile, Paul Robeson had gone to London to appear in *Showboat*. He made such a tremendous hit there that he refused to come back, although he was under contract to Mrs. Reagan, so Mrs. Reagan went to law. Paul's wife, Essie Robeson, came back to New York, but could not settle the matter, it seems, and was forced to flee over the Harlem roof tops with baby Paul in her arms, like Eliza in *Uncle Tom's Cabin*, in order to escape the clutches of Mrs. Reagan's process servers. But Essie Robeson got to the boat, escaped, and was off to England again. So then Mrs. Reagan went to London and sued Paul Robeson there. She won her case and got several thousand pounds, so it was said in Harlem, where the people Mrs. Reagan had under contract were paid what was due them on her return.

But the revue never went on. Delay and trouble broke

it up. So Mrs. Reagan went to Paris and married a French poet and lived in the south of France and no longer worried about show business.

Mrs. Reagan had bad luck with Negro shows. It was she who took *La Revue Nègre* to Paris, with Maude Russell, Claude Hopkins, settings by Miguel Covarrubias, and the then unknown Josephine Baker. Miss Baker, with her Charleston and her verve, stole the show from the more veteran Negro performers and overnight became the hit of Paris, stepping immediately from the chorus to stardom.

There is a story about Josephine Baker's first month in Paris, which the Parisians find very amusing. They say a wealthy and distinguished old Frenchman was so entranced with Miss Baker that he came every night to see *La Revue Nègre*. He sent daily bouquets of flowers to the dusky youngster from St. Louis, who could fling her limbs about in such amazing directions to the rhythm of Harlem music. He even went so far as to insist that Miss Baker accept the use of one of his town cars and a chauffeur in uniform. All of which Miss Baker accepted—but still paid the wealthy and elderly gentleman no mind. Finally, he asked her, in the best English that he could muster, just why she did not find his attentions to her liking.

Miss Baker naïvely replied: "But, monsieur, I thought you said you gave me all these things because you loved my art!"

Of course, after that she no longer had the town car nor the chauffeur nor the flowers from the same monsieur. But she did have many bids for her appearances in the various large theaters of Europe. She accepted one of these offers and left the American show to go to Berlin. And because she was under age, Mrs. Reagan could not prevent her going. With Josephine lost, the show was forced to close.

And that was the end of *La Revue Nègre*.

In those days, most of Harlem's actors were kept busy either on the Broadway stage, in night clubs, or in London or Paris. Aubrey Lyles, the comedian, rode up and down Seventh Avenue in a long red car with solid ivory trimmings. It was the first car Harlem had seen that could be turned into a sort of Pullman sleeper at will, the back seats sliding out to make a bed.

Another car that excited the colored world was that of Jules Bledsoe, who originated "Old Man River" in *Show Boat*. One day he appeared in the streets of Harlem with an expensive, high-powered motor, driven by a white chauffeur in livery. Mr. Bledsoe, who is dark, explained to the delight of Harlem that he had a white-uniformed chauffeur so that the public could tell which was the chauffeur and which the owner of the car.

Somewhat later, I recall a sincere but unfortunate attempt on Jules Bledsoe's part to bring "Art" to Harlem. He appeared in Eugene O'Neill's *The Emperor Jones* at the old Lincoln Theater on 135th Street, a theater that had, for all its noble name, been devoted largely to ribald, but highly entertaining, vaudeville of the "Butterbeans and Susie" type. The audience didn't know what to make of *The Emperor Jones* on a stage where "Shake That Thing" was formerly the rage. And when the Emperor started running naked through the forest, hearing the Little Frightened Fears, naturally they howled with laughter.

"Them ain't no ghosts, fool!" the spectators cried from the orchestra. "Why don't you come on out o' that jungle—back to Harlem where you belong?"

In the manner of Stokowski hearing a cough at the Academy of Music, Jules Bledsoe stopped dead in his tracks, advanced to the footlights, and proceeded to lecture his audience on manners in the theater. But the audience wanted none of *The Emperor Jones*. And their manners had been all right at all the other shows at the Lincoln, where they took part in the performances at will. So when Brutus continued his flight, the audience again howled with laughter. And that was the end of *The Emperor Jones* on 135th Street.

In those days Ethel Waters was the girl who could thrill Harlem. Butterbeans and Susie could lay them in the aisles. Jackie Mably could stop any show. Snakehips was a permanent "solid sender," and Louis Armstrong a killer!

But who wanted *The Emperor Jones* running through the jungles?

Not Harlem!

POETRY

I think it was at a party at 17 Gay Street in the Village, where Dorothy and Jimmy Harris lived, that I first heard people talking about New Mexico and Taos, and about writers and artists heading west to the desert and the Indians. It was about that time, too, that I first met Genevieve Taggard, Robert Wolf, and Ernestine Evans. And heard Eli Siegel read "Hot Afternoons There Have Been in Montana."

I met a lot of very exotic and jittery writers and artists of that period, too. And the more exotic and jittery they were, the more they talked of heading for Taos and the desert and the Indians. So I began to wonder what the Indians would think about their coming and if they would drink as much in Taos as they did in the Village. When

I got back to Washington, after one of my prize-money trips to New York, I was walking home from work one night when this poem came to me. I named it "A House in Taos."

RAIN

Thunder of the Rain God:
    And we three
    Smitten by beauty.

Thunder of the Rain God:
    And we three
    Weary, weary.

Thunder of the Rain God:
    And you, she and I
    Waiting for nothingness.

Do you understand the stillness
Of this house in Taos
Under the thunder of the Rain God?

SUN

That there should be a barren garden
About this house in Taos
Is not so strange,
But that there should be three barren hearts
In this one house in Taos—
Who carries ugly things to show the sun?

MOON

Did you ask for the beaten brass of the moon?
We can buy lovely things with money,

You, she and I,
Yet you seek,
As though you could keep,
This unbought loveliness of moon.

WIND

Touch our bodies, wind.
Our bodies are separate, individual things.
Touch our bodies, wind,
But blow quickly
Through the red, white, yellow skins
Of our bodies
To the terrible snarl,
Not mine,
Not yours,
Not hers,
But all one snarl of souls.
Blow quickly, wind,
Before we run back into the windlessness—
With our bodies—
Into the windlessness
Of our house in Taos.

It was a strange poem for me to be writing in a period when I was writing mostly blues and spirituals. I do not know why it came to me in just that way, but I made hardly a change in it after I put it down.

A year or so later from Lincoln University, during my first term there, I submitted the poem to *Palms,* as an entry in Witter Bynner's Intercollegiate Undergraduate Poetry Contest. It was given the First Award of one hundred and fifty dollars and published in *Palms* in 1927. Then amusing things began to happen. I did not know anybody in Taos, nor had I ever been there, but the Greenwich Villagers all seemed to know people there and even houses that the poem fitted, and I received a number of gossipy and amusing letters about it from folks I had never met. In one letter there was even a series of snapshots of what the writer claimed to be the very house of my poem—Mabel Dodge Luhan's house in Taos.

At that time, I had never heard Mrs. Luhan's name, nor did I know she had married an Indian, or that Jean Toomer had been a guest in her home. The red, yellow, and white of my poem came from the Indian corn colors of the desert. Three was a mystic number. The rain, sun, moon, and other nature words I used in contrast with the art-houses being built by the exotics from the Village.

Years later, when I met Mrs. Luhan in Carmel, the first thing she said to me was: "My house is not a bit like that." And she invited me to come and see for myself.

In New York in the summer of 1926, I wrote a poem called "Mulatto" which was published in the *Saturday Review of Literature*. I worked harder on that poem than on any other that I have ever written. Almost every night that summer I would take it out of the table drawer and retype it and work on it, and change it. When I read it one night at a gathering at James Weldon Johnson's, Clarence Darrow said it was more moving than any other poem of mine he had read. It was a poem about white fathers and Negro mothers in the South.

From the time when, as a small child in rompers in Lawrence, I had played with a little, golden-haired boy whose mother was colored and whose father, the old folks whispered, was white, and when, as this boy grew up, he went over into the white world altogether, I had been intrigued with the problem of those so-called "Negroes" of immediate white-and-black blood, whether they were light enough to pass for white or not. One of my earliest poems was:

CROSS

My old man's a white old man
And my old mother's black.
If ever I cursed my white old man
I take my curses back.

If ever I cursed my black old mother
And wished she were in hell,
I'm sorry for that evil wish
And now I wish her well.

My old man died in a fine big house.
My ma died in a shack.
I wonder where I'm gonna die,
Being neither white nor black?

The problem of mixed blood in America is, to be sure, a minor problem, but a very dramatic one—one parent in the pale of the black ghetto and the other able to take advantage of all the opportunities of American democracy. Later I presented one phase of this problem in my play, *Mulatto*, on Broadway. And I have written several short stories about it.

My second book of poems, *Fine Clothes to the Jew*, I felt was a better book than my first, because it was more impersonal, more about other people than myself, and because it made use of the Negro folk-song forms, and included poems about work and the problems of finding work, that are always so pressing with the Negro people.

I called it *Fine Clothes to the Jew*, because the first poem, "Hard Luck," a blues, was about a man who was often so broke he had no recourse but to pawn his clothes—to take them, as the Negroes say, to "the Jew's" or to "Uncle's." Since the whole book was largely about people like that, workers, roustabouts, and singers, and job hunters on Lenox Avenue in New York, or Seventh Street in Washington or South State in Chicago—people up today and down tomorrow, working this week and fired the next, beaten and baffled, but determined not to be wholly beaten, buying furniture on the installment plan, filling the house with roomers to help pay the rent, hoping to get a new suit for Easter—and pawning that suit before the Fourth of July—that was why I called my book *Fine Clothes to the Jew.*

But it was a bad title, because it was confusing and many Jewish people did not like it. I do not know why the Knopfs let me use it, since they were very helpful in their advice about sorting out the bad poems from the good, but they said nothing about the title. I might just as well have called the book *Brass Spittoons,* which is one of the poems I like best:

BRASS SPITTOONS

Clean the spittoons, boy!
> *Detroit,*
> *Chicago,*
> *Atlantic City,*
> *Palm Beach.*
Clean the spittoons.
The steam in hotel kitchens,
And the smoke in hotel lobbies,
And the slime in hotel spittoons:
Part of my life.
> *Hey, boy!*

> A nickel,
> A dime,
> A dollar,
> Two dollars a day.
> Hey, boy!
> A nickel,
> A dime,
> A dollar,
> Two dollars
> Buys shoes for the baby.
> House rent to pay.
> Gin on Saturday,
> Church on Sunday.
> My God!
> Babies and gin and church
> and women and Sunday
> all mixed up with dimes and
> dollars and clean spittoons
> and house rent to pay.
> Hey, boy!
> A bright bowl of brass is beautiful to the Lord.
> Bright polished brass like the cymbals
> Of King David's dancers,
> Like the wine cups of Solomon.
> Hey, boy!
> A clean spittoon on the altar of the Lord,
> A clean bright spittoon all newly polished—
> At least I can offer that.
> Com'mere, boy!

Fine Clothes to the Jew was well received by the literary magazines and the white press, but the Negro critics did not like it at all. The Pittsburgh *Courier* ran a big headline across the top of the page, *LANGSTON HUGHES' BOOK OF POEMS TRASH*. The headline in the New York *Amsterdam News* was *LANGSTON HUGHES—THE SEWER DWELLER*. The Chicago *Whip* characterized me as "The poet lowrate of Harlem." Others called the book a disgrace to the race, a return to the dialect tradition, and a parading of all our racial defects before the public. An ironic poem like "Red Silk Stockings" they took for literal advice:

> Put on yo' red silk stockings,
> Black gal.
> Go out and let the white boys
> Look at yo' legs.
>
> Ain't nothin' to do for you, nohow,
> Round this town—
> You's too pretty.
> Put on yo' red silk stockings, gal,
> An' tomorrow's chile'll
> Be a high yaller.
>
> Go out an' let de white boys
> Look at yo' legs.

Benjamin Brawley, our most respectable critic, later wrote: "It would have been just as well, perhaps better, if the book had never been published. No other ever issued reflects more fully the abandon and the vulgarity of its age." In the Negro papers, I believe, only Dewey Jones of the Chicago *Defender* and Alice Dunbar-Nelson of the Washington *Eagle* gave it a sympathetic review.

The Negro critics and many of the intellectuals were very sensitive about their race in books. (And still are.) In anything that white people were likely to read, they wanted to put their best foot forward, their politely polished and cultural foot—and only that foot. There was a reason for it, of course. They had seen their race laughed at and caricatured so often in stories like those by Octavus Roy Cohen, maligned and abused so often in books like Thomas Dixon's, made a servant or a clown always in the movies, and forever defeated on the Broadway stage, that when Negroes wrote books they wanted them to be books in which only good Negroes, clean and cultured and not-funny Negroes, beautiful and nice and upper class were presented. Jessie Fauset's novels they loved, because they were always about the educated Negro—but my poems, or Claude McKay's *Home to Harlem* they did not like, sincere though we might be.

For every Negro intellectual like James Weldon Johnson, there were dozens like Eustace Gay, who wrote in the Philadelphia *Tribune,* of February 5, 1927, concerning my *Fine Clothes to the Jew*: "It does not matter to me whether every poem in the book is true to life. Why should it be paraded before the American public by a Negro author as being typical or representative of the Negro? Bad enough to have white authors holding up our imperfections to public gaze. Our aim ought to be to present to the general public, already mis-informed both by well-meaning and malicious writers, our higher aims and aspirations, and our better selves."

I sympathized deeply with those critics and those intellectuals, and I saw clearly the need for some of the kinds of books they wanted. But I did not see how they could expect every Negro author to write such books. Certainly, I personally knew very few people anywhere who were wholly beautiful and wholly good. Besides I felt that the masses of our people had as much in their lives to put into books as did those more fortunate ones who had been born with some means and the ability to work up to a master's degree at a Northern college. Anyway, I didn't know the upper class Negroes well enough to write much about them. I knew only the people I had grown up with, and they weren't people whose shoes were always shined, who had been to Harvard, or who had heard of Bach. But they seemed to me good people, too.

So I didn't pay any attention to the critics who railed against the subject matter of my poems, nor did I write them protesting letters, nor in any way attempt to defend my book. Curiously enough, a short ten years later, many of those very poems in *Fine Clothes to the Jew* were being used in Negro schools and colleges.

[handwritten annotation: 3. Washington emphasized trade skills and jobs. Langston Hughes saw the Harlon Ronaissance as a temporary escape from the plight of Blackmer]

NIGGER HEAVEN

The strange inability on the part of many of the Negro critics to understand irony, or satire—except the obvious satire of George S. Schuyler's *Black No More*—partially explains the phenomenon of that violent outburst of rage that stirred the Negro press for months after the appearance of Carl Van Vechten's *Nigger Heaven*.

The use of the word *nigger* in the title explains the rest of it. The word *nigger* to colored people of high and low degree is like a red rag to a bull. Used rightly or wrongly, ironically or seriously, of necessity for the sake of realism, or impishly for the sake of comedy, it doesn't matter. Negroes do not like it in any book or play whatsoever, be the book or play ever so sympathetic in its treatment of the basic problems of the race. Even though the book or play is written by a Negro, they still do not like it.

The word *nigger*, you see, sums up for us who are colored all the bitter years of insult and struggle in America: the slave-beatings of yesterday, the lynchings of today, the Jim Crow cars, the only movie show in town with its sign up FOR WHITES ONLY, the restaurants where you may not eat, the jobs you may not have, the unions you cannot join. The word *nigger* in the mouths of little white boys at school, the word *nigger* in the mouths of foremen on the job, the word *nigger* across the whole face of America! *Nigger! Nigger!* Like the word *Jew* in Hitler's Germany.

Countee Cullen's poem "Incident" [1] captures with great power the meaning of *nigger* for most black Americans—except that that meaning extends far beyond the child world, as the poem indicates. Cullen says:

> Once riding in old Baltimore,
> Heart-filled, head-filled with glee,
> I saw a Baltimorean
> Keep looking straight at me.
>
> Now I was eight and very small,
> And he was no whit bigger,
> And so I smiled, but he poked out
> His tongue and called me, "Nigger."
>
> I saw the whole of Baltimore
> From May until December:
> Of all the things that happened there
> That's all that I remember.

[1] From *Color*, by Countee Cullen (New York: Harper & Brothers).

So, when the novel *Nigger Heaven* came out, Negroes did not read it to get mad. They got mad as soon as they heard of it. And after that, many of them never did read it at all. Or if they did, they put a paper cover over it and read it surreptitiously as though it were a dirty book—to keep their friends from knowing they were reading it. And they held meetings to denounce it all across America. At one meeting in the Harlem Public Library, the crowd saw a large white-haired old gentleman in the back they thought was Carl Van Vechten. They turned on him in verbal fury. Astonished, the old gentleman arose stammering in amazement: "Why, I'm not Carl Van Vechten."

Carl Van Vechten was distressed at the reactions his book provoked in the Negro press. He had not expected colored people to dislike it. Certainly in the novel he had treated the Negroes of Harlem much better, for instance, than he had treated his own home folks in *The Tattooed Countess*. But I doubt if any of the more vociferous of the Negro critics had ever read *The Tattooed Countess*, so, naturally, they didn't know that. I doubt if any of those critics had ever read any book of Mr. Van Vechten's at all, or knew anything about his style. If they had they could not then have written so stupidly about *Nigger Heaven*.

Perhaps, like my *Fine Clothes to the Jew*, Mr. Van Vechten's title was an unfortunate choice. A great many colored people never did discover that the title was an ironical title, applying to segregated, poverty-stricken Harlem the words used to designate in many American cities the upper gallery in a theater, which is usually the only place where Negroes may buy tickets to see the show —the *nigger heaven*. To Mr. Van Vechten, Harlem was like that, a segregated gallery in the theater, the only place where Negroes could see or stage their own show, and a not very satisfactory place at that, for in his novel Mr. Van Vechten presents many of the problems of the Negroes of Harlem, and he writes of the people of culture as well as the people of the night clubs. He presents the problem of a young Negro noveiist faced with the discriminations of the white editorial offices. And he writes sympathetically and amusingly and well about a whole rainbow of life above 110th Street that had never before been put into the color of words.

But Mr. Van Vechten became the goat of the New Negro Renaissance, the he-who-gets-slapped. The critics of the left, like the Negroes of the right, proceeded to light on Mr. Van Vechten, and he was accused of ruining, distorting, polluting, and corrupting every Negro writer from then on, who was ever known to have shaken hands with him, or to have used the word *nigger* in his writings, or to have been in a cabaret.

Some of the colored critics, evidently thinking I did not know my mind, accused Mr. Van Vechten of having brought about what they felt were the various defects of my *Fine Clothes to the Jew.* But the truth of the matter was that many of the poems in the book had been written before I had heard of or met Mr. Van Vechten, and they were not included in my *Weary Blues,* because scarcely any dialect or folk-poems were included in the *Weary Blues.* And, although I did shake hands with Mr. Van Vechten once upon being introduced to him at the N.A.A.C.P. party in 1924, it was many months before I saw him again. The blues, spirituals, shouts, and work poems of my second book were written while I was dragging bags of wet wash laundry about or toting trays of dirty dishes to the dumb-waiter of the Wardman Park Hotel in Washington.

Margaret Larkin in *Opportunity* was the first critic to term my work proletarian, in her review of *Fine Clothes*. Since high school days I had been writing poems about workers and the problems of workers—in reality poems about myself and my own problems. And, contrary to the accusations of the critics, after I came to know Carl Van Vechten, I never heard him say: "Don't write poems about workers." Or in any way try to influence me in my writing.

What Carl Van Vechten did for me was to submit my first book of poems to Alfred A. Knopf, put me in contact with the editors of *Vanity Fair*, who bought my first poems sold to a magazine, caused me to meet many editors and writers who were friendly and helpful to me, encouraged me in my efforts to help publicize the Scottsboro case, cheered me on in the writing of my first short stories, and otherwise aided in making life for me more profitable and entertaining.

Many others of the Negroes in the arts, from Paul Robeson to Ethel Waters, Walter White to Richmond Barthe, will offer the same testimony as to the interest Van Vechten has displayed toward Negro creators in the fields of writing, plastic arts, and popular entertainment. To say that Carl Van Vechten has harmed Negro creative activities is sheer poppycock. The bad Negro writers were bad long before *Nigger Heaven* appeared on the scene. And would have been bad anyway, had Mr. Van Vechten never been born.

SPECTACLES IN COLOR

Strangest and gaudiest of all Harlem spectacles in the '20's, and still the strangest and gaudiest, is the annual Hamilton Club Lodge Ball at Rockland Palace Casino. I once attended as a guest of A'Lelia Walker. It is the ball where men dress as women and women dress as men. During the height of the New Negro era and the tourist invasion of Harlem, it was fashionable for the intelligentsia and social leaders of both Harlem and the downtown area to occupy boxes at this ball and look down from above at the queerly assorted throng on the dancing floor, males in flowing gowns and feathered headdresses and females in tuxedoes and box-back suits.

For the men, there is a fashion parade. Prizes are given to the most gorgeously gowned of the whites and Negroes who, powdered, wigged, and rouged, mingle and compete for the awards. From the boxes these men look for all the world like very pretty chorus girls parading across the raised platform in the center of the floor. But close up, most of them look as if they need a shave, and some of their evening gowns, cut too low, show hair on the chest.

The pathetic touch about the show is given by the presence there of many former "queens" of the ball, prize winners of years gone by, for this dance has been going on a long time, and it is very famous among the male masqueraders of the eastern seaboard, who come from Boston and Philadelphia, Pittsburgh and Atlantic City to attend. These former queens of the ball, some of them aged men, still wearing the costumes that won for them a fleeting fame in years gone by, stand on the sidelines now in their same old clothes—wide picture hats with plumes, and out-of-style dresses with sweeping velvet trains. And nobody pays them any mind—for the spotlights are focused on the stage, where today's younger competitors, in their smart creations, bid for applause.

Harlem likes spectacles of one kind or another—but then so does all the world. On Sunday afternoons in the spring when the lodges have their turnouts, it is good to stand on the curb and hear the bands play and see the women pass in their white regalia with swinging purple capes, preceded by the brothers in uniform, with long swords at their sides and feathered helmets, or else in high hats, spats, and cutaway coats. Once I saw such a lodge parade with an all-string band leading the procession, violins and mandolins and banjos and guitars playing in the street. It was thrilling and the music was grand.

Since Harlemites almost all work in the daytime, many of the Harlem funerals take place at night so that the friends and lodge brothers of the deceased may attend. Sometimes at ten or eleven at night, you hear a funeral march filling the air on Seventh Avenue and see a long, slow-moving procession following somebody to his last home.

The Florence Mills funeral was on a Sunday afternoon, and it was a beautiful procession, with the chorus girls from her show marching all in gray, and an airplane releasing flocks of blackbirds overhead.

The Countee Cullen wedding was another spectacle that had Harlem talking for a long time—the wedding of the leading lyric poet of the Negro Renaissance to Yolande DuBois, the daughter, and only child, of the leading old-guard Negro writer, Dr. W. E. B. DuBois. It was the social-literary event of the season, and very society. I was an usher—by virtue of being a poet. It was an Easter-time wedding, held at dusk in the church pastored by Countee Cullen's father, one of the largest Negro churches in the world, but it didn't begin to hold the crowd. The first floor was given over to holders of engraved invitations, and the balcony to the general public, and both were packed to capacity.

The bride had been teaching in Baltimore, and her bridesmaids all came from Maryland in a special car, looking very charming and pretty. We held a rehearsal of the wedding on Good Friday and it was my job to escort the bride's mother to her seat. Unfortunately, I didn't own a pair of tails, so I had to rent a set. In the rental shop the suit looked black, but once outside, it looked rusty green. It was one of those cheap, dull blacks that had faded with time, and the trousers were stove-piped. I felt very self-conscious in a green, rented pawnshop dress suit, so I said to myself: "I will never go into society again if I have to rent my clothes." But, nevertheless, I enjoyed being in the wedding.

In the waning days of the New Negro Renaissance, in the same church where our leading poet was married, there occurred a series of the most amazing revivals ever seen in Harlem, conducted by the Reverend Dr. Becton. Dr. Becton was a charlatan if there ever was one, but he filled the huge church—because he gave a good show. He had a small jazz band with him, playing church music in syncopated time, and they would begin to play early in the evening so that the congregation would be in a good mood by the time the Reverend Dr. Becton arrived.

About nine, in a long car with liveried chauffeur and a lighted cross on the hood, Dr. Becton would appear with two valets. He would enter the church by the side door and, without looking to the right or left, proceed straight to the altar in his long black overcoat. He would come forward to the edge of the platform, and, in full view of the audience, silently commune with God, eyes shut and head back, for perhaps five minutes. Then he would open his eyes and say fervently: "I couldn't wait to commune with God! Oh, no! Friends, I couldn't wait."

Then one valet would step forward and take his hat, another his coat, the first, his gloves, the second would hand him a handkerchief, and he would then take charge of the service, which would go on until midnight, with intervals of preaching and praying, broken only by having the audience rise to sing, or to demonstrate who were Christians and who were sinners, or to parade to the altar and put down their money.

The Reverend Dr. Becton, I thought, was a very bad preacher, running back and forth across the platform, mouthing inanities and whistling for God, but he could make people shout, nevertheless. And the stirring rhythms of his excellent gospel swing band would cause many to rise and dance in the aisles for joy.

A great many white people came to watch him put on his show, and churches anywhere in the East fortunate enough to have him grace their rostrums for a month or two were sure to come out of the red. For, besides the collections at the altar, Dr. Becton had an envelope system, called "The Consecrated Dime—A Dime a Day for God." And every Sunday he would give out his envelopes. And every Sunday he would collect hundreds of them from the past week, each with seventy cents therein, from the poor working men and women who made up the bulk of his congregation. Every package of dimes was consecrated to God—but given to the Reverend Dr. Becton.

Dr. Becton lived in a fine house in Harlem, with his business manager, his secretaries, his valets, and most of the members of his jazz band. The furnishings were of the finest, from an old established Fifth Avenue shop. There were luxurious drapes at the windows, with the sign of the cross woven in them. There was a private chapel where Dr. Becton prayed at dawn before a lighted cross. And he slept in a specially built bed with two transparent crystal crosses in the bed-panels at head and foot—crosses that gave out a soft glow as he slept, lighted, he said, by God. Those members of his congregation, most faithful in contributions and attendance, would, on occasion, be shown through this house.

As his popularity in Harlem grew, Dr. Becton started a magazine. It was not a bad magazine, and it paid higher rates for material than any Negro magazine in America, because most of them pay nothing. It paid *Nation* or *New Republic* rates. He bought an article of mine and one or two poems. One day he sent the editor of the magazine to ask me if I would accept a post on his staff in a literary capacity. He requested that I come to talk to him about it. And that is how I happened to see his house.

I had dinner with him and his staff, a very good dinner, and afterwards he took me into his private study, which was simple enough, evidently not embellished for public consumption. There he told me of his desire to make of his magazine and the various other leaflets and papers he planned to get out, not only well-printed publications, but intelligent and interesting ones, stressing, of course, the religious life, but not entirely.

The Reverend Dr. Becton told me he had been a student of behavioristic psychology for a long time—that was why he had his audience get up and down so much, to rest them and hold them longer at his services. And thus (I knew) he was able to take up more collections in one evening than if the people started to drift out early. (He preferred to have them drift to the altar with a dime.) He said he knew the effects of music and rhythm on the human emotions, for he had made a study of audiences and their reactions, and he knew how to handle them. Now, he was looking for someone who was clever with the written word to do with people through the printed page what he could do with them in person. During his talk with me, never once did he mention God. In the quiet of his study, he talked business, God being, no doubt, for public consumption.

I did not take the job, but it would have been interesting to know Dr. Becton better and to find out what he really thought of those hundreds of poor people who daily gave into his keeping a Consecrated Dime for God.

But I never saw him again. A few years later he was shot and killed in Philadelphia, some say by racketeers. But he was given a grand funeral, attended by a great many saints and sinners. And his memory lives on.

LINCOLN UNIVERSITY

At the height of the Negro Renaissance, I was a student at Lincoln University, spending my week-ends and holidays in New York. Lincoln is a college and theological seminary primarily for men of color, although white students may attend, too, if they wish. It was established in 1854, by John Miller Dickey, a Presbyterian minister in Oxford, Pennsylvania, because there was then no college in the North especially for Negro youth, and he felt that there should be one.

"A race enlightened in the knowledge of God will eventually be free," he preached. "Kindle the lamp of religious knowledge. It will surely light them to an everlasting position among the people of the earth."

Lincoln is located in the rolling hills of Pennsylvania, forty miles from Philadelphia through the Quaker country on the highroad heading toward the Maryland border and Jim Crow. In spring, its campus is beautiful and green and there are tall old trees everywhere, and from its dormitory windows a view of farm lands for miles around is to be seen. Down the campus road a piece there is a tiny village of a dozen houses, with a general store and a railroad station. Four miles away by train or road is Oxford.

I liked Lincoln very much. But just as I like America and still find certain things wrong with it, so I found several things wrong with Lincoln. When I first went there, it had an all-white faculty teaching an all-Negro student body. And, other than the football coach, no Negro had ever, in all its seventy years, held a professorial position at Lincoln, a college for, as its catalogue states, the training of Negro leaders. There was an unwritten official color line that said no Negro could teach on that faculty. And no one of its alumni had ever been asked to join the Board of Trustees. How then could they be training Negro leaders? That worried me, for surely out of all the Negro leaders they had trained, some one would be capable of serving on the Board of Trustees of the college, or of coming back to the campus as a teacher.

Most of the professors on the faculty were elderly, kind, religious old gentlemen, graduates of Princeton in the '80's. Some of them, like Professor Labaree, Professor Wright, and Dean Johnson, were excellent teachers, but others were merely mediocre. And between faculty and students there were practically no social or comradely relations of any kind. From chapel in the morning until classes were over in the afternoon, we saw our teachers only in the classrooms. After that until the next morning they disappeared into their houses bordering the campus, leaving the main yard and the dormitories entirely to the students—which gave student life a certain freedom not enjoyed by most Negro colleges. Indeed, dormitory life was entirely student-controlled—and sometimes highly hilarious.

Hazing was terrific. Incoming freshmen were given the paddling of their lives practically every night, from the opening of classes until the holidays. They were called *dogs,* made to roll pencils with their noses, to clean the sophomores' rooms, to "assume the angle" for paddling, and to write insulting letters to their girl friends. At Thanksgiving, just before the annual big game, in the dead of night, all freshmen were seized and their heads shaved bald.

Fraternity initiations occasionally sent agonized howls into the darkness around the countryside, whole woods and fields being available for the ordeal of brotherhood. The manhood rites of an African tribe could hardly have required more strength of the aspirants. When I was initiated, because I was a poet with my first book published and my name in the papers, each of my brothers-to-be was inclined to think every other brother would let me off easy.

The result—each and every brother laid on with such a heavy hand, applying so many licks to be sure the poet would be well initiated, that I could scarcely walk for a week.

"A New Negro, huh?" Wham!

"The boy poet, heh?" Wham!

"So nobody else'll beat you, heh?" Wham!

"Letting you slip by easy, are they?" Wham! Wham! Wham!

I was well initiated all right!

Water-throwing was an institution, too, at Lincoln, in defiance of faculty rules. We used the fire buckets in every dormitory hallway for the delightful purpose of drenching our fellow students. Whenever an unsuspecting student, preferably a dressed-up one, was entering or leaving the building—the most desirable were those leaving for a week-end in Philadelphia—somebody in an upper-story window would let him have it with a full bucket of water on his head, or perhaps two or three buckets from the sides. Well aimed, they could drench you to the skin.

Sometimes, by accident, a passing faculty member would get a soaking, since the front walk ran near the dormitories. And then there would be a quietus on water-throwing for a long while.

In winter there were snowball fights, a pond in the village for skating, a barn of a gymnasium for basketball, and movies in the chapel on Saturday nights. There were movies in nearby Oxford every night, but Negroes had to occupy the last rows on the side in the theater, so few of the Lincoln students went. As in most colleges, most of a student's spare time was spent in bull-sessioning. Nobody having much money, there was little gambling. As long as prohibition lasted, however, there was a campus bootlegger or two—some enterprising student with enough cash to lay in a supply of hooch for resale after a trip to Baltimore or Philadelphia.

In my junior year a group of upper classmen organized a Sportsmen's Club, the initiation fee being the contribution of something that the committee considered valuable to the club, said contribution to be stolen by the neophyte à la Robin Hood from anywhere on the campus. Rip Day, a husky Harlem incorrigible, was the president and I was on the organizing committee. The committee began by deciding to steal our president's room from him and make a club out of it. So, in the middle of the night, Rip was forcibly removed, bed and baggage, and placed in another classmate's room to lodge. Not wishing to set a bad example, the president acquiesced—and then proceeded to think up all manner of deviltry himself. We proceeded to list the most attractive couches, sofas, chairs, tables, silken pillows, and floor lamps to be found in the various dormitory rooms, and neophytes were ordered to secure them. In the case of very difficult jobs, the club as a whole would condescend to aid. It took the entire club, one pitch-black night, to steal into the silent prayer room of the chapel and remove the organ, since we decided we needed music during our club meeting.

Of course, no one was admitted to the club room except members, who had to know various secret signals and passwords even to enter that end of the dormitory hallway. When all was ready and our club completely furnished, we planned to hold open house—from which *we* would be absent, so that the students could scramble over their missing belongings. But that reception never came off. Over-ambition brought us to our end too soon.

We decided that the barren walls of the club room

needed the attractive faces of pretty women to make it more to our liking, so neophytes and club members alike were ordered to scour the dormitories for the loveliest pictures of the prettiest women to be found—not magazine pictures, but real pictures of attractive girl-friends and sisters of our schoolmates. Those bringing a picture already framed received an extra mark of merit on the club roster.

Then it was that trouble began. Boys began to miss their favorite girls' pictures from their dressers and desk tops. (And with the spring track-meet coming on, there would be some tall explaining to do if the girls showed up on the campus for a visit.) One aspirant to membership in the Sportsmen's Club was caught leaving a room with the photograph of a football man's brownskin lovely only partially concealed in the covers of a biology notebook. The football man fell upon the would-be Sportsman with a vengeance and took his picture back. By then, however, our walls were lined with beauties, ranging from blonde high-yellows to chocolate-browns. So one more or less didn't matter. But by that time the campus was in an uproar. A missing overstuffed chair, bought in a second-hand store, might be taken as a joke, but *not* a missing girl-friend's picture. By now, prayer meeting night had rolled around, too, and the divinity faculty discovered only an empty space where the organ had been. Somehow they suspected the Sportsmen's Club.

Irate lovers and irate theological professors got together and descended upon the club room. And that was the end of the Sportsmen's Club! Well, spring had come, anyhow, when the young ladies would be arriving to watch the sprinters. Other amusements would be available.

There were four hundred men at Lincoln pursuing their

studies—and only a few colored girls in the nearby village. However, for the games on the campus, and the Glee Club concert, young ladies—often chaperoned by their mothers —would come out from Philadelphia, Baltimore, or even New York, or from nearby Cheney Teachers' College. The old dormitories had no guest rooms, nor even lobbies to entertain guests, so the hospital house was given over to the students for that purpose. But it was very small and inadequate.

There was, of course, a rule against young men having ladies in their rooms after dark, but nobody paid it any attention. Some of the visiting mothers, who could not find their daughters for hours, must have complained because, one spring, hired chaperons suddenly appeared in the dormitories for the first time in history—nice, old, village colored women, whose duty it was to sit at the bottom of the steps near the front door and see that no young ladies entered after sundown. The boys soon got rid of these paid guardians of respectability by dropping giant firecrackers boom! bang! down the well of the staircase.

The following day, after the firecrackers, one of the elderly professors in the theological seminary assailed the entire student body at chapel, calling us all "libertines and lickertarians." The students demanded an apology on the grounds that it wasn't so. But by that time the college year was at an end, anyhow, and everyone went off to get jobs for the summer in the big cities, where there were plenty of girls.

FLOOD ON THE MISSISSIPPI

In the spring of 1927, I was invited to read my poems during commencement week at Fisk University in Nashville, Tennessee, and the week following at a Y.W.C.A. conference in Texas. I had never been in the South before, nor had I ever been offered such attractive fees for the reading of my poems, so I accepted both invitations, leaving Lincoln immediately after examinations.

I had heard of Fisk largely through the famous Fisk Jubilee Singers, and I was anxious to see that distinguished old institution of Negro learning in the Southland. My visit there was a delightful one. For the first time I stood before a large audience of my own people, reading my poems, and I was thrilled, because they seemed to like those poems—poems in which I had tried to capture some of the dreams and heartaches that all Negroes know.

While I was at Fisk, the headlines in the papers grew bigger and bigger about the Mississippi rising in flood. And then the river broke its banks. The Y.W.C.A. officials wired me that it was impossible to hold their conference in Texas, because too many of the delegates were from the flooded regions and could not come. With the fee from my Fisk engagement and the settlement the Y.W.C.A. made for their cancelled agreement, I decided to spend the summer traveling in the South. First I went to Memphis to see Beale Street.

On the train between Nashville and Memphis, a party

of Fisk students with whom I was traveling played an amusing joke on me. They knew it was difficult for Negroes from the North to get used to the Jim Crow customs of the South, or to know exactly what one might or might not do. I learned, for instance, that in Nashville there were certain parks Negroes could not enter or cross. If a park lay between you and your destination, you could not walk through the park as a white person might do. Being colored, you had to go *around* the park. I knew, of course, that Negroes were compelled to use Jim Crow waiting rooms at the railroad stations, and ride in the Jim Crow car up next to the engine. And I rather expected to see a lynching every day; but about such subtleties as parks, I was ignorant.

However, the South is not entirely as bad as it is painted, although I did not know that my first week there. So on the way to Memphis, I sat in the dusty Jim Crow car and discussed my thoughts and apprehensions with the students. The sun was very bright and the cinders from the engine flew in the windows, so I put on a pair of smoked glasses that I carried to protect my eyes.

Shortly the train stopped at a small station to water the engine, and we had time to get out and stretch our limbs, and buy ice cream cones from a platform vendor. While I was standing on the platform, some of the Fisk students came cautiously up to me and whispered in my ear: "Mr. Hughes, don't you know the white folks down South don't allow Negroes to wear smoked glasses?" Quickly I snatched my glasses off and looked around to see if any white folks had noticed me wearing them!

The students laughed loudly, then I knew it was only a joke. But I had heard *true* stories of cities where colored people were permitted to drive only second-hand cars; and other cities where they had to step off the sidewalk when a white man passed; and towns with signs up:

> NIGGER DON'T LET THE SUN
> GO DOWN ON YOU HERE

so I thought maybe it might be possible that there was also a feeling against colored people wearing dark glasses to protect their eyes from the sun. But it was only a joke, like that famous Mississippi sign:

> DARKIE, READ AND RUN!
> IF YOU CAN'T READ, RUN ANYHOW!

which was probably invented in vaudeville.

I was disappointed in Beale Street, and it was not until several years later when I visited it in company with W. C. Handy that that feeling was somewhat removed. Portions of Fifth or Lenox Avenues in New York's Harlem were, I thought, equally tough, equally colorful, and quite as colored as the famous Memphis thoroughfare. So I went on down to Vicksburg, Mississippi.

By now, the waters of the river were raging, and it was possible to go to Vicksburg only by a roundabout way. The main thing I remember about the town is a river front café with marvelously misspelled signs on the wall:

> ALL FIGHTIN MUS BE DID OUTSIDE

and another:

> IF YOU WANTS TO PLAY THE DOZENS GO HOME

and

> WHEN YOU EAT, PAY ER RUN
> CAUSE MR. BOSS GOT HES GUN

The papers said a vast camp for flood refugees had been established in Baton Rouge, and that thousands of Negroes and whites who had never been out of the plantation country before were being housed there. The Negro papers said the flood was a blessing in disguise, rescuing hundreds of black field hands and their families from peonage. I felt like going to talk with these field hands, so I struck out for Baton Rouge.

I found Baton Rouge a charming city to look at, but very southern in its prejudices against Negroes. And the treatment of the flood refugees there, according to race, was and is a classic example of Dixie today.

The white refugees were brought down the river to the city in steamers with cabins and covered decks to protect them from the elements, while the Negroes were transported on open flatboats, exposed to the wind and weather.

In Baton Rouge, the Red Cross had housed the whites in a group of tree-shaded buildings that were former government barracks, I believe. The Negroes were housed in an open field in small tents, where the mud was ankle deep when it rained.

The whites were given three hot meals a day, the Negroes, two. The whites received regular rations of tobacco, snuff, and candy. The Negroes got what was left over, if any, of these delicacies.

The Negroes, some of them, had horrifying tales to tell of forced labor at the point of a gun on levees that finally gave way; of terrified whites fleeing in all the available boats and leaving their black workers to find the way to safety as best they could; of hair-raising nights on roofs or knolls or flood surrounded portions of the levee, fighting back snakes and little wild animals that sought refuge there, too.

Most of the refugees could not read or write; most of them had never seen a city before; some of them had never been off the plantations where they were born; some of them, grown, had never had ten dollars at once in their lives.

"But are you going back to the plantations?" I would ask.

The camp was guarded and the Negroes would look at the guards; they had no money; they knew nowhere to go; they would generally say: "Yes, suh, I reckon we is."

Baton Rouge depressed me terribly; so, having the money to go away, I went. I bought a ticket for New Orleans.

The day before I left, I stayed at the colored refugee camp all day. Near sundown I was sitting on a pile of dirt from the ditches of the improvised drainage system, talking to a field hand of perhaps thirty, short, powerfully built, with a face dark as Africa. A little distance away, near one of the tents, his wife sat on a box, playing with three small children. She was a good-looking, brownskin girl in a blue flowered dress.

"She's mighty proud o' herself cause she's got one of them dresses out o' the barrel that come this mornin'." the field hand said.

It was not a bad dress to be from an old clothes barrel, and she looked good in it as she sat laughing with the young ones.

"Your kids?" I asked, nodding toward the three children.

"Sho is," he said. "All boys."

Two of the children were quite dark, but the skin of one of them was an ivory-yellow, near white. A curious contrast, two dark, one light. I think he read my thoughts.

" 'Course," he said, hunching over on the pile of dirt, "one chile truthfully ain't mine."

"Oh," I said.

"That little one yonder, the meriney, belongs to de overseer. But I treats him like it's mine."

NEW ORLEANS—HAVANA

In New Orleans, I wanted to live on Rampart Street, the leading Negro street, so I found a room not far from the railroad station, with a lady who rented out rooms, both transient and permanent.

On Saturday nights, her second-floor flat was very gay, because she held fish frys there and sold home-brew, and sometimes had so many transient couples wanting rooms temporarily that she rented mine until I was ready to go to bed. There was no piano, but she played marvelous blues records on an old victrola: Blind Lemon Jefferson, Lonnie Johnson, and Ma Rainey. And sometimes a wild guitar player would come in off the street and plunk a while, providing somebody bought him a drink or two. In Baton Rouge and New Orleans I heard many of the blues verses I used later in my short stories and my novel.

In the district where I lived there were some amazing voodoo shops and drug stores that seemed to deal almost exclusively in magic medicaments with strange names, good for whatever might ail you. Roots and herbs and powders that had much more power, the vendors said, than ordinary roots and herbs. There was one window on Poydras Street, displaying more than fifty conjur and voo-doo preparations: High John The Conqueror Root, Go-and-Stay Powders, Love Lucky Load Stone, black cats' bones, various kinds of incense, and tall, black luck candles. Signs announced: Good Business Water, 25¢; White Dove's Blood, 50¢; Follow Me Seeds, 10¢; Genuine Cala-bar Spirit Beans Cheap.

I bought some Wishing Powder and I think it brought me luck, because the next day, quite unexpectedly, I found myself on the way to Havana.

I was down at the docks, watching them unload bananas from the West Indies off a United Fruit boat, when I noticed, tied up at the next pier, a small, rusty freighter named the *Nardo*, with all the hatches open and the winches rattling, looking as though she were ready to put out to sea shortly since there didn't seem to be much cargo left on her dock. I walked along beside the *Nardo* under the swinging cargo nets, wondering where she voy-aged to, and feeling a bit homesick for a job on a boat myself.

Leaning over the rail I noticed a wizened Filipino steward.

I yelled: "Hey, Steward, don't you need a mess boy?"

He beckoned me to come up on deck. With all the noise of loading going on, he couldn't hear me, but nevertheless he knew what I said.

"Glad you come," he said. "I need one mess boy. I take you go see Captain now."

And in a few minutes I was signed up for a trip to Havana and back. It was just what I wanted—a short trip that would still allow me a week or so in New Orleans on the return, before having to go North to college.

The entire steward's department on the *Nardo,* with the exception of myself, was composed of Filipinos and Chinese. The crew were mostly Spaniards, with a few Americans thrown in. They were not quite so rough and rowdy a bunch as the fellows I had worked with on the S.S. *Malone* to Africa. On the New Orleans-Caribbean runs, the crews were frequently in port, and so had plenty of opportunities to let off steam. Sometimes the *Nardo* went to Jamaica, or Haiti, sometimes to Panama, sometimes to Norfolk or New York. Had I not had to return to Lincoln in October, I would have spent the winter on the *Nardo.*

The Chinese cooks and I became good friends. For themselves they prepared food Chinese style, usually fish and herbs and rice. And I almost always ate with them, when I had finished waiting on my sailors and firemen in the fo'c'sle.

In Havana I went with the Chinese to visit friends, who lived in a single enormous room with about forty other Chinese, all sleeping on straw mats on tiered shelves, packed in at night side by side like sardines in a tin. In the center of the room was a common pipe with a stem three or four feet long. Whoever wished, and whenever he wished, could squat down beside the pipe and take a puff or two. It wasn't opium, only some sort of musty tobacco with a very strong smell.

We bought red Chinese whiskey, flavored with lichee nuts, in brown clay jugs. Then we went to a house of pleasure exclusively for Orientals, although the girls were Cuban. The house had a large, dusky patio and the rooms opened all around the patio. A girl sat in the doorway of each room, rocking or fanning, or doing fancy work or smoking, and the men moved silently from doorway to doorway, looking, as one would move from cage to cage in a zoo. It was very quiet, because the girls and the men did not speak the same language, so there was little verbal communication.

Sometimes ten or fifteen Chinese would be standing before the door of an attractive girl, just standing and looking, not saying a word, the girl calmly rocking or fanning as though quite unobserved. If one of the men decided to enter, she would rise from her rocker and close the door behind him. Then the others would move on, to stand in a ring before another girl's doorway, circling thus around and around that big dreary patio in a kind of mass silence. It was the most depressing brothel I have ever seen.

The sailors' cafés on San Isidro Street did not seem very amusing either. The weather was terrifically hot that August and everybody sort of lifeless from the heat, and not much dancing. Bad little orchestras played *rhumbas* and *sones,* but nobody bothered to move from the tables. It was too hot even to get drunk.

CREOLES AND CONJUR
wwwwwwwwwwwwwwwwwwwwwwwwwwwwwwwwwwwwwww

Once back in New Orleans, I hated to quit the S.S. *Nardo,* but another trip would have made me late for classes. I decided to spend the rest of August in New Orleans and was lucky enough to find a room in the old French Quarter in the home of a colored woman married to a Mexican. It was just a block from the Cathedral, in a house that must have been at least a hundred years old.

All the floors were solid stone. The steps and balconies had railings of twirling ironwork, and none of the rooms had windows, only tall shuttered doors opening into the patio or onto the long balcony off the second floor.

In the center of the patio was a well with a bucket and a hand roller for pulling the water up.

It was a picturesque house. But like most picturesque things out of the past, not very comfortable, only beautiful to look at. Cockroaches as large as mice came out of the cracks of the walls after dark and scraped their rasping feet over the stone floors. The patio was airless and the heat lay like a blanket and everybody left their doors wide open at night, and some of the roomers snored like frogs. Mosquitoes zoomed and hummed. And at dawn, the lady of the house got up and began to wash and clean and sing and cook in the patio, so there was no sleeping after the sun rose.

She was a stout, dark woman, who made very good coffee and a lot of it, for everybody in the house, so with the coffee and the sun and the singing and the bustle every morning, I found myself up early and out in the street rambling through the Vieux Carée.

One day I was in the old St. Louis Cemetery, with its tombs one on top of another above ground, when a couple of dark caretakers, sitting in the shade behind one of the tombs, hailed me. In English that had a decidedly strange accent, they asked me if I wanted to go in on a bottle of wine. I said: "Sure."

One of them scrambled up, figured out the exact amount each one had to contribute, and off he went for the wine. I noticed an empty bottle already on the ground, beside some bones from a tomb they must have been cleaning. They were short, very black fellows, who spoke Creole to each other. They were the first real Creoles I had met. In Louisiana, it seems, a Creole is anyone, white, black, brown, or mulatto, who speaks the Creole patois or who comes from certain parishes where that patois is the local language.

These grave diggers, or rather grave attendants, since they did not have to dig, were merry fellows, much in love with wine, and given to telling very funny jokes in Creole, because they would laugh and laugh. And they did not know enough English to explain to me what they were laughing about. But when the wine was drunk, they showed me all the famous tombs, including the tomb of Marie Laveau, where many black candles are burned and crosses made in memory of the high priestess of voodoo whose bones lie therein.

They had very little reverence for the tombs they were tending. One of them said to me in an attempt at English that I cannot reproduce: "All this folks got this great big tombs, they gonna have mighty hard time gettin' out from under when de Judgement Day comes. How they gonna get out from under all this stone? Can you tell me?"

I couldn't, so we went off to have supper in a nearby tavern for colored Creoles. I ate there often after that and came to know several Creoles pretty well. Even once or twice I was invited to their homes, and on one occasion to a party. The ordinary non-Creole colored people of New Orleans told me that was rather unusual, because the Creoles did not mix much, or show hospitality toward the English-speaking Negroes "across Canal Street." The non-Creoles said that the Creoles were a very dangerous people, given to the use of knives, and the Creoles said the same about the others. But I had a good time with all of them.

No sooner had I got off the train than I ran into Zora Hurston, walking intently down the main street, looking just as if she was out to measure somebody's head for an anthropological treatise. I didn't know she was in the South, and she didn't know I was either, so we were very glad to see each other. Right off we went to eat some fried fish and watermelon. Then she took me to see Dr. Williams and his daughter, Lucy Ariel, a talented pianist and poet.

Miss Hurston was bound North, too. She had her own car, so we decided to travel together, stopping on the way to pick up folk-songs, conjur, and big ole lies, for Miss Hurston was on a collector's trip for one of the folk-lore societies. Blind guitar players, conjur men, and former slaves were her quarry, small town jooks and plantation churches, her haunts. I knew it would be fun traveling with her. It was.

We stopped at Tuskegee and made speeches on writing to the summer school students—which was our only contact with formal culture all the way from Mobile to New York. Then we went to Macon, Georgia, where Bessie Smith was singing in a small theater. But you didn't have to go near the theater to hear Bessie sing. You could hear her blocks away. Besides, she practised every morning in the hotel where we lived, so we met her and got to know her pretty well.

Bessie said: "The trouble with white folks singing blues is that they can't get low down enough."

From Macon we went to Savannah and met a little woman who was out shopping for a second-hand gun to "sting her husband up a bit." She told us where the turpentine workers and the dock workers hung out, and we got acquainted with some and had supper with them. We

CREOLES AND CONJUR 297

asked them to sing some songs, but the songs they sang we had heard before and they were not very good songs. Miss Hurston said you had to live with people a long while, as a rule, before you might accidently some day hear them singing some song you never heard before, that maybe they had learned away off in the backwoods or remembered from childhood or were right then and there engaged in making up themselves.

"You can't just sit down and ask people to sing songs for you and expect them to be folk-songs, and good ones, and new ones," said Miss Hurston. It seldom happens that way. But it was fun having supper with the stevedores from the Savannah docks.

In Georgia, we visited an excellent Negro school at Fort Valley and met Mr. and Mrs. Hunt in charge, but at that time the school was closed and we saw only the buildings. Then we got wind of a famous conjur-man away off in the backwoods, so we decided to go see him. We were warned not to go on a week-end, for then the cars and wagons of Negroes and whites alike filled his cabin yard, and you might wait all day and not have a chance to talk with him.

We went in the middle of the week, driving over the red clay roads. It was not hard to find his cabin, because everybody along the road seemed to know him. We drove up in the early afternoon and a tall, red-skinned, middle-aged man received us, the conjur-man himself. There was nothing especially distinguished about the man either in appearance or personality. He was quiet and pleasantly serious and asked us, in a southern drawl, what our trouble was.

Miss Hurston said that she had a cousin in Brooklyn who was working against her, trying to keep her from coming back North because that cousin feared that some of the money from a piece of property left to the family might come to her. That cousin was working to put harm in her way, and in my way, and something awful might happen to us if we did not find protection.

The conjur-man picked up his huge apocryphal Bible and began to read from it. He then rose and darkened the room, after having laid out various chalks and powders on a nearby table. When the room was quite dark, he touched Miss Hurston on the forehead and on the breast with a piece of chalk that left white marks. He sprinkled water and mumbled an incantation. Then he gave us each a small stone to hold. He struck a match and put it to the stones and each stone began to blaze. He told us to move the stones in the form of a cross. After the stones had burned a while, he spoke in tongues, performed other simple rites behind our backs, and then raised the curtains and opened the door and charged us seventy-five cents. He said everything would be all right, but if we wanted further safeguards, to give him five dollars and he would continue the rites for a month for us—until there would be no possibility of harm coming from our Brooklyn cousin. We said we did not feel we needed the additional protection, and he agreed it was not absolutely necessary, since any and all of his charms were effective. So we went away.

Miss Hurston, who had visited a great many conjur-men, said that he was a poor one without power, using tricks like the burning sulphur-stones to amaze and confound people. We did not understand why he had such a reputation in that part of Georgia, where even some of the medical doctors were complaining about his having taken their patients away from them. Yet I guess if you really believe in a burning sulphur-stone dripping a cross, it might perhaps be good for what ails you.

OLD HAT
∿∿∿∿∿∿∿∿∿

While we were in Georgia, I visited the plantation where Jean Toomer had lived, and, so we were told, had got much of his material for *Cane*. We talked with some of his distant relatives. One of the old men there had on his head a marvelous patchwork hat of felt, patched over and over with varicolored bits of leather, linoleum, canvas, and baize where the holes of time had worn through. The entire hat was wonderfully weather-stained and dirty. The old Negro looked like something out of *Uncle Remus*. Indeed like Uncle Remus himself.

I coveted his hat. It seemed to me like the quaint soul of labor in the Old South, "caroling softly souls of slavery." It seemed to me like early dawn on the Georgia plum trees and sunlight in the cotton fields. So, after much dignified bargaining (for I had to overcome his entrenched resistance), I traded my new straw hat for it and brought the octogenarian's hat back with me to New York. There I put it in a safe-deposit vault in a Fifth Avenue bank, where, thanks to a patron, my manuscripts were stored, and also my grandmother's shawl, in which Sheridan Leary had been killed with John Brown at Harpers Ferry.

I don't know now why I considered that old hat so valuable—except that it was quaint and folk-like in the manner of the spirituals and the blues. So I wrapped it in tissue and put it securely in my locked suitcase in the vault.

That winter I had no reason to go to the safe-deposit for anything. But the following spring I went there to look up some notes in the suitcase for my first novel. It was Saturday morning and the elegant, guarded, triple-locked chamber was crowded with well-dressed people, inspecting securities or getting out their week-end jewels. The attendant handed me my suitcase. As I opened it, to my utter consternation, out came a great cloud of moths, filling the room! They rose in a dusty horde toward the ceiling and then gradually began to settle in flocks on the astonished heads and fashionable fur-pieces of the fine ladies in the vault and to get into the hair of various old gentlemen cutting coupons. Other insects merely drifted toward the guards.

As the bank's clients fought off the moths in indignant amazement, I quickly closed the suitcase, rushed out and took a taxi to the middle of Central Park. There I dumped everything on the grass and backed away as more and more insects continued to flutter into space.

Then I had to go over each leaf in every notebook, and each sheet of paper piece by piece, brushing off moth eggs for fear they would turn to eating up the manuscripts next—for they had eaten my old hat to a powder, leaving only a varicolored dust.

It was weeks before I took that suitcase back to the bank. I was ashamed! And when I did take it, redolent with camphor balls, I took it very early in the morning, sneaking in, lest I see some of the ladies and gentlemen there who might remember my moths and cower in panic.

INTERRACIAL CONFERENCE

During my sophomore year at Lincoln, I contributed to the college paper, took part in intra-mural track, and read my poems with the Glee Club at Princeton University.

That year, too, the college quartette and some of our students were invited to attend a Y.M.C.A. conference at Franklin and Marshall College, at Lancaster, Pennsylvania, and I was asked to read my poetry. It was my first inter-racial conference. Since then, I've discovered that an awful lot of hooey revolves around interracial conferences in this country. In Europe people of all races meet and eat and drink and talk and dance and do whatever they are meeting to do without self-consciousness. But here, when there are Negroes and whites present together, there is often an amazing amount of gushing, of blundering, of commiserating, of talking pro and con, of theorizing and excusing, and somebody is almost sure to bring up the question of intermarriage, and then everyone looks intense, interested, and apprehensive.

There is always the matter of where the Negroes are to sleep, too, and where they are to eat. When one has been in Europe or in Mexico where these things never come up, and one can sleep or eat anywhere, no matter what one's complexion, such considerations seem doubly stupid.

Once at the Hill School, a fashionable boys' preparatory school in Pennsylvania, Alain Locke and I were asked to appear on a morning program devoted to Negro literature. Afterwards we were invited to luncheon. Later I learned that the whole seating arrangement of the boys' dining hall had been disturbed, a special table allotted to us, and the boys asked to volunteer as to who would be willing to sit beside a Negro! Such a procedure seemed to me absolutely amazing—especially in the light of Dr. Locke's having represented the United States as a Rhodes Scholar at Oxford, his wide travel background, and his important contributions to American life.

"Who will volunteer to sit beside a Negro?"

At Franklin and Marshall, however, the students were less self-consciously cordial to their guests from Lincoln, hospitably sharing dormitory space with them and seats in the dining hall. And I don't believe we discussed intermarriage. But we did talk about the sociological aspects of the Negro problem, and about the hard times Negro students had finding jobs, and about the Jim Crow Y.M.C.A. system in America, and prayer, and the church, as well as a great many other problems that concern all Christian students as a whole. And the Lincoln University Quartette sang spirituals.

On the last day of the conference, when they were drawing up resolutions, it seemed to me there might as well be one really *practical* resolution regarding Negroes somewhere on the list. (I have always been an opponent of the general and the vague.) So since we were meeting on the campus of Franklin and Marshall, and since that college seemed to have an unwritten rule barring Negro students from attendance, and since there were a number of young Negroes graduating every year from high schools in Lancaster, who had to go away to more distant cities to further their education, I thought it would be fitting and proper for us, as a student conference, to see if we could get at the root of that matter *right there* on the campus where we were in session—as to why Negro citizens could not attend *that* college.

A resolution of such a nature involving a definite task, but of local scope, it seemed to me, would have an immediate practical value, and give the Franklin and Marshall students something concrete to do.

But I could get no action on such a resolution at all! Everybody shied away. And the white director of our conference—an adult professional Young Men's Christian Association leader—said regarding this problem in his final talk to the assembled delegates: "There are some things in this world we must leave to Jesus, friends. Let us pray!"

So they prayed. And the conference ended.

NOT WITHOUT LAUGHTER

Maybe everybody is sentimental about his college days. Certainly I loved Lincoln. My years there were happy years, jolly and full of fun. Besides I learned a few things. And I wrote *Not Without Laughter*.

The ideas for my first novel had been in my head for a long time. I wanted to write about a typical Negro family in the Middle West, about people like those I had known in Kansas. But mine was not a typical Negro family. My grandmother never took in washing or worked in service or went much to church. She had lived in Oberlin and spoke perfect English, without a trace of dialect. She looked like an Indian. My mother was a newspaper woman and a stenographer then. My father lived in Mexico City. My granduncle had been a congressman. And there were heroic memories of John Brown's raid and the underground railroad in the family storehouse.

But I thought maybe I had been a typical Negro boy. I grew up with the other Negro children of Lawrence, sons and daughters of family friends. I had an uncle of sorts who ran a barber shop in Kansas City. And later I had a stepfather who was a wanderer. We were poor—but different. For purposes of the novel, however, I created around myself what seemed to me a family more typical of Negro life in Kansas than my own had been. I gave myself aunts that I didn't have, modeled after other children's aunts whom I had known. But I put in a real cyclone that had blown my grandmother's front porch away. And I added dances and songs I remembered. I brought the boy to Chicago in his teens, as I had come to Chicago—but I did not leave behind a well-fixed aunt whose husband was a mail clerk.

I wrote the book during the summer following my junior year at Lincoln. The authorities said I might remain in the empty dormitory and write. For two weeks I didn't do anything. But the time passed like two days. Then suddenly I began with the storm, and my characters seemed to live in the room where I worked. Their chairs and tables were there, too, and the lamp. Then I wrote out short histories for all my characters as they came to life—how old they were, where born, things that had happened to them, and what might happen to them. Also why.

These sketches and outlines I tacked on the wall above the table where I worked. Then I began the second chapter. At first, I did a chapter or two a day and revised them the next day. But they seemed bad; in fact, so bad I finally decided to write the whole story straight through to the end before re-reading anything. This I did in about six weeks. Then I went to Provincetown for a vacation before classes opened in the fall.

All that winter, my senior year, I re-read and re-worked my novel. The following summer, after graduation, I again stayed on the campus in a big, empty theological dormitory all alone. I began to cut my novel, which was far too bulky. As I cut and polished, revised and re-wrote, the people in the book seemed to walk around the room and talk, to me, helping me write. Aunt Hager and Annjee and Jimboy were there. And an oil light burned on my table—as in Kansas.

That night when Harriett ran away to join the carnival was almost more than I could stand. I knew I would miss her. (I had never really had an aunt who ran away to join a carnival, but I wanted to have one. And there wasn't really any oil light in the dormitory.)

At the end of the summer the book was not finished, but I thought it was, so I went to Canada. When I came back to New York and read it, it seemed so bad it made me sick. So I went to work once more. I couldn't bear to have the people I had grown to love locked up in long pages of uncomfortable words, awkward sentences, and drawn-out passages. I began to cut and re-write, page after page. I was lucky now to have a sympathetic and excellent typist, Louise Thompson, who must have done certain pages over for me so often she could have recited by heart their varying versions.

So all that winter in New Jersey I worked on the novel. Finally it had to go to the printer. Galley proofs came. Page proofs. And at last it was on the stands: *Not Without Laughter*. Distributed to San Francisco and Melbourne, Bombay and London, Tokio and Paris. Listen, Aunt Hager! Listen, Harriett! Listen, Annjee! Listen, Jimboy!

Hey, Benbow! I wanted to make you as wonderful as you really are—but it takes a lot of skill in words. And I don't know how.

I went to Far Rockaway that summer and felt bad, because I had wanted their novel to be better than the published one I had given them; I hated to let them down.

ALMA MATER

During my senior year—to the neglect of my Greek—I did one other thing besides my novel that interested me greatly. For Professor Labaree's course in sociology each graduating student had to turn in a paper on some phase of American life. I chose to do a survey of the campus on which I studied. Food, living conditions, social life, academic standards, and race relations between the Negro student body and the white faculty were all to be covered. Menus studied over a period of time as to their dietary value, dormitories checked daily, each student and teacher interviewed on questions vital to the college life—so much material, in fact, that two other students were assigned to help me, once the study was outlined.

There was something I wanted to prove. So I checked on menus and whether or not there were any bedbugs on the beds, simply to get around to that.

During my years at the college I had sat in on many student bull-sessions, and over and over I had heard Lincoln's own peculiar color line discussed: the fact that there was an all-white faculty for an all-Negro student body. Over and over I heard many students agree that it was better so, that there was something inherently superior in white teachers that Negro teachers did not have. I wanted to prove that the students believing this were wrong, and that Lincoln was fostering—unwittingly, perhaps—an inferiority complex in the very men it wished to train as leaders of the Negro race. I wanted to show that the color line is not good on campus or off.

Of course, I did not say so, but that was in the back of my head. So I began to gather data on the matter, quite sure that the data would not lie. It didn't.

My survey showed that sixty-three per cent of the members of the junior and senior classes preferred that Lincoln have an all-white faculty. The reasons given were various: that Lincoln was supported by "white" philanthropy, therefore whites should run the college; that favoritism and unfairness would result on the part of Negro teachers toward the students; that there were not enough Negro teachers available; and that things were all right as they were, so why change? Three students even said they just didn't like Negroes. Two said they did not believe Negro teachers had the interest of students at heart. Another said members of his own race were not morally capable!

These comments I tabulated carefully. In my paper commenting on the results of my survey, I wrote:

"63% of the members of the upper classes favor for their college a faculty on which there are no Negro professors. And, since I have never heard otherwise, I judge that the faculty of Lincoln University itself supports this attitude. Yet it seems to me the height of absurdity for an institution designed for the training of Negro leadership to support and uphold, on its own grounds, the unfair and discriminatory practices of the American color line. And the fact that 81 members of the Senior and Junior classes at this college can themselves approve of such a situation, and give reasons for their approval which express open belief in their own inferiority, indicates that the college itself has failed in instilling in these students the very quality of self-reliance and self-respect which any capable American leader should have—and the purpose of this college, let us remember, is to educate 'leaders of the colored people.'

"There is a mixed faculty at Fisk, and certainly the work done there is quite on par with Lincoln. Tuskegee has an *all-Negro* faculty, as have many other schools dependent upon white philanthropy. And certainly with men like Charles S. Johnson, Westley, Locke, Brady, and Just in the teaching fields, besides large numbers of colored graduates every year from the best Northern universities, it is stupid to say that there are no capable Negro teachers available. Not an all-Negro faculty—possibly not even a predominantly colored faculty is to be desired, but certainly *one* of our eleven professors might well belong to the race from which all of the 323 resident students of this institution come.

"Student-faculty relationships outside the class-room, while friendly, do not seem to be in any way free or intimate. There is a tendency on the part of the students to avoid relations with the faculty or members of their families, and what cultural contacts come to the students from the faculty are, therefore, almost solely by way of the class-room. Few individual students ever enter a faculty home unless it be on a matter of class-room business, by special invitation, or else to work there. Faculty-student relations at Lincoln are confined almost wholly to curricular activities."

And that was true. The same line that cuts across American life, dividing the white from the non-white, cut across the life at Lincoln: the dark students in their dormitories on the campus, the white teachers in their houses across the road—meeting a few hours a day for classes, and that was just about all.

When I entered Lincoln there was an all-white Board of Trustees, and an all-white faculty. Kind, gentle, missionary-minded people, most of them, personally sweet and likable. But there was no course in Negro History being given, none in Negro Literature, and none in Negro Education (the problems peculiar to the segregated Southern schools where most of the young men who became teachers would teach). Among the alumni there was a growing agitation for a Negro member of the Trustee Board, and for Negro members of the faculty. But among the students the most vocal were opposed to these reforms.

My survey created a sensation on the campus. A portion of it leaked out to the newspapers, inaccurately. Letters came in from Southern schools saying they would not employ Lincoln men to teach, coming as they did from a student body that did not believe Negroes capable of teaching themselves.

One of the famous old grads of Lincoln, in objecting to the baldness with which the facts of my survey were presented, said to me at graduation: "Young man, suppose I told the truth to white folks. I never could have built the great institution I've built for my race." (And he has created a large and much needed institution for the Negro population in a great Middle Western city.) He continued: "You don't get things out of white folks that way." His implication was that "things are got out of white folks" by flattery, cajolery, good-natured begging, lying, and general Uncle Toming—not by truth.

"I don't agree with you," I said.

"After you've been out of college awhile, you'll agree, young man," he answered. "You'll agree."

He walked away. I looked at him crossing the campus, famous, well-to-do—the kind of a man the graduation speakers told us to look up to.

I felt bad, confused, puzzled. I had never thought much before about the nature of compromise. For bread how much of the spirit must one give away? He had his great buildings, serving hundreds of black people denied the same service elsewhere in the city where he lived. And maybe those buildings would stand there a long time on their cornerstone of lies.

I began to think back to Nat Turner, Harriet Tubman, Sojourner Truth, John Brown, Fred Douglass—folks who left no buildings behind them—only a wind of words fanning the bright flame of the spirit down the dark lanes of time.

The old grad has his buildings, just as Booker T. Washington had Tuskegee. Yet how heavily the bricks of compromise settle into place!

But Lincoln today is not the Lincoln of my survey. In ten brief years many changes have been made. There are Negro members of both the faculty and the Board of Trustees. It is a mixed faculty now, Negro and white—which is the way it seems to me all the faculties of all the universities of America should be.

EXTRA PAGE

After I had finished my survey, I added a kind of poetic foreword to precede the various pages of statistics my associates and I had gathered and the twenty-six pages of comment I had prepared. A poetic foreword has no place in a sociological survey, but, nevertheless, I put it there as a kind of extra flourish. This was the

FOREWORD

In the primitive world, where people live closer to the earth and much nearer to the stars, every inner and outer act combines to form the single harmony, life. Not just the tribal lore then, but every movement of life becomes a part of their education. They do not, as many civilized people do, neglect the truth of the physical for the sake of the mind. Nor do they teach with speech alone, but rather with all the acts of life. There are no books, so the barrier between words and reality is not so great as with us. The earth is right under their feet. The stars are never far away. The strength of the surest dream is the strength of the primitive world.

This meant, I suppose, that where life is simple, truth and reality are one.

PATRON AND FRIEND

While I was at Lincoln, I spent several pleasant weekends in the spring or fall with Joel and Amy Spingarn at their country place, Troutbeck, that had once been the old farm of John Burroughs, the naturalist, where his trout pool is still preserved. I met the Spingarn sons and daughters, who were also in college or prep school. And I saw the beautiful medieval virgin in wood that Mrs. Spingarn had brought from Europe. She had there, too, a tiny hand press, and later published a small volume of my poems, in a limited edition on hand-made paper, a collection of lyrics called *Dear Lovely Death*.

The Spingarns were charming, quiet people. Joel Spingarn told me much about the early days of the National Association for the Advancement of Colored People, in which he had a great interest as one of the founders and later as its President. He told me, too, about his long acquaintanceship with Dr. DuBois and other Negro leaders. And his brother, Arthur, who has one of the largest collections of Negro books in America, often spoke of the work of the older Negro authors like Chesnutt, my fellow Clevelander, and of others at the beginning of our literary history, of whom, until then, I had never heard.

During my years at Lincoln, on one of my week-end visits to New York, a friend took me to call on a distinguished and quite elderly white lady who lived on Park Avenue in a large apartment, with attendants in livery at the door and a private elevator-landing. I found her instantly one of the most delightful women I had ever met, witty and charming, kind and sympathetic, very old and white-haired, but amazingly modern in her ideas, in her knowledge of books and the theater, of Harlem, and of everything then taking place in the world.

Her apartment was many floors above the street and there was a view of all New York spread out beneath it. Her rooms were not cluttered with furniture or objects of art, but every piece was rare and beautiful. When I left, after a delightful evening, she pressed something into my hand. "A gift for a young poet," she said. It was a fifty-dollar bill.

From Lincoln, I wrote her and thanked her for the gift. In reply, she asked me to dine with her and her family on my next trip to New York. At dinner we had duck and wild rice. And for dessert, ice cream on a large silver platter, surrounded by fresh strawberries. The strawberries were served with their green stems still on them, the tiny red fruit being very pretty around the great mound of ice cream on the silver platter.

Carefully, I removed the green stems and put them on the side of my plate. But when I had finished eating the berries and ice cream, I noticed that no one else at the table had left any stems on the plates. Their ice cream and all was gone. I couldn't imagine what they had done with their stems. What did one do with strawberry stems on Park Avenue? Or were these a very special kind of strawberry stem that you could eat? Or had I committed some awful breach of etiquette by removing my strawberry stems by hand and putting them in plain view of everyone on the side of my plate? I didn't know. I was worried and puzzled.

As the Swedish maids warmed the finger bowls, my curiosity got the best of me and I asked my hostess what had everyone else done with the strawberry stems. She smiled and replied that no one else had taken any—since they were all allergic to strawberries!

In the living room after dinner, high above Park Avenue with the lights of Manhattan shining below us, my hostess asked me about my plans for the future, my hopes, my ambitions, and my dreams. I told her I wanted to write a novel. She told me she would make it possible for me to write that novel. And she did by covering the expenses of my summer, so that I need do no other work during vacation.

That was the summer when I wrote a draft of *Not Without Laughter*. Then I went for a short vacation at Provincetown, where I saw the Wharf Players performing a version of Donald Ogden Stewart's *Parody Outline of History*. I liked the wide sandy beaches of Cape Cod, but I did not like Provincetown very much, because it was hard for a Negro to find a place to sleep, and at night the mosquitoes were vicious.

During my senior year at Lincoln, I rewrote my novel. And at graduation I was given a generous monthly allowance by my patron, who had read both drafts of the book, had helped me with it, and found it good. Then began for me a strange and wonderful year of economic freedom, starting with a boat trip up the Saguenay River to see the northern lights. (The boat trip would have been pleasant had I not been the only Negro on board in the midst of a crowd of Middle-Westerners and Southerners. The steward refused to give me a sitting in the dining-saloon except after all the whites had eaten. So I got off the boat somewhere in the wilds of Canada and came back to Montreal by train. The company refunded my money.)

In the fall I spent a few weeks with Jasper Deeter at Hedgerow Theater, writing my first play, *Mulatto*. Then I settled in Westfield, New Jersey, near New York, where I made the final revisions of my novel.

My patron (a word neither of us liked) was a beautiful woman, with snow-white hair and a face that was wise and very kind. She had been a power in her day in many movements adding freedom and splendor to life in America. She had had great sums of money, and had used much of it in great and generous ways. She had been a friend of presidents and bankers, distinguished scientists, famous singers, and writers of world renown. Imposing institutions and important new trends in thought and in art had been created and supported by her money and her genius at helping others. Now she was very old and not well and able to do little outside her own home. But there she was like a queen. Her power filled the rooms. Famous people came to see her and letters poured in from all over the world.

I do not know why or how she still found time for me, and many others like me, young and just starting out on the big sea of life. Or how she arranged her very full day to include so many people and so many things. Or how she never forgot the tiniest detail of what she had worked for or planned with anyone. She was an amazing, brilliant, and powerful personality. I was fascinated by her, and I loved her. No one else had ever been so thoughtful of me, or so interested in the things I wanted to do, or so kind and generous toward me.

For years this good woman had been devoted in a mild way to the advancement of the Negro and had given money to Negro schools in the South. Now she had discovered the New Negro and wanted to help him. She was intensely excited about each new book, each new play, and each new artist that came out of the Negro world.

Everything born to Negroes in those days of the '20's, she knew about. For a woman as old as my grandmother would have been had she lived, she still kept up with everything from Duke Ellington to the budding Marian Anderson.

Still, Negroes occupied but one corner in that vast and active mind of hers. She was deeply interested in a great many things other than Negroes. One of the outstanding American achievements of this century, heralded on the front pages of the world's newspapers, came into being partly through this woman's aid. But, due to her own wish, her name was nowhere mentioned in connection with it, for she never permitted a credit line concerning anything she did, or a dedication to herself of any book she helped to bring to being.

Concerning Negroes, she felt that they were America's great link with the primitive, and that they had something very precious to give to the Western World. She felt that there was mystery and mysticism and spontaneous harmony in their souls, but that many of them had let the white world pollute and contaminate that mystery and harmony, and make of it something cheap and ugly, commercial and, as she said, "white." She felt that we had a deep well of the spirit within us and that we should keep it pure and deep.

In her youth she must have been an amazing person, indeed—and certainly one of America's finest representatives of great wealth. I cannot write about her more fully now because I have no right to disclose her name, nor to describe in detail her many and varied activities. I can only say that those months when I lived by and through her were the most fascinating and fantastic I have ever known.

Out of a past of more or less continued insecurity and fear, suddenly I found myself with an assured income from someone who loved and believed in me, an apartment in a suburban village for my work, my brother in school in New England and no longer a financial difficulty to my mother, myself with boxes of fine bond paper for writing, a filing case, a typist to copy my work, and wonderful new suits of dinner clothes from Fifth Avenue shops, and a chance to go to all the theaters and operas and lectures, no matter how expensive or difficult securing tickets might be. All I needed to say was when and where I wished to go and my patron's secretary would have tickets for me.

That season I went to the Metropolitan, to concerts at Carnegie Hall, to the hit plays and latest musicals, often with my patron. Together we heard *Sadko,* saw the first *Little Show, Berkeley Square,* and *Blackbirds.* We heard Madame Naidu speak, and General Smuts. We saw the Van Goghs. We drove through Central Park in the spring to see the first leaves come out.

It was all very wonderful. Park Avenue and Broadway and Harlem and New York! But when I had finished my novel and it went to press, I didn't feel like writing anything else then, so I didn't write anything. I was tired and happy, having completed a book, so I stopped work.

I didn't realize that my not writing a while mattered so much to the kind and generous woman who was caring for my welfare. I didn't realize that she was old and wanted quickly to see my books come into being before she had to go away. She hadn't told me that I must always write and write, and I felt sure she knew that sometimes for months, a writer does not feel like writing. That winter I did not feel like writing because I was happy and amused. (I only really feel like writing when I am unhappy, bored or else have something I need very much to say, or that I feel so strongly about I cannot hold it back.) That winter I didn't seem to need to say anything. I had had my say in the novel—spread over almost two years in the saying. Now I was ready for the first time in my life really to enjoy life without having to be afraid I might be hungry tomorrow.

Of course, I felt bad sometimes because I couldn't share my new-found comfort as fully as I might have wished with my mother, who was working as a cook in a rest home in Atlantic City. And in Cleveland we had relatives who were having a pretty hard time getting along at all, for the depression had come. But at least the burden of my kid brother's care had been lifted from my mother. He was happy and well fed in New England, not running the back alleys of Atlantic City.

I always felt slightly bad, too, when I was riding in the long town-car that belonged to my Park Avenue patron—and most other Negroes (and white folk) were walking. I would never occupy the car alone if I could help it. But sometimes she would insist, if it were very late, that I be driven to Harlem—or to the ferry, if I were going to Jersey—in her car. At such times I felt specially bad, because I knew the chauffeur did not like to drive me.

He was a rather grim and middle-aged white man, who, probably in all his career as a chauffeur, had never before been asked to drive a Negro about. At least, I felt that in his attitude toward me when I was alone in the deep, comfortable back seat of the car (where I didn't want to be) with him driving me to Harlem. I would have preferred to ride in front with him, talk with him, and get to know him, but he never gave me a chance. He was always coldly polite and unsmiling, drawing ceremoniously up to the curb in front of my Harlem rooming house, getting out and opening the door for me, but never looking pleasant, or joking, or being kind about it. I felt bad riding with him, because I knew he *hated* to drive me, and I knew he had to do it if he wanted to keep his job. And I dislike being the cause of anyone's having to do anything he doesn't want to do just to keep a job—since I know how unpleasant that is. So often, I would ask my patron's chauffeur simply to drop me at the nearest subway entrance.

But I remember once an amusing situation developed on a certain occasion when I was going out of town on a mid-winter lecture trip. I had been delayed at luncheon on Park Avenue, and so was late getting to the train. There was a terrific blizzard with heavy snow, and, fearing that in a taxi I might be too late for the train, my hostess sent not only her car and chauffeur with me to the station, but her secretary as well to help me get my ticket and have the baggage checked.

The secretary was a tall New England spinster, very efficient and pleasant, and not at all ungracious like the chauffeur. But the funny thing was that when the long town-car drew up to the ramp in the Pennsylvania Station and a dozen colored red caps that I had gone to college with rushed up to take the baggage and saw me get out with the secretary—as a white chauffeur held the door—the red caps were gleefully amazed.

As the secretary rushed ahead to get the Pullman reservation, several of the red caps I knew shook hands and asked me where I was going, and my college friends slapped me on the back in their usual friendly manner and demanded: "Since when the swell chariot, Lang?" But the chauffeur closed the door with a bang, jumped back into the car, and whirled away.

New York began to be not so pleasant that winter. People were sleeping in subways or on newspapers in office doors, because they had no homes. And in every block a beggar appeared. I got so I didn't like to go to dinner on luxurious Park Avenue—and come out and see people hungry on the streets, huddled in subway entrances all

night and filling Manhattan Transfer like a flop house. I
knew I could very easily and quickly be there, too, hungry
and homeless on a cold floor, anytime Park Avenue got
tired of supporting me. I had no job, and no way of making a living.

During the winter Zora Hurston came to Westfield
from one of her many trips into the deep South, and there
began to arrange her folk material, stacks and stacks of it—
some of which later appeared in *Mules and Men*. Together
we also began to work on a play called *Mule Bone,* a Negro
folk comedy, based on an amusing tale Miss Hurston had
collected about a quarrel between two rival church factions. I plotted out and typed the play based on her story,
while she authenticated and flavored the dialogue and
added highly humorous details. We finished a first draft
before she went South again, and from this draft I was
to work out a final version.

Zora, a very gay and lively girl, was seriously hemmed in
in village-like Westfield. But those backing her folk-lore
project felt that she should remain quietly in a small town
and not go galavanting gaily about New York while engaged in the serious task of preparing her manuscripts. So
she was restless and moody, working in a nervous manner.
And we were both distressed at the growing depression—
hearing of more and more friends and relatives losing jobs
and becoming desperate for lack of work.

In the midst of that depression, the Waldorf-Astoria
opened. On the way to my friend's home on Park Avenue
I frequently passed it, a mighty towering structure loom-
ing proud above the street, in a city where thousands were
poor and unemployed. So I wrote a poem about it called
"Advertisement for the Waldorf-Astoria," modeled after an

ad in *Vanity Fair* announcing the opening of New York's greatest hotel. (Where no Negroes worked and none were admitted as guests.)

The hotel opened at the very time when people were sleeping on newspapers in doorways, because they had no place to go. But suites in the Waldorf ran into thousands a year, and dinner in the Sert Room was ten dollars! (Negroes, even if they had the money, couldn't eat there. So naturally, I didn't care much for the Waldorf-Astoria.) The thought of it made me feel bad, so I wrote this poem, from which these excerpts are taken:

ADVERTISEMENT FOR THE WALDORF-ASTORIA

Fine living à la carte!!

LISTEN, HUNGRY ONES!

Look! See what *Vanity Fair* says about the
    new Waldorf-Astoria:
    "All the luxuries of private home. . . ."
Now, won't that be charming when the last flop-
    house has turned you down this winter?
    Furthermore:
"It is far beyond anything hitherto attempted in the hotel
    world. . . ." It cost twenty-eight million dollars. The
    famous Oscar Tschirky is in charge of banqueting. Alex-
    andre Gastaud is chef. It will be a distinguished back-
    ground for society.
So when you've got no place else to go, homeless and hungry
    ones, choose the Waldorf as a background for your rags—
(Or do you still consider the subway after midnight good
    enough?)

ROOMERS

Take a room at the new Waldorf, you down-and-outers—
    sleepers in charity's flop-houses.

They serve swell board at the Waldorf-Astoria. Look at this
menu, will you:

GUMBO CREOLE
CRABMEAT IN CASSOLETTE
BOILED BRISKET OF BEEF
SMALL ONIONS IN CREAM
WATERCRESS SALAD
PEACH MELBA

Have luncheon there this afternoon, all you jobless.
　　Why not?

Dine with some of the men and women who got rich off of
your labor, who clip coupons with clean white fingers because your hands dug coal, drilled stone, sewed garments,
poured steel to let other people draw dividends and live
easy.

(Or haven't you had enough yet of the soup-lines and the
bitter bread of charity?)

Walk through Peacock Alley tonight before dinner, and get
warm, anyway. You've got nothing else to do.

NEGROES

Oh, Lawd! I done forgot Harlem!

Say, you colored folks, hungry a long time in 135th Street—
they got swell music at the Waldorf-Astoria. It sure is a
mighty nice place to shake hips in, too. There's dancing
after supper in a big warm room. It's cold as hell on
Lenox Avenue. All you've had all day is a cup of coffee.
Your pawnshop overcoat's a ragged banner on your hungry frame. You know, downtown folks are just crazy about
Paul Robeson! Maybe they'll like you, too, black mob
from Harlem. Drop in at the Waldorf this afternoon for
tea. Stay to dinner. Give Park Avenue a lot of darkie
color—free—for nothing! Ask the Junior Leaguers to sing
a spiritual for you. They probably know 'em better than
you do—and their lips won't be so chapped with cold after
they step out of their closed cars in the undercover driveways.

Hallelujah! Undercover driveways!
Ma soul's a witness for de Waldorf-Astoria!

(A thousand nigger section-hands keep the roadbeds smooth
so investments in railroads pay ladies with diamond neck-
laces staring at Cert murals.)
Thank Gawd A'mighty!
(And a million niggers bend their backs on rubber plantations,
for rich behinds to ride on thick tires to the Theatre
Guild tonight.)
Ma soul's a witness!
(And here we stand, shivering in the cold, in Harlem.)
Glory be to Gawd—
De Waldorf-Astoria's open!

EVERYBODY

So get proud and rare back; everybody! The new Waldorf-
Astoria's open!
(Special siding for private cars from the railroad yards.)
You ain't been there yet?
(A thousand miles of carpet and a million bathrooms.)
What's the matter?
You haven't seen the ads in the papers? Didn't you get a card?
Don't you know they specialize in American cooking?
Ankle on down to 49th Street at Park Avenue. Get up
off that subway bench tonight with the *Evening Post* for
cover! Come on out o' that flop-house! Stop shivering
your guts out all day on street corners under the El.
Jesus, ain't you tired yet?

"It's not you," my benefactor said when she had read
that far. "It's a powerful poem! But it's not you."
I knew she did not like it.
I began that winter to feel increasingly bad, increasingly worried and apprehensive. Not all at once, but gradually I knew something was wrong. I sensed it vaguely,
intuitively—the way I felt in Mexico, when my father
would come home and find the bookkeeping not added up
right, and I could feel before he got home that it wasn't
added up right, even though I had worked on it all the

afternoon! So it was hard eating dinner with him in his bare, tiled dining room in Toluca, just as it became hard eating dinner on Park Avenue with people who had freshly cut flowers on the table while the snow fell outside.

NOT PRIMITIVE

That winter I had been in Cuba looking for a Negro composer to write an opera with me, using genuinely racial motifs. The lady on Park Avenue thought that Amadeo Roldan might do, or Arturo Cartulo. I could not find Cartulo, and Roldan said he wasn't a Negro. But Miguel Covarrubias had given me a letter to José Antonio Fernandez de Castro, person extraordinary of this or any other world. And José Antonio saw to it that I had a rumba of a good time and met everybody, Negro, white and mulatto, of any interest in Havana—from the drummers at Marianao to the society artist and editor of *Social,* Masaguer.

But I came back to New York with no Negro composer who could write an opera.

More and more tangled that winter became the skein of poet and patron, youth and age, poverty and wealth—and one day it broke! Quickly and quietly in the Park Avenue drawing-room, it broke.

Great wealth had given to a woman who meant to be kind the means to power, and a technique of power, of so mighty a strength that I do not believe she herself knew what that force might become. She possessed the power to control people's lives—pick them up and put them down when and where she wished.

She wanted me to be primitive and know and feel the intuitions of the primitive. But, unfortunately, I did not feel the rhythms of the primitive surging through me, and so I could not live and write as though I did. I was only an American Negro—who had loved the surface of Africa and the rhythms of Africa—but I was not Africa. I was Chicago and Kansas City and Broadway and Harlem. And I was not what she wanted me to be. So, in the end it all came back very near to the old impasse of white and Negro again, white and Negro—as do most relationships in America.

Then, too, I knew that my friend and benefactor was not happy because, for months now, I had written nothing beautiful. She was old and it took a great deal of strength out of her to worry about me, and she was, I think, a bit impatient with men who are not geniuses. (She knew so many great people.) So I asked kindly to be released from any further obligations to her, and that she give me no more money, but simply let me retain her friendship and good will that had been so dear to me. That I asked to keep. But there must have been only the one thread binding us together. When that thread broke, it was the end.

I cannot write here about that last half-hour in the big bright drawing-room high above Park Avenue one morning, because when I think about it, even now, something happens in the pit of my stomach that makes me ill. That beautiful room, that had been so full of light and help and understanding for me, suddenly became like a trap closing in, faster and faster, the room darker and darker, until the light went out with a sudden crash in the dark, and everything became like that night in Kansas when I had failed to see Jesus and had lied about it afterwards. Or that morning in Mexico when I suddenly hated my father.

Physically, my stomach began to turn over and over—and then over again. I fought against bewilderment and anger, fought hard, and didn't say anything. I just sat there in the high Park Avenue drawing-room and didn't say anything. I sat there and listened to all she told me, closed my mouth hard and didn't say anything.

I do not remember clearly what it was she said to me at the end, nor her face as the door closed, nor the elevator dropping down to the street level, nor my final crossing of the lobby through a lane of uniformed attendants.

But I do remember the winter sunshine on Park Avenue and the wind in my face as I went toward the subway to Harlem.

DIAGNOSIS

That evening I was invited to dinner at Louise Thompson's house in Harlem. There were other guests, and her mother had prepared a wonderful meal. Everybody was gay. But suddenly, in the midst of dinner, the conversation at table floated a million miles away from me, off into space. I could see everyone clearly, hear everything that was said, but I didn't seem to be there at all. Still, if anyone spoke to me or looked toward me, I nodded, answered something in a monosyllable, smiled automatically, and tried to keep on eating. But I couldn't eat any more. Not a mouthful. I felt as if I was going to die. And I didn't want to die right then and there at my friends' table, so I tried to wait until dinner was over.

As soon as dinner was over, I excused myself, saying I had forgotten I had an important appointment, and that

I would have to leave right away. Outside, I hailed a taxi and drove to my doctor's office in the Dunbar Apartments. It was about eight o'clock at night, clear and starry.

On entering the courtyard of the Dunbar Apartments, I met E. Simms Campbell and his aunt, Miss Allie Simms, coming out. I hadn't seen them for a long time. They spoke to me pleasantly and asked when I would come to dinner with them.

I said: "Sometime in the next two or three years."

I meant to say, two or three weeks. I knew I said *years*, but I couldn't correct myself. My voice seemed far away and the whole thought lost in such a void that I couldn't correct myself, although I was conscious of my error. So I left them standing there astonished and went on into my doctor's office.

The doctor was just about to leave. He asked me what was the matter, and I said I felt as if I had gone to the other world. He smiled, gave me some ammonia to drink, made me take off my clothes and stretch out on a long table covered with black leather. The coldness of the table and the sharpness of the ammonia water brought me back to life. And then I really felt very sick—the way I had felt in Mexico when my father said: "Hurry up," and anger like a tidal wave had laid me in my bed for a week.

Violent anger makes me physically ill, I guess, although I've only been that angry twice in my life. All that day I had kept trying not to feel angry or hurt or amazed or bewildered over the morning on Park Avenue—and I didn't feel any of those things consciously—for I had loved very much that gentle woman who had been my patron and I wanted to understand what had happened to us that she had sent me away as she did. But now I was violently and physically ill, with my stomach turning over and over each time I thought about that morning at all. And there was no rationalizing anything. I couldn't. The doctor felt my pulse and listened to my heart a long time. He took my temperature. Then he said he found nothing seriously the matter. He advised rest and a light diet.

"Have you been eating in cheap restaurants of late?" he asked.

No, I hadn't. I smiled. I had been eating very well. But I couldn't, for the life of me, tell the doctor about Park Avenue, or why I was ill. I couldn't open my mouth about it. At the very thought, nausea swept over me! I thought she'd liked *me*, my patron. But I guess she only liked my writing, and not even that any more.

I went home to New Jersey, but I couldn't sleep. The next day I couldn't eat. For a week or more I couldn't eat anything at all. So I went back to the doctor. He said I had better have some x-rays made to see what was the matter, since he could detect nothing. (And of course, all the while, I knew what was the matter, but couldn't say it, for if I did, the world started to float away.) So I went and had the x-rays.

The doctor suggested that I go to Rudolph Fisher for the x-ray photographs, but I knew that my writer-friend, Bud, would be full of clever witticisms of a sort that I could never find repartee for when I was in a normal state of mind, let alone now—with my mind in the far-off spaces and my stomach doing flops. So I went to another Harlem specialist I did not know.

He shared an office with a fellow doctor. He charged me a big fee, payable in advance. When he had the fee, he took a picture of my stomach and then gave me an enormous container of white liquid to drink, looked at me in the fluoroscope, and said to come back the following day exactly at noon, because the pictures had to be taken a certain number of hours apart, *exactly*.

The next day I went back and he took some more pictures and gave me some more white, chalky liquid to drink and said to be back at *exactly* six that evening for the final photographs. At six I was in his office—but no doctor. He had forbidden me to eat anything, so by now—the body being contrary—I had begun to have an appetite. I sat there wishing he would come so I could go drink some milk, at least. But he didn't come and seven o'clock was fast approaching. The doctor who shared his office asked me if I had had an appointment.

I said: "Yes, for six."

He said he had to lock up the office and go to dinner, but suggested that I run around the corner to the barber shop and see if the specialist was there, since he thought my doctor had probably gone for a hair cut.

Well, that made my stomach turn over again. I said I never knew a patient was supposed to go look for his doctor in a barber shop, especially when the doctor himself had made an explicitly stressed appointment for a certain hour.

This seemed to make the other physician mad. He said: "Well, you'll have to come back tomorrow, since it's time for me to go to dinner, and I'm going to lock up the office."

I said I was sorry, but I would not go until I had seen my doctor, and if he wished to lock me up in the office, all right!

About that time, however, the x-ray specialist came rushing in, and, without offering an apology or even donning his white coat, he took the final pictures, and seemed in a hurry to get away again. Perhaps he had a heavy date.

When my own doctor saw the plates, he said they showed

nothing physically wrong with my stomach. But since I still could take only a very light diet, puzzled, he advised me to have a laboratory examination, so he sent me to a group of specialists on 125th Street. They took samples of my blood, my urine, my spittle and whatever else there was about me to take, charged me a high fee—in advance—and a week later reported to my physician that I had a Japanese tapeworm.

My doctor was amazed to hear this, and began to look through books on Asiatic diseases. He said the laboratory diagnosis must be in error, but that we had better consult with a famous, but very busy, specialist who was a good friend of his on the staff of the hospital where they both served. Meanwhile, I kept on being sick.

Shortly, it was arranged that I see the famous white specialist, who kindly consented to check on my case for his colored colleague. And since I was a Negro, he would charge me only a modest fee. An appointment was made for me outside office hours. Ironically enough, the office of this celebrated specialist was on Park Avenue near my former patron's home, so I returned to familiar ground.

His fee (for a Negro) was ten dollars. As soon as I arrived, a nurse-secretary ushered me into a large room where the doctor was lying on a couch in an old dressing gown, looking very tired—no doubt from a hard day's practice. As I entered, he turned on his side and glanced up at me wearily. When I was about three feet from his couch, he said: "Stand still!"

I stopped. For a split second he looked me in the eye.

"You've got no Japanese tapeworm," he barked.

That was all. I was ushered out.

The nurse collected ten dollars.

LITERARY QUARREL

Of course, I knew I had no tapeworm all the time, so I decided to go home to Cleveland and get in bed. My mother then lived in three rooms in a basement on Carnegie Avenue, with my step-father and my brother. Very kindly my mother gave me the only bed and they slept on the davenport. My brother stayed with some cousins, because we had only two sleeping rooms and a kitchen.

By now my brother was no longer in school in New England. Work was scarce in Cleveland, and my mother and dad were not doing so well. We were all in a rather bad way. The doctor in Cleveland said it was my tonsils that were poisoning my system, so he took them out—and that took the last money I had. Strangely enough, I still wouldn't tell any of the doctors I was just upset and emotionally confused. I guess I enjoyed paying for attention. And certainly I felt better as soon as the last penny left from Park Avenue was gone.

But to cap the climax, while I was in Cleveland, I had my first literary quarrel—although, basically, it was not really a literary quarrel.

On the evening that I arrived in Cleveland, the Gilpin Players, America's oldest Negro theater group, were performing a new play and I went to see it, thinking it might ease my mind. After the performance I was talking with the director, Rowena Jelliffe, and she told me that she had just received an excellent Negro folk comedy by a talented young woman named Zora Hurston. I expressed interest, so she went on to tell me that it was about a quarrel between two rival church factions in the deep South, that it was a very amusing play, and that it was called *Mule Bone*. She said it had just been turned down by the Theatre Guild in New York, but that an agent had sent a rough draft to her with permission to try it out in Cleveland.

From her description and the title, I knew it was the same play Zora Hurston and I had worked on together. But it was not finished and it did not seem to me it should be produced in that form.

I tried to telephone Miss Hurston, but could not reach her. I wired her, but got no answer. I wrote her three letters, and finally she replied from New York. She said, yes, she had sent the play to *her* agent because she felt that if the play were ever produced I would only take my half of the money and spend it on a girl she didn't like. Besides, the story was her story, the dialogue her dialogue, and the play her play—even if I had put it together, and she didn't want me to have any part in it.

Girls are funny creatures! By now the Gilpin Players were worried and wished her permission in writing, which they tried to secure. An answer came from her agent, giving the Gilpins permission to continue. I agreed to make a final draft, so the play was put into rehearsal, pending a written agreement from Miss Hurston, who as yet had sent no business word. Finally, Miss Hurston wrote that she was driving out to Cleveland to see the rehearsals and would then sign the agreement. Shortly she arrived.

We had a long talk and she agreed that whatever her personal feelings were about other things, the production could go ahead.

But overnight she changed her mind—or, rather, before 12 P.M. She heard that the girl she did not like had been in town, so at midnight she called up Mrs. Jelliffe and said that never, under any circumstances, would she permit any of her work to be linked with mine, nor her name with mine, and that there could be no production of our play, *Mule Bone*. By that time the Gilpin Players had put a sizable amount of money into scenery and costumes for the play. So Mrs. Jelliffe requested a joint conference with me and Miss Hurston the following day. Nothing, she felt, could be settled over the phone at midnight.

Having recently had my tonsils out, I was forbidden by my doctor to leave bed, so the conference was called for my house. It was a cold and snowy day. Mr. and Mrs. Jelliffe arrived. Miss Hurston also came. But she would not talk about the play! Not at all. She would speak only of things that did not concern the drama in question, one way or another. She spoke passionately, long, and loud, until the Jelliffes begged to be excused. They went home. Miss Hurston then got the last word and left without saying good-bye to my mother, whom she had known for years. That made my mother angry, so she pursued Miss Hurston into the hall to give her a piece of her mind. I had to get up out of bed and restrain my mother. It was an exciting afternoon for a tonsillectomy patient.

That evening my fraternity brothers were giving a dance in my honor. I had informed them three days before that the doctor had forbidden me to leave my bed and that I could not come to any dance. But since it was all arranged, they went ahead with it just the same. In my honor, Miss Hurston, being a visiting celebrity, was invited to the party, since the brothers knew nothing of our literary quarrel. With a local young man, she went to the ball and told everyone how awful I was. Then she drove back to New York. As soon as I recovered my voice, I called up the local young man to tell him I meant to beat the hell out of him.

I never heard from Miss Hurston again. Unfortunately, our art was broken, and that was the end of what would have been a good play had it ever been finished—the first real Negro folk comedy—*Mule Bone*.

About that time, *Not Without Laughter* appeared and I received the Harmon Gold Award for Literature, given by the Federated Council of Churches—four hundred dollars and a gold medal. The week that I received the award, I wired Alain Locke, who knew the circumstances of our having written the play and had, I believe, seen a first draft. I asked him kindly to talk to Miss Hurston for me. Alain Locke wired back, YOU HAVE HARMON AWARD SO WHAT MORE DO YOU WANT. Exactly ten cooling words.

I could not go to New York to receive the award, so they sent it to me by mail—a medal and a check. I put the medal away in my trunk. With the four hundred dollars I went to Haiti.

I needed sun.

POSTSCRIPT

That spring for me (and, I guess, all of us) was the end of the Harlem Renaissance. We were no longer in vogue, anyway, we Negroes. Sophisticated New Yorkers turned to Noel Coward. Colored actors began to go hungry, publishers politely rejected new manuscripts, and patrons found other uses for their money. The cycle that had charlestoned into being on the dancing heels of *Shuffle Along* now ended in *Green Pastures* with De Lawd.

The generous 1920's were over. And my twenties almost over. I had four hundred dollars and a gold medal.

Up to the time I received the 1931 Harmon Award, I had never had that much money of my own at once in all my life. Four hundred dollars! I had never had a job that paid more than twenty-two dollars a week. Nor had I sold any of my poems or articles for more than seventy-five dollars (the top price paid once for a group of poems). Mostly I had received no income at all from my poetry (since I gratefully gave it away to anybody who would publish it) and very little from the few stories or articles I had written. My novel had just come out. My two books of poems had both gone beyond the first edition, but had by no means been best sellers. So as yet the big editors did not know my name, or gave no sign of knowing it. And my play, *Mulatto,* was unproduced.

Nevertheless, I'd finally and definitely made up my mind to continue being a writer—and to become a professional writer, making my living from writing. So far that had not happened. Until I went to Lincoln I had always worked at other things: teaching English in Mexico, truck gardening on Staten Island, a seaman, a doorman, a cook, a waiter in Paris night clubs or in hotels and restaurants, a clerk at the Association for the Study of Negro Life and History, a bus boy at the Wardman Park in Washington.

Then I'd had a scholarship, a few literary awards, a patron. But those things were ended now. I would have to make my own living again—so I determined to make it writing. I did. Shortly poetry became bread; prose, shelter and raiment. Words turned into songs, plays, scenarios, articles, and stories.

Literature is a big sea full of many fish. I let down my nets and pulled.

I'm still pulling.

OTHER BOOKS FROM PLUTO

NOTES OF A NATIVE SON
JAMES BALDWIN
With a new introduction by the author

Notes of a Native Son is James Baldwin's first
non-fiction book. Since its publication in 1955,
Baldwin has established himself as one of
America's foremost writers. These essays on life
in Harlem, movies, the protest novel and
Americans abroad are as relevant today as
when they were first written.

'A straight-from-the-shoulder writer, writing
about the troubled problems of this troubled
earth with an illuminating intensity that should
influence for the better all who ponder on the
things books say.' Langston Hughes, *The New
York Times*

192 pages
0 7453 0059 6   £3.95 paperback

A LONG WAY FROM HOME
CLAUDE McKAY

In this rich and rewarding autobiography,
Claude McKay, the Jamaican-born poet and
novelist, remembers the Harlem Renaissance,
the labour movement in Britain, meetings with
Radek and Trotsky in post-revolutionary USSR
and a formative trip to Africa.

McKay writes about meetings in the 1920s
and 1930s – with Frank Harris, George Bernard
Shaw, W.E.B. Du Bois, Isadora Duncan, Charles
Chaplin, H.G. Wells, Sinclair Lewis and many
more. He also describes his life among black
dock workers and sailors in Marseilles and
among Africans in Morocco, where he lived
until his return to the United States in 1934

Throughout this book, McKay voices a
militant black consciousness that shocked bien-
pensant society of the day. Today's reader will
warm to this early expression of 'Black is
beautiful'.

Claude McKay went to New York from
Jamaica in 1912. His novels *Banjo* and *Banana
Bottom* and his poems, including *Harlem
Shadows*, were central to Harlem Renaissance
in the 1920s. He died in 1948. *A Long Way From
Home* is his autobiography.

384 pages
0 7453 0082 0   £4.95 paperback

A DIFFERENT HUNGER
Writings on Black Resistance
A. SIVANANDAN
Introduction by Stuart Hall

A Different Hunger is a collection of essays by Sivanandan on the many aspects of black oppression. The opening essay, 'From Resistance to Rebellion', is a history of black struggle in Britain since 1958. It underlines the culture of oppression that produced the events of Brixton, Toxteth and Chapeltown in the summer of 1981.

Other essays consider the racism of the British state and the immigration and race policies of British governments since 1976; the international context, with particular reference to South Africa and the new international division of labour; and 'the liberation of the black intellectual', including essays on individuals such as James Baldwin and Angela Davis.

Sivanandan is director of the Institute of Race Relations.

'One of the most exciting and controversial political thinkers in Britain.' *Guardian*

192 pages
0 86104 371 5   £3.95 paperback

HOW CAPITALISM UNDERDEVELOPED BLACK AMERICA
MANNING MARABLE

Manning Marable's study of the evolution of the US black community, from slavery to the 1980s, is written in the tradition of Walter Rodney's *How Europe Underdeveloped Africa.*

He examines the effects of the twin structures of racism and capitalism, and the role of patriarchy on black women and the black community as a whole. He analyses the development of special groups: as well as black women, the black 'ghetto class', black prisoners, the black elite, and black entrepreneurs.

Finally, Marable looks at the black political leadership produced by this evolution, and outlines a new social vision and programme for black liberation in the 1980s.

354 pages
0 86104 710 9   £5.95 paperback

Pluto books are available through your local bookshop. In case of difficulty contact Pluto to find out local stockists or to obtain catalogues/leaflets (telephone 01-482 1973).
    If all else fails write to:

Pluto Press Limited
Freepost (no stamp required)
105A Torriano Avenue
London NW5 1YP